THE STORY OF THE ITALIANS IN AMERICA

Books by Michael A. Musmanno

VERDICT!
BLACK FURY
TEN DAYS TO DIE
AFTER TWELVE YEARS
LISTEN TO THE RIVER
WORLD WAR II IN ITALY
THE EICHMANN KOMMANDOS
THE SOLDIER AND THE MAN
CONSTITUTIONAL AMENDMENTS
JUSTICE MUSMANNO DISSENTS
ACROSS THE STREET FROM THE COURTHOUSE
THE STORY OF THE ITALIANS IN AMERICA

THE STORY
OF THE ITALIANS
IN AMERICA

—————————— MICHAEL A. MUSMANNO

DOUBLEDAY & COMPANY, INC., GARDEN CITY, NEW YORK, 1965

Dedicated

to the countless Italian immigrant pioneers who, despite want, hardship, and rebuff, never wavered in the faith which brought them to America to give of their brain, brawn, and Latin heritage in the building of a nation—a nation surpassing the glories of ancient Rome.

CONTENTS

LIST OF ILLUSTRATIONS

NOTE

For convenience to the writer and the reader, I will refer, generally, to all persons of Italian stock, whether in the past or present, as Italians. It would be awkward and tedious, in a book dealing exclusively with the Italian people, to keep referring to American children of Italian forebears as Italian-Americans. Even a five-generation American of Irish ancestry is properly referred to as an Irishman. The word Italian here, when it applies to a native-born American of Italian ancestry, will be used in the same sense.

ACKNOWLEDGMENTS

I am grateful to Giovanni Schiavo for the valuable assistance I derived from his splendid work, *Four Centuries of Italian-American History*. The entire Italian community of America should be indebted to Mr. Schiavo for his dedicated and stupendous labors in digging out of old records, books, and documents much of the history of the Italian in early-day America.

I express my particular appreciation to Dr. J. Robert Spence, Instructor in the Fine Arts Department of the University of Pittsburgh for his observations and suggestions, after reading the part of my manuscript dealing with the fine arts.

I am also appreciative of the time given by Professor Sergio Pacifici of the City University of New York to that portion of the book dealing with Italian literature.

I owe a deep sense of gratitude to Victor A. Arrigo of Chicago, a scholar of vast erudition, for recommendations offered after reading the entire manuscript.

I thank the Architect of the United States Capitol, who, through his staff, supplied me with valuable information and data on the Italian artists who contributed their talents to decorating the Capitol.

I am under obligation to Mrs. Laura Fermi for her suggestions on my discussion of the epochal work of her husband, the illustrious scientist Enrico Fermi.

I thank Joe DiMaggio and Lester J. Biederman of the Pittsburgh *Press* for reading that portion of the manuscript which deals with baseball. I am indebted to Al Abrams, sports editor of the Pittsburgh *Post-Gazette* for his suggestions on the entire section dealing with sports.

I acknowledge with gratitude the helpful suggestions offered by

Harold Cohen, drama editor of the Pittsburgh *Post-Gazette*, on the figures discussed in the pages on the theater, motion pictures, and the general entertainment field.

I appreciate the kindness of Dr. Martin Engel, Professor of History and Fine Arts of the Carnegie Institute of Technology for reading the pages on sculpture, architecture, and painting, of Professors Joseph Morice, Severino Russo, and W. G. Storey of the Department of History, Duquesne University, for their attention to the pages on education, of Hal C. Davis, President of Musical Society Local 60, American Federation of Musicians, for reading the sections on music and labor leaders, and of Frank Cantelmo, Managing Editor of *Il Progresso*, for supplying me with a list (which we both know is far from complete) of outstanding Italian businessmen.

I appreciate the comments offered by Miss Veronica Volpe, Food Editor of the Pittsburgh *Press*, on the pages devoted to Italian food.

My greatest debt is owed to the attendants at the Carnegie Library in Pittsburgh and in the Congressional Library in Washington for assistance in locating material and books for me.

THE STORY OF THE ITALIANS IN AMERICA

Italy

SWITZERLAND

AUSTRIA

FRANCE

L. Maggiore

L. Como

L. Di Garda

UDINE

TORINO

MILAN

VENICE

TRIESTE

Po R.

YUGOSLAVIA

GENOA

BOLOGNA

FLORENCE

Ligurian Sea

SAN MARINO

Adriatic Sea

CORSICA

Tyrrhenian Sea

Tiber

PESCARA

ROME

NAPLES

SASSARI

SARDINIA

Mt. Vesuvius

BARI

I. CAPRI

BRINDISI

CAGLIARI

PALERMO

MESSINA

CATANZARO

Mt. Etna

REGGIO

MEDITERRANEAN

SICILY

CATANIA

AFRICA

SEA

1 THE BOOT

If one, with imagination, pores over a map of the world, he will detect in the outlines of various geographical divisions a striking resemblance to familiar objects and even a suggestion of historical figures. But without exercising any imagination at all, he will see that Italy resembles a boot, and, what is more, that it has all the detailed characteristics of a boot. It presents the perfect toe, the faultlessly shaped heel, the arched instep and the knee expansion of a cavalier's boot. At the properly designated spot there appears even the telltale spur with which the rider has prodded the steed of history over the highways of the centuries, galloping into the farthest reaches of man's domains, taking to them the initiative, learning and culture of the ancient Latin civilization, as well as the daring and genius of modern Italy.

This Italian boot has traveled on horseback, ship, and land, and, wherever it has touched the earth's surface, it has left memorable imprints. But nowhere did the bootprints sink so deeply and leave their mark so permanently as in America. Christopher Columbus wore the Italian boot as he paced the deck of the *Santa Maria* and then beached his landing craft at San Salvador. That boot trudged through the sands of Cuba, Jamaica, Puerto Rico, and other islands of the West Indies, as well as the northern coast of South America.

Giovanni Caboto (known in history as John Cabot) drew on that same boot as he prepared to climb the gangplank of his ship, the *Matthew*, in which he discovered the northern stretches of the western hemisphere. Columbus and Cabot were followed by Amerigo Vespucci who, tramping in the same identical boot, explored both continents of the hemisphere. He then described in such illuminating and fascinating language the new lands marked by his, Columbus', and Cabot's footprints, that cartographers and historians resolved to append his name to the whole new world—and thus "America" was born. Recent research reveals also that Vespucci was the first European to sight what later became Cape Canaveral and is now Cape Kennedy.

Giovanni da Verrazano, while wearing the never-changing Italian boot, with its seemingly magical powers of discovery, drew aside the veils that had concealed New York Bay. He cut through the surf and gave to the world the island now universally hailed as the most fabulous of all water-circumscribed land, Manhattan.

The Italian boot made the first circumnavigation of the earth in Magellan's fleet, worn by Antonio Pigafetta, who gave to the world the most detailed and authoritative history of that epochal, globe-blazing voyage. Alessandro Malaspina, similarly shod, headed a scientific expedition which in 1791 surveyed the Pacific coast from Alaska to Mexico.

The discoverer's boot and the explorer's boot in America were followed by the boot of colonization. Then, as the wheels of time turned, the islands of the West Indies and the continents of the Americas vibrated to the tramp of military boots, settlers' boots, planters' boots, farmers' boots, and fishermen's boots hailing from the mother boot of Italy.

Mingling with the cadence and rhythmic lilt of the boots of colonization, cultivation, and civilization, there could also be heard by the chronicler of events the soft tread of the sandals of missionaries as they carried the water of the gospels into the arid deserts of aboriginal lands, at the same time delivering the learning and the paraphernalia of European enlightenment into the settlements of the primitive Indians. Perhaps the first of these missionary colonizers was the Italian Fra Marco da Nizza who arrived in what was then known as New Spain (Mexico) in 1531. The Spanish conquistadors, for whom the glitter of gold had, like an aura, always encircled the compass which had guided them to the new world, had heard vaguely of a land to the northeast where gold was so abundant that the natives plated the walls of their temples with it.

Undoubtedly each person who retold the tale gilded it with the brush of his own fancy until Coronado, governor of what is now Northern Sonora and Chihuahua, Mexico, mentally pictured the inhabitants of the faraway land using golden cooking utensils and sleeping on golden beds. He turned to Fra Marco da Nizza, who probably knew more about the surrounding terrain than any other white person, since he had established numerous missions in that area of the new world, and asked him to make a preliminary exploration. The Italian priest set out on his journey, armed with only a cross, his sole companion a Negro named Estevanico. They scaled snow-capped mountains, forded turbulent streams and jogged over burning deserts, penetrating as far north as what is now Phoenix, Arizona. Poor Estevanico was not to return. He was slain by Indians and Fra Marco reported to Coronado that he had seen people ornamented with pure pearls and turquoise and had learned of a place called Cibola where gold was as plentiful as pebbles.

Coronado quickly mounted an imposing expedition, and set out for the land of the yellow nuggets with Fra Marco as his guide. A Sicilian, Francesco Rojo, enthusiastically joined the bustling caravan, supplying his own "arms and horses." Alas, El Dorado turned out to be a mirage, the creation of unlettered romanticism. The ambitious enterprise, however, was not without fruitful achievement. The men pushed forward as far north as the overawing Grand Canyon and the plains of what is now Kansas, laying foundations for thriving settlements to follow.

Fra Marco's zeal for conversion and exploration found its counterpart in his countryman Father Eusabio Chino, who sailed from Genoa in 1678, tarried in Spain for a couple of years, and landed eventually in the vast western lands of the American continent, where he performed missionary work among the Indians of northern Mexico and southern Arizona.* A scholar of note, he published before his departure for America a pamphlet which enjoyed great popularity, on the "Great Comet" which had just appeared.

* From now on, for convenience, I will use the current names of geographical areas, although obviously they were not so known in the time that I am writing about.

Mixing tremendous practicality with his works of faith, Father Chino poured into the baptismal font the formulas for economic and social self-sufficiency. He taught the Indians advanced agriculture; he instructed them in carpentry, masonry, and animal husbandry. He built for them houses and ranches with the same eagerness he erected churches and chapels to the glory of God. Fearing no danger and shrinking from no hardship, he picked his way through deep valleys, suffered the blistering heat of the deserts, climbed high mountains amid fog and snow, and fought against hunger, thirst, and sleep to reach his objectives. The notion prevailed in the late 1600s that Lower California was an island. It was Father Chino who, by sea voyages and land exploration, proved to the skeptics that it was a peninsula.

Raising and corraling vast herds of cattle, he pioneered the American cattle industry in the southwest. Professor H. E. Bolton of the University of California has called Father Chino the "cattle king of his day and region," explaining with appropriate eulogy that the energetic priest never possessed for himself a single animal.

On February 14, 1965, at impressive exercises in the Capitol at Washington, the State of Arizona dedicated a statue of Father Chino, under the name of Father Kino (the Spanish phonetic spelling), to be placed in the Hall of Columns, House of Representatives. A large contingent from Trento, Italy, near where Father Chino was born, attended the ceremony which was graced by the presence of the Italian, Spanish, and Mexican ambassadors, together with Governor Samuel P. Goddard, Jr., and Senator Carl Hayden of Arizona.

Father Salvaterra, a countryman from Milan, assisted Father Chino in his ambitious program for the colonization and evangelization of California and carried on his work after Father Chino's death.

When Hernando de Soto, the discoverer of the Mississippi River, made his historic march from Florida to Oklahoma, three Italian engineers accompanied him. Two of them, according to a report made by the U. S. De Soto Expedition Commission, were a Genoese engineer called Maestro Francisco and a calker from Sardinia, who "turned out to be among the most essential members of the expedition since they were relied upon in building bridges during the march and constructed the boats in which the survivors finally escaped to Mexico."

Italian military engineers worked with the Spanish conquistadors to fortify their acquired realms from pirates who roamed the Main.

One of these engineers, Giovanni Battista Antonelli, urged in 1529 the building of a canal through the Central American isthmus, in Nicaragua. In 1589 another Antonelli designed the famous Morro Castle in Havana.

Italian as well as Spanish priests and missionaries were much sought after by the French and Spanish explorers because, aside from the pacifying influence they might exert over the native Indians, they were usually energetic scholars who had reduced to writing and maps what they had learned in their pilgrimages, which often preceded the advance of the colonizing pioneers. Many brave disciples of the Church were slain by the Indians before their amicable intentions were understood.

An Italian friar, Brother Mengozzi, was killed by Indians in February 1571, on the banks of the Rappahannock in Virginia. Father Gesù de Lombardi met death at the hands of the Hopi Indians in Arizona around 1679. In 1695 Indians in Southern California killed Father Saverio Saetta. Father Francesco Gressani of the Society of Jesus narrowly escaped death when he was tortured and sold into slavery for a trinket or two by the New York Iroquois in 1664. He later escaped and returned to his missionary work, continuing all the while his scholastic labors in mathematics and astronomy. So far as can be ascertained, he was the first European to describe in sparkling prose that roaring, splashing spectacular phenomenon of nature, the delight of honeymooners and the mecca of tourists—Niagara Falls.

It was also here at Niagara in 1679 that another Italian, this time a soldier, Enrico Tonti, built the *Griffin*, the first large vessel to cleave the waters of the Great Lakes, stupefying the natives with its wide decks and high canvas spread and striking terror to their hearts by its five mounted cannon. The builder and master of the *Griffin* was as much a terror to the Indians on land as on water. His right arm ended with an iron hand, the original having been blown off by a grenade in the Sicilian wars. In close combats he swiped this metallic member across the faces of the foe, breaking heads and knocking out teeth with such facility that the Indians, ascribing to him supernatural powers, called him Thunder Arm.

Second in command to the famous French explorer, Robert La Salle, Tonti built the first white settlement in Illinois. From here he set out to blaze trails through the great wildernesses, heading for the Gulf Coast. On his journey he faced a thousand hardships and risks, fighting wild animals and at times equally wild aborigines. He slept on frozen ground and slashed his way through flooded canebrakes with a hatchet, always advancing to tame a primitive continent.

On April 9, 1682, with La Salle, he entered the delta of the Mississippi and here the two resolute explorers performed a ceremony which raised an epochal curtain on America's destiny in the West. Planting a huge cross and unfurling the flag of France, they proclaimed all the vast lands drained by the mighty Mississippi to belong to King Louis XIV. Thus was staked out the Louisiana Territory which, through the courage and wisdom of Thomas Jefferson, became the Louisiana Purchase. And thus, an Italian pioneer participated in the weaving of the continental fabric which was to add thirteen new states to the Union, exceeding in territory the original thirteen states by over 500,000 square miles.

At the confluence of the Arkansas and Mississippi Rivers, Enrico Tonti founded, in 1686, a trading station, named Arkansas Post, the first European settlement in Arkansas. He is regarded by many Arkansans as the founder of their state.

Enrico's brother, Alfonso Tonti, carrying on in the same audacious Tonti tradition, founded, with a few other brave spirits, the city of Detroit and for twelve years ruled as its governor. Theresa Tonti, the first white person born in Detroit, was his child.

A general impression prevails among those who have given no study or but little thought to the relevant historical data, that, after the Italian discoverers and explorers of the fifteenth and sixteenth centuries had reboarded their ships, weighed anchor, unfurled their sails, and disappeared into the mists from which they had first emerged, no other Italians strayed from their sea-locked boot. Further, that the Italians steadfastly remained in that boot producing progeny until the population reached explosion point. Then the boot, like an upturned cornucopia, poured out its flood of humanity, inundating the American continent with dark-eyed *paisani*, who performed all the manual and menial work the older Americans spurned. It is thus assumed among the uninformed that for the three-hundred-year period between the discoverer-explorer epoch and the post-Civil War era, the Italians in no way participated in the military, economic, and political development of America. They will concede that, following the Civil War, the Italians contributed considerable muscle to the American giants of industry, commerce, and wealth, but they cling to the notion that somehow the Italians were, all along, unassimilable outlanders. The same fantasy prevailed with regard to the Irish. Bob Considine, in his excellent book *It's the Irish* wrote:

> The Irish who came to America, eventually like a tidal wave, were unique in two respects. They were the first, really, to suffer segregation and discrimination. And, of course, they were the first to do something about a symbolic and neatly printed sign they read in the windows of Boston, New York and elsewhere: MAN WANTED. NO IRISH NEED APPLY.

I was born in Pennsylvania, but it was assumed that that did not make me an American, since my father and mother were born in Italy. I must here interpolate a story of my childhood. At twelve years of age I fell in love with a very pretty girl who had recently arrived from England and sat at a desk across the aisle from mine in the country schoolhouse of Stowe Township, Pennsylvania. One day I asked her if I could help her with her homework. I would do anything, I said to her, to make her life in America a happy one, as she had now filled the world with happiness for me. It was not long until I was accompanying her home, carrying her books, and writing her notes of adoration.

One day I decided that when I grew up, Penelope Worthington should be my wife. I realized that she would have many suitors, so it behooved me to let her know far in advance of my intentions. I felt rather timid about popping the question myself, so I got my boyhood chum, Arthur Young, to deliver the message.

The next day, while the school bell was ringing, he reported. "Mike," he said, "I talked to Penelope and she said she loves you, she thinks you're wonderful and smart and she likes to listen to you talk. But she says she can never marry you because you are a foreigner."

I was born in America; she had been here seven months. She was an American, I was a foreigner. The school bell seemed to be tolling my funeral. I did not even attempt to argue the question with her because I accepted what everybody said and believed. Italians were foreigners.

But they were not foreigners in the eyes of the founders of our country. As early as 1789 the historian David Ramsey wrote: "The Colonies which now form the United States may be considered as

Europe transplanted. Ireland, England, Scotland, France, Germany, Holland, Switzerland, Sweden, Poland, and *Italy* furnished the original stock."* Nor did the Italians themselves look upon America as a foreign land.

Angelo Flavio Guidi, in his charming monograph "Washington and the Italians," tells the moving story of the last days of the Father of our Country. After describing the Italian mantelpiece at Mount Vernon and how Washington cherished its artistic design with its sentimental attachments, Guidi relates:

> By that fireplace wherein burned the logs from Virginia woods, Washington was wont to sit while conversing with his family or with the soldiers and statesmen that called on him.
>
> By that hearth he lingered for the last time that evening when, wet and covered with sleet, he returned home and retired, never to rise again. His last glance was for that mantelpiece. His eyes rested on the carved forms he so much loved, envisaging their beauty with an Italian sentiment, full of fondness—then he saw no more.
>
> Many Italians had fallen by his side, *fighting for a country they did not consider foreign,* without ever seeing again all that they had loved back home; the grief of not having seen once again, and the grief of having never seen were equal.
>
> In the silence of the tomb, Glory united the Leader of the Victorious Army of America and First President of the United States with the dauntless heroes, forgotten or unknown, who had fallen fighting for America, asking for naught. All of them had fought for the greatest boon to humanity:—Freedom.†

Mr. Guidi states that poring over the regimental lists of the Continental Army, the first Italian name he encountered was that of Captain Cosmo de Medici, attached in 1777 to the Light Dragoons of North Carolina. Then he found James Bracco, a lieutenant in the Seventh Regiment of Maryland (killed in action at White Plains), B. Tagliaferro, a captain in the Second, Virginia, and a subaltern of George Washington; Nicola Tagliaferro or Talliaferro, second lieutenant in the Sixth, Virginia; Colonel Richard Talliaferro, who fell at the Battle of Guilford Court House, and of whom Governor T. M.

---

* All italics in book mine, unless otherwise noted.
† *Italy and the Italians in Washington's Time.* Prepared under the auspices of Casa Italiana of Columbia University, New York City, Italian Publishers, New York, 1933.

Holt said in 1893 on the occasion of the dedication of the monument erected on the battlefield where he fell: "He sealed his service with his blood. He gave his young life that you and I might be free." Then there was Ferdinando Finizzi, who was present at the surrender of Cornwallis at Yorktown, having served in Washington's army from 1777 on.

Guidi also spoke of Francesco Monte, lieutenant in the First Infantry. In the register of the "Massachusetts Soldiers and Sailors of the Revolutionary War," he found Stefano Almero, in the artillery; Giuseppe Amo; Eduardo Casa; Michele Cazzale; Giuseppe Cova, barnstable; Vincenzo Curria, bugler with Colonel Sheldon of the Light Dragoons. And then there were De Luce Francesco, who took part in the battle of Dorchester; Giorgio de Luke, ill in a military hospital in October 1777; Marescho Giacomo Battista; Giovanni Norile; Tito Patamia; Giovanni Rosso, who fought at Ticonderoga; Francesco Sisso; Giovanni Scotto; Giovanni Virtualo; Giullo Francis; Giovanni Guitta; Giacomo Batta Laguario; Giovanni Meloda. Among the officers of the West Orange Regiment he saw the name of Giovanni Poppino, later transferred as a lieutenant to the Florida Regiment. Mr. Guidi explains that in the "Complete Army and Navy Register of the United States from 1776 to 1887," only officers were listed and "that therefore many names of mere Italian privates in the American Revolutionary Army will never be known."

In his scholarly and exhaustive work *Four Centuries of Italian-American History,** Giovanni Schiavo relates:

Two regiments recruited mostly in Italy came over in 1779, the Third Piemont, with 473 men, and the Thirtieth Du Perche, with 1064 men. (Pascol, A., *Histoire de l'Armée*, 4 vols., Paris, 1853, II, 226.) Another regiment, the Royal Italien, is also said to have come over. Five members of the Scalvini family are said to have enlisted in said regiment and to have fought for our independence. One of them, Alessandro Scalvini, was introduced to George Washington, according to Amy Bernardy, an Italian writer who taught in Massachusetts not many years ago.

Mr. Schiavo says he is of the belief that Major John Belli, Deputy Quarter Master General of the United States Army from 1792 to

* *Four Centuries of Italian-American History*, by Giovanni Schiavo, Vigo Press, 4th ed., 1957.

1794 was a native either of Italy or of Italian Switzerland. Many Italian sailors abandoned their native ships when they arrived in New York, Philadelphia, Baltimore, Boston, or Savannah, in order to sail on vessels flying the flag of the newest republic in the world. Mr. Guidi explains that it was impossible for him to obtain the names of these sailors since the lists of the crews were often lost. He did, however, discover that the American *Tyrannicide* carried as members of its crew Antonio DeMani and Giovanni Forti; the *Protector* a Martino Mattia; the *Deana* a Martini Giovanni Battista.

In appraising the esteem America bestowed on Italy from the very beginning, it is revealing that of the first five warships commissioned by the Continental Congress, three were named after famous Italians of the sea: Christopher Columbus, John Cabot, and Andrea Doria.*

* Doria was a Genoese admiral who as late as his eighty-fourth year was fighting the Barbary pirates.

2 CRUSADING FOR AMERICAN FREEDOM

American independence was not achieved alone by muskets on land and cutlasses at sea. Many pens stormed the heights of tyranny and released the light of knowledge and understanding, inspiring and strengthening the colonists in their mighty endeavor toward ultimately breaking completely from the British monarchial yoke. One of those sharp pens was wielded by Philip Mazzei,* a scholar, doctor, and agriculturist from Poggio a Caiano, Italy, who, arriving in Virginia in 1773, was welcomed by prominent colonists, including George Washington.

Benjamin Franklin, who had known Mazzei in London, invited him to America to conduct agricultural experiments, and Mazzei sailed, accompanied by fourteen Italian farmers, laden with seeds, plants, and agrarian equipment. Jefferson donated to him two thousand acres of land for his experimental farm. Here Mazzei grew vineyards and produced vegetables which had never seen light before in the New World, but the climate of the colonies required the cultivation of something far more important, the Tree of Liberty, and so Mazzei

* For most of the discussion on Philip Mazzei, I am indebted to Giovanni E. Schiavo and his vast research on the subject, *One of America's Founding Fathers,* Vigo Press, 1951, to *Philip Mazzei, Friend of Jefferson,* by Richard Cecil Garlick, Jr., Johns Hopkins Press, 1933, and to Victor Arrigo in Chicago.

bent his tremendous energies to political arboriculture. He addressed himself at once to the writing of pamphlets and newspaper articles, exhorting the colonists to sever all ties with England.

Although familiar with the English language, since he had lived sixteen years in London, Mazzei often wrote in his native Italian, which Thomas Jefferson translated into English. It could well be that as Jefferson rendered Mazzei's Dantean idiom into his own classic prose, some of Jefferson's original thoughts slid down the pen into the ink which formed the words now attributed to Mazzei. There could have been a further reason for employing Mazzei as the vehicle for Jefferson's revolutionary ideas, since Mazzei used a *nom de plume* ("Furioso"). In any event, it is certain that some telling language in Mazzei's articles strikingly resembles phrases immortalized in the Declaration of Independence. In his book *A Nation of Immigrants*, President John F. Kennedy said: "The great doctrine, 'All Men Are Created Equal,' incorporated in the Declaration by Thomas Jefferson, was paraphrased from the writings of Philip Mazzei." The relationship between Jefferson and Mazzei was so close that when the Declaration was taking final form in Philadelphia, Jefferson sent what he termed an "original" copy to Mazzei in Virginia.

Shortly after his arrival Mazzei was elected member of a Virginia county committee which carried on correspondence with the other twelve colonies, on the subjects of interdependency and collective independence. He also appealed to influential friends in Europe to support the American cause. As a result of Mazzei's exhortations, the Grand Duke of Tuscany ordered the printing in a Florentine newspaper of the "Declaration of the Causes and Necessity of Taking Up Arms, in America," and removed all duties on the American Commerce "to give it encouragement." In the fall of 1776 the Grand Duke declared himself "zealously in favor of America."

Mazzei worked with his Virginian confreres in the formation of the Virginia Constitution. On June 29, 1776, he wrote Patrick Henry giving his observations on the "English constitution, endeavoring to prove the weak basis & heavy errors of it," and offering recommendations "in regard to the nature of the best Government which may be easily established by us, an opportunity that no people (by what we know from histories) ever had before."

An excellent speaker, he exhorted public audiences on the impelling necessity of resisting and overcoming British tyranny. When the "shot heard round the world" echoed over Mazzei's experimental farm, he seized a musket and presented himself to Patrick Henry as a volunteer in the Independent Company of Albemarle which the distinguished Virginian patriot was recruiting. At the same recruiting spot he found Thomas Jefferson and Carlo Bellini, destined later to become Secretary for Foreign Affairs for Virginia, and then a professor of romance languages at the College of William and Mary. However, the British withdrew before Henry's forces could go into action, and the company disbanded. In 1777 Mazzei volunteered for regular enlistment in the Continental Army but Patrick Henry dissuaded him from this service, insisting that his pen and voice were vitally needed in the moral battle for aid from Europe. That year Mazzei sailed as Virginia's special envoy to seek funds across the seas for American independence and to represent it abroad in good public relations. Of this mission Thomas Jefferson wrote to Richard Henry Lee:

> I have been led the more to think of this from frequent conversations with Mazzei whom you know well and who is well acquainted with all those countries. . . . His connections in Tuscany are good, his acquaintances with capital men there, in Rome, and Naples great. . . .

As the ship which was to bear Mazzei to Europe cleared the Virginian capes, a British privateer drew up alongside and demanded his custody, with that of several others, but Mazzei had thrown overboard all identifying documents so that the British, after detaining him for a couple of months, released him. In Paris, Mazzei, with tongue and pen, helped in no small degree to condition the French into later making common military cause with the Americans.

In 1783 he returned to Virginia, called on George Washington, attended a dinner given for Lafayette, and visited with James Monroe at a session of the Continental Congress in New York. When he left America for the last time, it was like a lover parting from his sweetheart. He wrote Madison:

> I am about to depart, but my heart remains behind. When I think what I felt in crossing the Potomac I am ashamed of my weakness. I do not know what may happen when Sandy Hook disappears from my sight. But I know that wherever I go I shall always work for the well-being and progress of the country of my adoption.

In his declining years Mazzei lived in Pisa, proudly recounting the loyalty that had made him an American citizen in 1777 and writing the first history of the American colonies and their valiant and triumphant battles for freedom.* When he passed away in 1816 Thomas Jefferson paid him the tribute:

> His esteem in this country was very general; his early and zealous cooperation in the establishment of our independence having acquired for him here a great degree of favor.

While Mazzei was battling for the cause of independence in Virginia, William Paca, a great-grandson of one of the early Italian settlers of Maryland, was fighting the battle in Maryland. Documentary evidence abounds that many Italians were living in Maryland long before 1649. In that year the Maryland legislature enacted a law declaring that persons of "French, Dutch or *Italian* descent" were authorized by law to buy and sell land.

William Paca, who served in the Maryland Legislature and the Continental Congress, was one of the bold patriots to renounce allegiance to the British crown and affix his name to the immortal Declaration of Independence. Later he became Chief Justice of the Maryland Court of Appeals and from 1782 to 1786 was governor of the state.

On July 18, 1937, William S. Paca, great-great-grandson of the illustrious patriot, wrote a letter to the New York *Times* in which he spoke of William Paca's Italian origin. He explained that the name was originally spelled Pacci and that some of his forebears had gone to England from Italy and then to America:

> I am now 74 years old and can distinctly recall having seen some of the great brass-bound chests that were used in importing silks, laces and other finery for the ladies from English and Italian ports.

An article in the Baltimore *Sun* dated July 3, 1904, recounted:

* In 1937 the curator of the Congressional Library discovered among an accumulation of pamphlets from the library of Thomas Jefferson a brochure which contained the minutes of "The Constitutional Society," which met in June 1874 to discuss the formation of a federal constitution. Among the members of the society were such names as John Blair, James Madison, James Monroe, John Marshall, Edmund Randolph and Philip Mazzei, he being the only non-Anglo-Saxon name in the distinguished list. In his *Memoirs* Mazzei discusses this organization and how he proposed John Blair as its president.

A tradition in the Paca family gives its origin as Italian and of the same ancestral blood as that of Pope Leo XIII. . . . Robert Paca, the original settler in Maryland, came by way of England, but having made no effort to locate his residence there, it is sufficient to know that he was never naturalized in the province, but was as early as 1651 granted a tract of 490 acres of land in Anne Arundel county for transporting nine men into the Province, according to the conditions of plantations. . . . Robert Paca married the daughter of one of the commissioners appointed by Oliver Cromwell to govern Maryland. By her he had one son, Aquila, who became High Sheriff of Baltimore county 1762–3, and later member of the House of Burgesses.

Giovanni Schiavo advances the interesting suggestion that Robert Paca called his first son Aquila in honor of the Aquila family, related in marriage to the Paca family of Benevento and Naples.

Although most of the fighting in the Revolutionary War ranged up and down the Atlantic seaboard, one crucial battle brought the young Americans and the old British face to face west of the Alleghenies. The outcome of that battle accomplished more than any other single event to advance the flag of the United States westward across the continent. On December 6, 1927, President Coolidge said to Congress:

"The historic character and the importance of the Vincennes victory are too little known and understood: they gave us not only the Northwest Territory, but by means of that the prospect of reaching the Pacific."

The Northwest Territory comprised what are now the states of Ohio, Indiana, Illinois, Michigan, and Wisconsin, and part of Minnesota. If one will visualize the original thirteen colonies as a soldier, with his feet as Florida and his head as Maine, facing the Atlantic, one will see the Northwest Territory as a bear clinging to his back, impeding and tormenting him at every movement. Had the bear not been dislodged it could have forced the Continental Army into a two-front war, which could only have been disastrous to the Americans.

If General George Rogers Clark deserves, as he richly does, the credit for relieving American forces facing the enemy on two fronts, he shares that credit with Giuseppe Maria Francesco Vigo, full-blooded Italian, who supplied him with military material and military intelligence which made the glorious Vincennes victory possible. Judge John Law wrote in his book *The Colonial History of Vincennes* (1839):

> I have accurately and critically weighed and examined all the results produced by any contest in which we were engaged during the Revolutionary War; in my opinion, for the immense benefits acquired and the signal advantages obtained for it by the whole Union, it was second to no enterprise undertaken during that struggle. The whole credit of this conquest belongs to two men, General George Rogers Clark and Colonel Francis Vigo.

Francis Vigo, who was born in Mondovi, Italy, in 1747, arrived in New Orleans at the age of twenty-seven. With characteristic Latin energy, he at once plunged into the fur trade, traveling up and down the Mississippi, dealing with the Indians, penetrating into the deepest forests, and, in a short time, attaining such a reputation for initiative and practical results that the Spanish governor of the territory in St. Louis, De Leyba, became his silent partner in the fur business, a lucrative one. Vigo, who was a natural linguist, speaking, in addition to his native Italian and Piedmontese, Spanish, English, French, Choctaw, Chickasaw, and Shawnee, made St. Louis his headquarters and added the Ohio River valley to his fur-procuring domain.

Passionately devoted to the cause of American independence, he called on Clark at his camp in Kaskaskia where Clark was working out plans for driving the British from the Northwest Territory. Captain Helm, commanding the American forces in Fort Vincennes, had just notified Clark by courier that he desperately needed provisions and ammunition. Vigo at once volunteered to help Helm, since he was well known in Vincennes and could draw at will on traders in the region.

Clark appointed Vigo his agent, supplying him with a letter to that effect, and Vigo set off in his pirogue (a hollowed-out tree canoe) for the arduous and long journey down the Mississippi to its confluence with the Ohio, up the Ohio and then over the Wabash to Vincennes. While vigorously paddling toward his distant destination General Hamilton, commanding the British forces in the Northwest Territory, swept into Fort Vincennes and made Helm prisoner. By this bold stroke Hamilton saw himself conquering one-third of the American continent for King George. The prospects were promising.

Before reaching his destination, Vigo was captured by a British officer, with Indian allies, and was hauled before Hamilton. On the way to the British general, Vigo thrust into his mouth, chewed up, and swallowed the document signed by Clark which would have warranted Hamilton under military law to hang Vigo as a spy.

With the self-incriminating fatal evidence in his intestines, Vigo indignantly protested his arrest to Hamilton, asserting that he was a Spanish subject. Hamilton, fearing to offend the Spanish sovereign and turn him into an enemy, released Vigo from immediate custody but confined him to the limits of the fort. Several weeks later he allowed him to leave after first exacting the promise that on his way back to St. Louis, Vigo would do nothing injurious to the British interests. During his detention Vigo, with the acute observational faculties of an Indian scout, had acquired extensive knowledge of the fort's defenses. He also had obtained detailed information on the deployment of British forces throughout the entire Northwest Territory.

Vigo maintained his promise not to injure British interests on his way to St. Louis, but, once in that city, and unburdened of his pledge, he at once moved swiftly by pirogue and on horseback to Kaskaskia, where he briefed Clark on the whole Vincennes situation. Clark excitedly heard him out and decided to attack at once, before Hamilton could recruit more Indians and before his Detroit militia would arrive. After that first flush of enthusiasm, however, he dropped his arms helplessly to his side. He had no equipment, supplies, or ammunition for an expedition of this magnitude. Vigo seized the general by the shoulders and entreated him not to worry. Clark could draw on Vigo's St. Louis bankers for everything he needed. In several days Kaskaskia hummed with activity as food, equipment, ammunition, and uniforms poured into the camp on the wagons of Vigo's patriotism and generosity. In addition he recruited on his own a company of French soldiers. He purchased a keel boat which he mounted with two cannons and loaded with forty men devoted to him personally.

Vigo's many fur-trading forays into this territory had familiarized him with the topography and terrain and, even though much of the area was now covered with snow, swamps, and floods, obliterating landmarks, Vigo could see beneath the seasonal obscuring blankets the traversable routes and paths he knew as well as the lines in the palm of his hands.

And so the expedition marched, sailed, paddled, and sloshed through 240 miles of storm-tossed, hostile-Indian-infested land. The men waded through water that reached to their ankles, knees, and waists. They lay down in slush and mud for an occasional rest so that some measure of strength would remain for the eventual surprise attack, to which Clark and Vigo were with iron-willed determination leading them. At night the soldiers often had to erect scaffolds to keep their powder dry for the decisive battle ahead.

Finally in the early days of February 1779 the mud-ice-encrusted and almost famished warriors descended on Fort Vincennes with the fury of an avalanche, overwhelming Harrison as he complacently sat in his cannon-protected fort playing cards and reading into them the glory that was to be his in having conquered one-third of the continent for King George III.

On February 25, 1779, Harrison surrendered, the pestiferous bear was pulled off the Continental's back, and Yorktown was assured.

Vigo's monumental contribution to the success of the American arms in the Revolution led to many honors. After being made a United States citizen he was commissioned a colonel in the Indiana militia. In 1789 President Washington summoned him to Carlisle, Pennsylvania, where the great president conferred with him regarding defensive measures in the western part of the country. In 1802 he became a member of the State Assembly at Vincennes and in 1832 the county of Vigo was created in his name.

And so, Colonel Vigo lived out his life in his adopted country rich with distinction and awards, but poor in worldly goods. The moneys he had expended for the success of the Vincennes expedition had left him impoverished and when he passed into the next world he possessed no more than was his when he was born. His estate could not muster even twenty dollars to pay for his funeral expenses. In his will he had provided a legacy of five hundred dollars with which to buy a bell to be hung in the courthouse of the county which had been named after him. That bell never rang until a hundred years after Liberty had first been proclaimed by the immortal bell in Philadelphia. It was not until 1876 that the heirs of Colonel Vigo could purchase the Vigo bell when the United States Supreme Court decreed that Vigo's heirs were entitled to the sum of $49,898.60 from the federal treasury, for moneys expended by him in behalf of the United States.

It should be noted at this point that at the time of the American Revolution and for nearly a century to follow, Italy was not a united nation but a land composed of kingdoms, duchies, provinces, and city-states under foreign rulers, with an occasional semi-independent republic. Thus the inhabitants of Italy were not always referred to as Italians. More often they were called Sardinians, Venetians, Neapolitans, and so on. And then it often happened they were listed as nationals of the power which at that time was holding sovereignty over their home state, thus being mistakenly referred to as Austrians, Spaniards, and Frenchmen. This, added to the inadequate record-keeping of the period, together with the loss of books and documents in battle action, probably explains why not more soldiers and sailors of early American history were recorded as Italians. However, it cannot be doubted that whenever Italians saw the chance to plunge into any enterprise dedicated to the objectives of the United States, they did so enthusiastically and with supreme vigor.

In 1804 Commodore Edward Preble, commanding the American Squadron in the Mediterranean, sailed into the harbor of Siracusa, Sicily. Departing a few days later, he carried an additional crew member, Salvatore Catalano, who had enlisted to serve as pilot on the *Intrepid*, a sixty-ton vessel commanded by Stephen Decatur, who had been selected to execute one of the most daring exploits ever recorded in the annals of naval warfare. For some years the Tripolitan pirates had been seizing vessels whose masters refused to pay tribute as they sailed through the Mediterranean. The United States which, with other countries, had been drawing money from its treasury for this "protection," finally rebelled against the odious practice (Millions for Defense but Not a Penny for Tribute!) and went to war against the freebooters. In that year, 1804, the American frigate, the *Philadelphia*, fired on pirate vessels, which scurried for cover into the fortified harbor of Tripoli.

The American commander, with an intrepidity which outdistanced his navigational caution, pursued the ocean villains into the harbor. Suddenly his vessel shuddered. It had struck a reef. The Tripolitans swarmed aboard, turned her heavy armament of forty guns into a floating fortress and from this vantage point dominated the Mediterranean. Consumed with wrath over this turn of events which had made of an American vessel a devastating force against Americans and civilization in general, Commodore Preble decided to attack the former United States warship. Preble envisioned a daring enterprise. He decided nothing less than sending a ship into the lion's mouth and destroying the lion before it could snap its jaws shut.

To head this seemingly quixotic enterprise he chose young Lieutenant Stephen Decatur. Decatur realized at once that what he needed more than anything else was a pilot familiar with the treacherous waters and who knew the language of the treacherous foe. In addition, he had to be a man who recognized no fear of night, fire, shot and shell. Salvatore Catalano, a native Sicilian, met all these formidable requirements and volunteered to pilot the *Intrepid*.

A gale was sweeping the Mediterranean when Catalano with superb seamanship took the *Intrepid*, without superfluous tacking, directly to the Tripolitan port and audaciously maneuvered the craft to a point within shouting distance of the *Philadelphia*. Cupping his hands he shouted in the Tripolitan language to the master of the floating fortress that he had lost his anchors in the storm. "May I," he bellowed across the raging white-crested surf, "tie up to your ship for safety—for the night?"

The Tripolitan captain grumblingly assented and ordered his men to throw a line into the sea for the benefit of the storm-tossed *Intrepid*. Decatur, in his turn, cast a line from his vessel into the waters and ordered a small boat lowered to fasten together the ends of the two lines. With a continuing cable now stretching from the *Intrepid* to the *Philadelphia*, the Americans, by lying on their backs, and pulling with the strength of titans, sent their small ship rapidly gliding toward the frigate. As the ships were about to touch, the *Philadelphia* captain realized what was happening and shouted the alarm: "*Americanos!*"

The Americans, however, were now leaping to the decks of the *Philadelphia*, eighty-four of them, including Catalano, led by Decatur, swinging a cutlass with the others. The daring raiders slew twenty of the bewildered Tripolitan crew as they confusedly leaped from their bunks to battle. Overcoming all resistance, Decatur's men raced through the moored vessel, placing in strategic spots their explosives and inflammables. They threw torches at the fuses and as the

Tripolitan crew rallied to consolidate their counter-attack, the Americans fled to the bulwarks, vaulted to the *Intrepid*, cutting the lines and casting loose the grapnels just as the *Philadelphia* burst into a sheet of flame. Catalano seized the helm again and steered the *Intrepid* away from her staggering adversary, plowing through the blazing waters and away from the shore batteries which now went into action, churning the Mediterranean into a boiling cauldron.*

Lord Nelson, the world-famous naval hero, declared, upon hearing of this exploit, that it was the "most bold and daring act of the age." It does not require any imagination or Italianophile to state that this daring act could not have been successfully concluded without the intrepidity and skill of Salvatore Catalano. Decatur stated in his report to Commodore Preble:

> It would be unjust in me, were I to pass over the important services rendered by Mr. Salvatore Catalano, the pilot, on whose good conduct the success of the enterprise in the greatest degree depended.

Catalano later emigrated to the United States and served as a sailing master in the United States Navy until his death in 1846. His services included piloting on the historic "Old Ironsides," the USS *Constitution*.

* *Stephen Decatur*, by Cyrus Townsend Brady, Boston, Small, Maynard & Co., 1900. *The Romantic Decatur*, by Charles Lee Lewis, Philadelphia, University of Pennsylvania Press, 1937.

3 THE HERO OF TWO CONTINENTS

Italians have fought for the United States in every war in which she has pitted her might, honor, and destiny against those who would destroy her. Italian fighters for American freedom have been lowered into graves in nearly every one of the states, but those graves were not always marked nor "long remembered." Joseph Lametti landed in America from Modena, Italy, and enlisted in the New York State Militia. He fought in the War of 1812 and when he died in 1848 he was buried in the churchyard of St. Patrick's Old Cathedral in New York. It was not until 1930, one hundred and sixteen years after the termination of that second conflict with England, that the Society of the War of 1812 recognized by a suitable marker on Lametti's grave that he had offered his life in defense of his adopted country.

Of the many Italians who had migrated into the South in the early days of America, it is not unreasonable to suppose that some of them enrolled under the flag of Sam Houston as he led the fighting Texans to independence. One Propero Bernardi, who was enlisted as a soldier in Houston's army, received a thousand acres of land after his discharge in 1837. José Antonio Navarro, whose ancestors hailed from Corsica, was a delegate to the Texas Convention of 1836 and signed both the Texas Declaration of Independence and its first constitution. Another Italian, Joseph Avezzana, even served under the Mexican flag in its war for independence from Spain.

Giovanni Schiavo records the names of Italians who served with the American forces in the Mexican War of 1848–50. He lists a Navy Lieutenant Louis C. Sartori who later advanced to the rank of commodore; Midshipman Bancroft Gherardi who eventually achieved an admiral's epaulettes; William Trovillo; Lieutenant Charles Fiesca and Lieutenant Colonel Henry Forno in Louisiana regiments; Navy Surgeon N. C. Barrabino; Lieutenant Colonel Christian C. Nave in an Indiana contingent and Lieutenant John Phinizy in a Georgian regiment of volunteers.

What part did Italians play in the Civil War? Let us first look ahead fourscore years to World War II. In the early days of that global conflict, the Italian soldiers fighting for Mussolini were regarded generally as lacking in military spirit. John Gunther in his book D Day, which was a diary of his war experiences, wrote under date of July 23, 1943:

Lentini, Sicily . . . The enemy paratroops are Italian, it seems, so they cannot be serious.

Gunther's observation was not an unjust one. The Italian soldier had no heart in Mussolini's war. A story that went the rounds in those days had to do with a conversation between two Neapolitan soldiers in a foxhole. One said to the other: "I think we're going to lose this war." The other lamented: "Yes, I know, but when?"

There was more realism than humor in this remark because the men knew that even if they won with Hitler they would still lose as serfs under a Swastika despotism. Moreover, since practically every family in Italy had some near or distant relative in America, it was sheer lunacy to assume that the Italian soldier could willingly fight against the United States, a country which was, if not a second motherland, certainly a second childrenland. Thus, the Italian soldier in the short inglorious conflict between the Duce's dictatorship and American democracy wrestled with one problem, namely how to surrender—fast. I talked to many Italian prisoners who joyously spoke of their surrender to the Americans as a moral triumph.

The history of the Italian soldier going back to Caesar's days has been one of outstanding fortitude and courage. In World War I the victory of the Italians on the Piave destroyed the Austrian army completely, knocked her out of the war and thus left the German army, minus her redoubtable ally, a crippled foe on the western front.* General von Hindenburg said: "Italy's victory at the Piave won the war for France and England, whom we had on the run." Italy's sacrifice in blood to the Allied cause was a staggering one. Out of a population of thirty-four million, she mobilized five million soldiers, of whom 500,000 left their lives on the battlefield, 700,000 were permanently disabled, one million and a half were wounded.

Thus, when in World War II Italy finally extricated herself from the dictatorial vise of Benito Mussolini, she immediately allied herself with England, France, and the United States. The hitherto reluctant soldier of the African and Sicilian campaigns at once transformed into the restless and resistless warrior of the Apennines, fighting for freedom and liberation of his own land. During my service as Fifth Army liaison officer to the Legnano Division of the Italian Army under General Umberto Utili, many Italian officers, assuming I knew the plans of the Allied High Command, entreated me to persuade General Utili to let them lead the Legnano's attack so that their units could meet the enemy in head-on clash at the earliest possible moment. In this, they were personifying the spirit of the three most famous soldiers in military history, Julius Caesar, Marc Antony, and Napoleon Bonaparte—all Italian born. But there was one even greater, a soldier whose sword outshone those wielded by all the others because he unsheathed it not for imperial power, lands, riches, or personal aggrandizement. He fought for the liberty of man—Giuseppe Garibaldi.

In the first year of the Civil War, with the North smarting under the disaster of Bull Run, and Lincoln having to contend with the vacillating McClelland and other inexperienced generals, the great Civil War president offered Garibaldi a major-generalship and a Union army. Only months before, Garibaldi had achieved one of the most spectacular triumphs in the history of arms. With only a thousand men at his command, he sailed from Genoa in two ancient and battered ships to battle the Bourbon king of the Neapolitan kingdom (embracing Sicily and lower Italy) heading 130,000 superbly battle-equipped troops.

In red shirts, with bandana handkerchiefs about their necks and ponchos on their backs, the battle garb Garibaldi had evolved in

* *Italy's Part in the World War*, by Edgar Erskine Hume, *Atlantica*, March–April 1935.

South America, the men stormed ashore at Marsala, Sicily, on May 11, 1860, and routed the Bourbon troops at Calatafami, defeated them at Palermo, overwhelmed them at Messina, crushed them at Reggio, and finally decimated the remnants of the enemy, 40,000 strong, on the Volturno. The liberation of Italy, which had been merely a dream for centuries, was now acquiring flesh-and-blood reality.

Garibaldi, who was appropriately born on the Fourth of July, felt that tyranny, no matter where inflicted, was a personal affront to him, and that injustice, no matter upon whom visited, should be fought by the whole world. Ever since the dismemberment of the Holy Roman Empire, Italy had been a treasure house for the adventurers and monarchs of Europe to raid at their fancy. Cut apart by sword and bayonet, the parcels were taken by, or allotted to, varying powers depending on the military strength or diplomatic conniving of the conquerors.

In the early 1800s the revolutionary society, known as the Carbonari, sprang into being, its members pledged to wrest political independence from Bourbon, Habsburg and papal secular rule, which held four-fifths of Italy under foreign domination. Joining the Carbonari, the youthful Garibaldi dreamed of a day when Italy would be united and its capital grace the banks of the river where it had once gleamed triumphantly as the capital of the world. This dream gripped him as if in a trance and he murmured to himself: "Rome or Death."

He plotted with Giuseppe Mazzini, arch disciple of republicanism, to overthrow the Sardinian government, whose domain embraced Piedmont and Sardinia, but before the conspirators could act, the plot was discovered and Garibaldi fled to Marseille. Here newspaper headlines proclaimed that he had been court-martialed and sentenced to death.

Learning that tyranny was flying its black flag in Brazil he sailed for South America, where he joined the forces of the rebelling state of Rio Grande do Sul. Commanding a small vessel which he christened the *Mazzini*, he attacked an enemy ship four times the size of his own, and, by the fury of his onslaught, compelled the Brazilian master to strike his colors. He offered his prisoners one of three choices: to be held as prisoners, sent ashore, or to join up with Garibaldi. Unanimously they chose to fight with Garibaldi.

On land he recruited and trained a troop of horse marines, spreading terror among the imperialist forces. After a series of spectacular victories he passed into the service of Uruguay, which had revolted against Argentina. He organized the Italian Legion and smashed the enemy with sudden attacks, rapid mobility, and audacious charges, achieving Uruguay's independence. A grateful nation crowned him "The Hero of Montevideo." He now returned to Italy to battle again for the freedom of his homeland. Raising a volunteer army of three thousand he marched against the occupying Austrians.

In Rome the populace revolted and proclaimed a republic. Garibaldi leaped to its defense against the forces of France, Austria, Spain, and the Bourbon Kingdom of Naples which had joined together to destroy the republic. Garibaldi faced the investing columns at San Pancrazio, Palestrini, and Velletri and defeated them. But his forces being too small to cope with the attacking armies enveloping Rome from all sides, he assembled them in Saint Peter's Square. It was July 4, his birthday. Lifting his voice within the flanking gigantic colonnade, he spoke words that still tingle the spine:

> "Romans and Countrymen! Whoever wishes to carry on the struggle against the enemy, let him come with me. I can offer him neither money, nor lodging, nor food. I can only offer him, instead, hunger, thirst, forced marches, battles and even death. All who have the name of Italy, not only on their lips, but in their hearts also . . . let them follow me!"

Four thousand followed. But in the wake of those four thousand, sixty-five thousand of the enemy followed. Hotly they pursued him up the peninsula in what became known as the greatest manhunt in history, seeking the red-shirted general—dead or alive. Reaching the northern frontier Garibaldi could count at his side only a corporal's guard, the others having been dispersed, killed, or captured. His devoted wife, Anita, whom he had won on the pampas of South America, and who had fought at his side in all his battles, had accompanied him in the flight, but, overcome by fatigue, she fell mortally ill and expired in her grieving husband's arms. After lowering her into a hastily dug grave and noting the spot so that he could return to recover the body for burial in a place where he might also one day be buried, he made his way to the sea and took secret passage to Tunis, then to Gibraltar, then to England. Finally he sailed for America.

By this time the liberty-loving world rang with praise for liberty's famous fighter. The New York *Tribune* declared on July 30, 1850:

The ship *Waterloo* arrived here from Liverpool this morning bringing the world-renowned Garibaldi, the hero of Montevideo and the defender of Rome. He will be welcome by those who know him as becomes his chivalrous character and his services in behalf of liberty.

Immediately upon arrival he took out first citizenship papers to become a fully naturalized American. Then, like any other Italian immigrant, he started to work at once, obtaining employment in a Staten Island candle factory owned by Antonio Neucci, the celebrated inventor. Later he returned to seafaring, captaining ships which took him to many European ports; but with a price still on his head, he could not land on the soil of his beloved Italy.

In 1859, regardless of threat, he disembarked in Piedmont where King Victor Emmanuel II, now committed to the unification of Italy, placed Garibaldi in command of the Alpine Infantry, with which the red-shirted warrior charged the Austrians, scattering them like sheep before him, liberating the Alpine territory as far north as the frontier of Tirol, and thus incorporating all of Lombardy into the Sardinian kingdom.

Then followed his spectacular invasion of Sicily and Naples with his Thousand Red Shirts. His thrilling and dramatic triumphs elevated him to the pinnacle of frenzied hero-worship, and, could his head have been turned by royal glory, the people would have clapped a crown upon it. However, emulating the Roman general Cincinnatus, he retired to agricultural pursuits on the little island of Caprera in the Mediterranean, which became his permanent home. He called upon the Italian people to support King Victor Emmanuel II.

While unification had now become a reality, Venice and Rome were still under foreign rule. Tormented by this divisive situation Garibaldi quitted Caprera, descended into Sicily, recruited an army and marched on the Eternal City, but now King Victor Emmanuel, who had commitments with France, which had made of the papal states a French protectorate, opposed the man who had assured him a unified realm. He engaged Garibaldi in battle at Aspromonte and the liberator fell wounded.

Before Garibaldi marched on Rome, however, Abraham Lincoln offered him a major general's commission. The Civil War president had always displayed a lively interest in Italian affairs,* and he had responded with animated appreciation to the little republic of San Marino in northern Italy which in 1861 had conferred on him honorary citizenship in that state:

> Although your dominion is small, your state is nevertheless one of the most honored in all history. It has by its experience demonstrated the truth, so full of encouragement to the friends of humanity, that government founded on republican principles is capable of being so administered as to be secure and enduring.
>
> You have kindly adverted to the trial through which this republic is now passing. It is one of deep import. It involves the question whether a representative republic, extended and aggrandized so much as to be safe against foreign enemies can save itself from the dangers of domestic faction. I have faith in a good result.†

In pursuance of that faith he instructed Secretary of State William H. Seward to communicate with Garibaldi. Seward quickly directed our minister at Antwerp, Belgium, Henry S. Sanford:

> I wish you to proceed at once and enter into communication with the distinguished soldier of Freedom. Say to him that this government believes his services in the present contest for unity and liberty of the American People, would be exceedingly useful, and that therefore, they are earnestly desired and invited. Tell him that this government believes he will, if possible, accept this call, because it is too certain that the fall of the American Union, if indeed it were possible, would be a disastrous blow to the cause of Human Freedom, equally here, in Europe, and throughout the world. Tell him that he will receive a Major-General's commission in the Army of the United States, with its appointments, with the hearty welcome of the American people. Tell him that we have abundant resources, and numbers unlimited at our command, and a nation resolved to remain united and free. General Garibaldi will recognize in me, not

---

* On Lincoln's trip to Gettysburg to make his now immortal address, the Italian ambassador accompanied him on the train.
† Letter discovered by Representative Ernest R. Ackerman of New Jersey in archives of San Marino, photostatic copy of which was presented to President Hoover. (United Press)

merely an organ of the government, but an old and sincere personal friend.*

Sanford at once dispatched a messenger to Caprera with a letter asking Garibaldi if he would be disposed, "if not occupied in the defense of your own country," "to take part in the contest for preserving the Unity and Liberty of the American people." Garibaldi replied:

I should be very happy to be able to serve a country for which I have so much affection and of which I am an adoptive citizen, and if I do not reply affirmatively and immediately to the honorable proposition which your government through your agency has made to me, it is because I do not feel myself entirely free, because of my duties toward Italy.

Although Garibaldi's first devotion was to Italy he let it be known that he would gladly fight for the Northern forces in liberating the Negro slaves. The New York *Tribune* cheered:

Our Washington correspondent states positively that Garibaldi has offered his services to the national government, that the offer was promptly accepted, and the rank of Major-General tendered. Should the liberator of Italy revisit this country to take the field for freedom, he would be greeted with an enthusiasm beyond the power of words to express.

But the Italian people were still clamoring for the liberation of Rome. In Naples the people paraded and cried: "On to Rome and Garibaldi!" The liberal press of Italy, while applauding Garibaldi's declaration to fight in America, pleaded with him to remain in Italy until one flag alone floated over the peninsula. Petitions by the thousands reached Garibaldi, entreating him:

Do not leave for America. The people have faith in you. Our national unity has not yet been completed. You have laid its most solid foundation; you alone are able to complete the work!

On September 10, 1861, Garibaldi wrote the American consul at Antwerp:

I am sorry to be obliged to say that I cannot go at present to the United States. I have no doubt of the triumph of the cause of the Union; but if the war should by evil chance continue in your country,

* *Century Magazine*, Vol. LXXV, New Series: Vol. LIII, November 1907.

I will overcome all the obstacles which hold me back, and will hasten to come to the defense of that people which is so dear to me.

In the summer of 1862, after Garibaldi's ill-fated march on Rome, the American consul in Vienna wrote, urging him to offer his valorous arm in the struggle "which we are carrying on for the liberty and unity of our great republic." Garibaldi replied that as soon as his wounds healed "the favorable opportunity will have arrived in which I shall be able to satisfy my desire to serve the great American Republic, of which I am a citizen, and which today combats for universal liberty."

Garibaldi's wounds proved more serious than had at first been supposed. Three months passed before the bullet in his foot could be extracted. On October 15, 1862, he wrote the American consul stating that as soon as he recovered he would go to America and take with him "all the democrats of Europe to join us in fighting this holy battle."

By now, however, the matter had evolved into the competence of Secretary of War Stanton, who made no recommendation. Thus passed—by a combination of almost heart-breaking circumstances— an opportunity that might have placed in the affections of the American people an Italian crusader for liberty to keep company with the French hero Lafayette.

In 1870 when Prussia invaded France, Garibaldi beheld tyranny assaulting freedom, and offered his sword to Napoleon III, who gave him an army with which he defeated the Prussians at Châtillon, Autun, and Dijon. As an expression of gratitude the French elected him to their Chamber of Deputies where the great Victor Hugo, also a member, eulogized him on March 8, 1871:

"None of the powers of Europe came to our aid, and this man intervened, a power in himself. . . . His sword had already rescued a whole people (Italy) and it might have saved another. . . . I do not wish to wound any member of this Assembly, but I would say that he is the only one of the generals fighting for France who was not beaten."*

* *Victor Hugo*, by Matthew Josephson, Doubleday, Doran & Co., New York, 1942, p. 475.

In 1874 Garibaldi was elected deputy to the Italian Chamber of Deputies in Rome, the city that had been etched in his heart with the cry of his youth: "Rome or Death!"

He died in 1882, mourned by the freedom-loving world, his fighting life having spanned a longer period than that of any other soldier. The Encyclopaedia Britannica refers to him as "one of the greatest masters of revolutionary war." Elbert Hubbard in his charming short biography of Giuseppe Garibaldi,* said:

> The insurance company that might have insured his life when he was twenty would have made money on the transaction regardless of rate. Yet he was the hero of sixty-seven battles on land and sea, and engaged in more than two hundred personal encounters, where rifles, pistols, stilettos, swords or cudgels played their part. Behold the irony of Fate!

> No man was ever more detested, hated, feared,—no man was ever better loved. That he was a sternly honest, sincere man, singularly pure in motive and abstemious in habit, even his bitterest enemies do not dispute. . . . He refused bribes, declined honors, put aside titles, and died as penniless as he was born, and as he had lived. His life was consecrated to one thing—Liberty.

Although fate decreed that Garibaldi was not to command the army Lincoln offered him, many of his soldiers crossed the ocean and volunteered for service in the Union cause. The 39th New York Infantry adopted the name of the Garibaldi Guard and carried into battle, next to the Stars and Stripes, a flag that had waved at the head of Garibaldi's columns when they fought the four powers that had destroyed the Roman Republic. Mazzini's shibboleth in large letters fluttered on its folds: GOD AND THE PEOPLE!

Wearing plumed hats, blue trousers with red stripes and white leggings, the most colorful uniform in the Northern Army, the Garibaldi Guard smartly paraded before President Lincoln on July 4, 1861, receiving his admiring approval. Its list of officers included Colonel Alexander Repetti, Lieutenant Colonel L. W. Tinelli, Commissary W. P. Molo, Captain Cesare Osnaghi, Lieutenants Giovanni Coloni, Ignacio Allegretti, Ferdinando Maggi, Venuti, and Salviratti.

The Garibaldi Guard fought valiantly throughout the war from

* In *Little Journeys to the Homes of the Great*, edited by Fred Bann, William H. Wise & Co., New York, 1928.

Bull Run to Appomattox. The Italian newspaper *L'Eco D'Italia*, published in New York, reported how the Guard, fighting heroically at the Battle of Cross Keys, Shenandoah, Pennsylvania, on June 29, 1862, suffered severe casualties. On the Gettysburg battlefield at Cemetery Ridge one can see today a monument to the bold Garibaldi Guard which sustained heavy losses in repulsing Confederate charges.

When their Commander-in-Chief Abraham Lincoln fell under an assassin's bullet, Lieutenant Ferdinando Maggi of the Garibaldi Guard organized a large contingent of mourners in the sorrowful funeral procession in Washington. Wearing white gloves and black mourning sleeves, with a small picture of the martyred president on their breasts, the Guard, under fluttering American and Italian flags, marched down Pennsylvania Avenue.

Italians distinguished themselves in various military exploits in the Civil War. At least one hundred Italian officers commanded New York troops. One of them, Giovanni D. Nesi, won his second lieutenant bars when only eighteen and was later killed in action. The highest military award of the nation, the Congressional Medal of Honor, was won by three Italians. Joseph E. Sova, a saddler in the 8th Cavalry, received it for having risked his life in capturing the Confederate flag in the Appomattox campaign in Virginia. Orlando E. Caruana of the 51st Infantry was so cited because he

> brought off the wounded Color-sergeant and the colors under a heavy fire of the enemy at the battle of Newburn, N. C., and volunteered, being one of a party of four, to determine the position of the enemy, in which action his three comrades were killed, at the battle of South Mountain, Maryland.

The third recipient, Colonel Luigi Palma di Cesnola, galloped with clanking sword at General Sheridan's side in the tumultuous Shenandoah campaign. His citation told how di Cesnola "seeing his regiment fall back, rallied his men and accompanied them in a second charge at their head until he was desperately wounded and taken prisoner." Lincoln later breveted him a brigadier general.

Other Italians achieved general's stars: Enrico Fardella, Eduardo Ferrero, and Frances B. Spinola. Fardella was promoted from colonel in the 85th New York Infantry Regiment to brigadier general for distinguished services at Plymouth, North Carolina. General Ferrero fought in the battles of Bull Run, Antietam, South Mountain, and Fredericksburg. Spinola, who was a state senator in New York when the war began, resigned his office to recruit four regiments of soldiers which he commanded in the field. Leading a bayonet charge at the battle of Wapping Heights he was twice wounded.

In the lists of Navy personnel there appear the names of numerous Italians who participated in naval engagements against Confederate men-of-war. One Italian, Lieutenant Commander Bancroft Gherardi, transmitted orders as his commander, the celebrated Admiral Farragut, lashed to the mast of his ship, steamed into the fiery battle of Mobile Bay, crying out: "Damn the torpedoes, full speed ahead!" Gherardi later commanded several ships in the west Gulf blockade and still later became chief of the North Atlantic Squadron. After the war he was promoted to the rank of rear admiral.

The Indian Wars, which kept the United States Cavalry galloping between the Civil War and the Spanish-American War, found many Italians in the saddle attired in the picturesque blue uniform with yellow stripes, sombrero and ascot, made familiar to all America through motion pictures and television westerns. One Italian trumpeter, John Martini, even managed to get himself into the immortally famous 7th Cavalry Regiment of George Armstrong Custer. Providentially he missed the all-engulfing massacre at the Little Big Horn because General Custer committed him to a mission just before the breaking of the deadly storm of Cheyennes, Pawnees, and Sioux.

The regimental rosters of the Spanish-American War Expeditionary Forces reveal many Italian names. In the Cuban Pacification Expedition which followed the Spanish-American War, Pasquale Musmanno served in the 11th Cavalry. I know him well. He is my brother.

4 CIVILIAN LIFE IN EARLY AMERICA

The Italians who fought for America on land and sea demonstrated a devotion that was ardent, but no more zealous than that of those who followed civilian pursuits in this land of their choice. The facts wholly refute the prevailing notion of the latter nineteenth century, and the early twentieth, that Italians in America performed only menial work. In point of reality there was scarcely a field of activity —industrial, architectural, artistic, and professional—in which Italians were not intensely active from the very beginning. Even in the colonial days and the first years of the republic, Italian doctors, merchants, teachers, architects, and engineers were exceedingly diligent in serving the American public.

The founders of our country held Italy and Italians in high esteem, Thomas Jefferson, Benjamin Franklin, and others among them, reading and speaking the Italian language. George Washington's eyes rested upon many a canvas of Italian panoramas gracing the walls of his beloved Mount Vernon. In 1794 when he was seeking an outstanding technician to build the military fortifications at Baltimore, Alexandria, and Norfolk, he selected for this operation of magnitude Major J. J. U. Rivard, an Italian Swiss engineer.

The Italians were everywhere recognized as skilled craftsmen. Governor Berkeley of Virginia, wrote in 1671:

Of late we have begun to make silk and so many mulberry trees are planted, that if we had skillful men from Naples or Sicily to teach us the art of making it, in less than an age, we should make as much silk in a year as England did yearly expend three-score years since.

Italians from Piedmont settled in Georgia and planted mulberry groves, launching the silk industry in that region. In 1657 some three hundred Piedmontese workers settled in Delaware.*

In 1635 Peter Caesar Alberti landed in New Amsterdam and started a tobacco plantation. In 1622 Italian glassworkers made their appearance in Virginia. Paolo Busti, who arrived in America from Milan in 1800, took up, in Pennsylvania and New York, the active management of the Holland Land Company owning some five million acres, which vast realm, through Busti's skillful planning and developing, evolved into American villages, towns, and cities.

Large numbers of Italians arriving on the eastern seaboard prior to 1850 rode stage coaches and plodded across deserts with thousands of native-born easterners, to follow the mirage of riches hovering over the highly romanticized gold fields of California. Most of them failed to find in the ground the yellow dust they eagerly sought, but they discovered that by planting in that same soil the seeds of grapes, they could pluck from the resulting vines purple nuggets which crushed easily into liquid gold. And the great wine industry of California was born.

There was scarcely a trade, calling, art, service, or profession in America, there was barely a venture on the continent in which the Italians did not eagerly participate even before the inundation from southern Europe which began in the second half of the 1800s. Although here in limited numbers, the Italians formed an integral part of the nation. They were essential pieces in the great mosaic, without which the image of America would have been incomplete, if not distorted; they formed part of the warp and woof of the fabric of social, cultural, scientific, and industrial America. All this makes rather inexplicable the superior attitude manifested by certain segments of the native population toward the Italians of a later period.

I was born into that later doleful era, and I was to experience many heartaches in witnessing discrimination in this land dedicated to nondiscrimination and of which Philip Mazzei had written in 1773:

* *The Italians Among Us*, by Albert Q. Maisel, *Reader's Digest*, January 1955.

Tutti gli uomini sentono per natura egualmente liberi e indipendenti. Quest' eguaglianza è necessaria per costituire un governo libero. Bisogna che ognuno sia uguale all'altro nel diritto naturale. La distinzione dei ranghi n'è sempre stata come sempre ne sarà un efficace ostacolo. . . .

The translation:

All people are by nature born equally free and independent. This equality is necessary in order to constitute a free government. It is necessary that each person be equal to every other person in natural law. The distinction of classes has always been and will always be an obstacle. . . .

Yet, when I became a lawyer and represented Italians in court, I had to, at times, in order to protect my clients, ask jurors on their *voir dire* the wholly absurd but unfortunately necessary question: "Do you have any prejudice against Italians?" And, sad to relate, there were a few who replied in the affirmative!

There abided no such prejudice or sense of discrimination in the early settlers who built the durable foundations of this republic. The very Capitol of the United States, unquestionably the most eye-entrancing capitol in the world, achieved in no small measure its architectural and artistic grandeur because of Italian influences and Italian artists. Its great shining dome, hanging like a huge bell in the sky, follows the lines of the dome designed by Michelangelo for St. Peter's Church in Rome. Great columns in the graceful edifice, statues, paintings, and frescoes beyond the counting, are the handiwork of gifted artists from Italy, among whom the early ones came to America at the bidding of Thomas Jefferson, who insisted that the mother house of this new nation should be a house of beauty as well as of democracy. Senator John O. Pastore of Rhode Island, in a speech delivered in Cleveland in August 1963, said:

"Where our Senate Building now stands, there stood, a century and a half ago, the cabins of the Italian sculptors and artists who were helping to create our Capitol Building, whose overwhelming beauty is the admiration of the world."

One of those sculptors, Giuseppe Franzoni, executed for the House of Representatives a statue of Liberty and various figures representing agriculture, art, science, and commerce. His American eagle, occupy-

Columbus leaving Palos

Here we see Columbus not as a steel engraving, but as a human being, accomplished mariner and mystic dreamer, all combined into the great navigator whose faith resulted in the discovery of America. The model chosen by the artist Joaquín Sorolla y Bastida was the Duke of Veragua, a descendant of the famous Admiral.

COURTESY, THE MARINERS MUSEUM, NEWPORT NEWS, VA.

"While stands the Colosseum, Rome shall stand;
When falls the Colosseum, Rome shall fall;
And when Rome falls—the world."
Byron—*Childe Harold*

Cathedral of Milan

Its intricate and stupendous marble beauty earned for it the description "Frozen Music."

Venice

Festa on the Grand Canal at the
famous Rialto Bridge.
COURTESY, CULVER PICTURES.

Leaning Tower of Pisa

Should it ever fall, its marble confetti will sprinkle regret throughout the artistic world.

Philip Mazzei, friend of Thomas Jefferson. President Kennedy said: "The great doctrine, 'All Men are Created Equal,' incorporated in the Declaration of Independence, was paraphrased from writings of Philip Mazzei." COURTESY, JOHN HOPKINS PRESS.

William Paca, signer of the Declaration of Independence, Governor and Chief Justice of Maryland.
FROM THE COLLECTIONS OF THE MARYLAND HISTORICAL SOCIETY.

ing twenty-five feet on the frieze of the Hall, drew from Benjamin H. Latrobe, the architect of the Capitol, the stirring praise:

"I do not feel that there has been carved in stone or in any other medium an eagle of such noble proportions and so well defining an American eagle as this work of Giuseppe Franzoni."

Tragically, Franzoni's magnificent creations, except the "cornstalk columns," disappeared in the British-ignited flames that destroyed the Capitol in 1814. Another sculptor, Giovanni Andrei, who had arrived with Franzoni, was sent to Italy by the American government to procure the carving of the Corinthian capitals, now surmounting the columns of Conglomerate marble in the Statuary Hall, formerly, until 1857, the Hall of the House of Representatives.

In 1816 two other Italian artists arrived, Carlo Franzoni, younger brother of Giuseppe, and Francesco Iardella. No visitor today to Statuary Hall can fail to be struck by the captivating elegance of that sculptural magnificence known as the Car of History, the work of Carlo Franzoni. A female figure (Muse Clio), with a tablet in her hand records the passing events as she rides in a winged chariot, one wheel of which forms the dial of a clock. It can well be imagined that many a congressman in the early days of the Republic, especially in periods of crisis, dramatically dwelt on the passing of time by pointing to the Franzoni clock (as it was called) and the need for action, of which future generations would be proud, as they read of that action recorded by History.

Francesco Iardella executed the tobacco capitals in the small rotunda just north of the main rotunda of the Capitol. Another Italian artist, Pietro Bonanni, decorated the ceiling of the House Chamber, now Statuary Hall, taking for his model the dome of the Pantheon in Rome. The craftsmanship that went into this work was so dexterous that the coffers appeared three-dimensional.

Up until 1958, when it was temporarily removed because of the extension of the East Front of the Capitol, the first work of art that caught the eye of the tourist as he mounted the vast and majestic stone steps leading to the Rotunda was the free-standing "Discovery Group" (Columbus holding a globe aloft with a female figure at his side) by Luigi Persico, who carved it in Italy. Persico also sculpted the statues of "War" and "Peace" in the Central Portico, East Front.

His sculptural study, "America, Justice and Hope," dominates the pediment over the Rotunda east entrance. It merits special attention because Persico executed it from a design traced by President John Quincy Adams.

The artist whose work covers more space in the Capitol and is more intimately identified with its artistic sublimity than that of any other was Constantino Brumidi, who has been appropriately termed "the Michelangelo of the United States Capitol." He landed in New York on September 18, 1852, coming directly from his frescoes in the Vatican. If, by some unimaginable cataclysm, all his paintings in the Capitol were to disappear, the Capitol would, to a considerable extent, be artistically impoverished. His breathtaking frescoes in the circular ceiling of the dome 180 feet above the Rotunda floor cover 4664 square feet of concave surface. In order to impart to the figures lifelike dimensions to those looking up from below, Brumidi had to paint them two to three times their natural size. He worked from a suspended cage whose motive power he supplied and whose directions he guided into the dizzying heights by a complicated system of ropes. For months he worked lying on his back.

In addition to his stupendous frescoes, which include six large patriotic and allegorical groups, Brumidi peopled the Capitol with portraits of America's giants of democracy. In corridors, in the President's Room, committee rooms, and reception rooms, one will find Benjamin Franklin, Thomas Jefferson, John Hancock, Henry Clay, Andrew Jackson, Horatio Gates, Alexander Hamilton, Roger Sherman, Robert Morris—all from the miraculous brush wielded by Constantino Brumidi. In his historical scenes one experiences the drama of the landing of Columbus, the debarkation of the Pilgrims, Washington at Valley Forge, the Storming of Stony Point, the Boston Massacre. In one corner of his vast fresco, Washington at Yorktown, which is in the House of Representatives Dining Room, the artist appended proudly the inscription: "C. Brumidi, Artist, Citizen of the U.S."

Brumidi's genius was as uncontained as the angels, cherubim, and birds which flew from his brush and ornamented ceilings, walls, corners, and stairways in the vast edifice of the nation's citadel of democracy. A passageway in the Senate Wing is known as the "Brumidi Corridor." He performed his wizardry during the administrations of six presidents: Franklin Pierce, James Buchanan, Abraham Lincoln,

Andrew Johnson, U. S. Grant and Rutherford B. Hayes—most of the time at eight dollars a day. It was Senator Jefferson Davis, later president of the Southern Confederacy, who had the pay increased to ten dollars a day. In the latter periods of Brumidi's artistic dedication, he was paid separately for each work performed, but no amount of money could adequately match the artistic supremacy he brought to the Capitol. Monetary remuneration was never his goal. He explained: "My one ambition and my daily prayer is that I may live long enough to make beautiful the Capitol of the one Country in the World in which there is liberty."

At seventy-two years of age, Brumidi began the tremendous work of painting in basso relievo the frieze of the Rotunda, a belt 9 feet wide circling the Rotunda 58 feet above the floor, the circumference being 300 feet. Although this work is wall-flat fresco, it has sculptured sharpness. Brumidi's designs called for a dramatic panorama of American history. While re-creating the touching scene of William Penn making peace with the Indians, an accident befell him. The support on which he was standing slipped from beneath his feet and he fell, but, seizing a rung of a ladder he held on, suspended in mid-air. The hand that had tightly grasped the brush that had brought back to life in color and form heroes of the past and had reproduced scenes to inspire present and future generations, clung tenaciously to the precarious anchorage long enough for workmen to come to his rescue and pull him back to safety. The fearful damage, however, had been done. The shock of the fall and the exhaustion resulting from a quarter century's toil had taken their toll. He died within five months.

On February 23, 1880, four days after his death, Senator Voorhees of Indiana paid beautiful tribute to him on the floor of the Senate:

"Mr. Brumidi was engaged at the time of his death on what he regarded as the greatest work of his life. He was unfolding with the magic of genius in the Rotunda of the Capitol the scroll of American history, from the Landing of Columbus to the present day. He earnestly desired to live long enough to complete this vast conception. . . . At no distant day some memorial will be erected in some appropriate place in this Capitol to his memory. He who beautifies the pathway of life, who creates images of loveliness for the human eye to rest upon is a benefactor of the human race. He will be crowned by the gratitude of his own and of succeeding generations.

In the older countries of Europe where the profession of art has a higher rank than here, Brumidi would have had a public funeral and his remains would have been deposited in ground set apart for persons of distinction. In England he would have had a place and a tablet in Westminster Abbey.

It matters little, however, whether we or those who come after us do anything to perpetuate his memory. The walls of this Capitol will hold his fame fresh and ever increasing as long as they themselves shall stand."

After this magnificently eloquent and merited tribute, Brumidi was put in the ground and forgotten. For seventy years his body lay in the melancholy shadows of indifference and neglect. It was not until 1950, when Mrs. Myrtle Cheney Murdock, wife of an Arizona congressman, located, after considerable search, Brumidi's untended grave in the Glenwood Cemetery in Washington, that interest on Capitol Hill was rekindled in the Italian immigrant who had given without reserve of his genius and energies to this beloved land of his choice. The following year Congressman Murdock introduced a bill, calling for the modest appropriation of two hundred dollars to buy a marker for the artist's grave. Congress doubled the appropriation and provided a fund for taking perpetual care of the last resting place of Constantino Brumidi, who, like the statue of Freedom which surmounts the dome of the Capitol, was modeled in Italy, and who shall live forever more in the very heart of the most beautiful capitol in the world.

After Brumidi's death, the decorating of the frieze was continued by Filippo Costaggini, painting from Brumidi's designs. When he died in 1904, there was a thirty-foot gap still left which was painted by the distinguished New York artist Allyn Cox.

Among the other Italian artists who toiled to give to the American Capitol the classic adornment which places it in the class of a perpetually enduring artistic monument were Antonio Capellano, sculptor: bust of Washington, East Central Portico, bas relief, "Preservation of Captain John Smith," above Western entrance Rotunda; Peter Cardelli, sculptor: ornaments and capitals in restoration following 1814 fire; Enrico Causici, sculptor: "Liberty and Eagle," plaster statue above frieze, Statuary Hall, bas reliefs, "Daniel Boone and

Indians," "Landing of Pilgrims," above South Door Rotunda; Gaetano Cecere, sculptor: relief portraits above remodeled House Chamber Gallery doors; Vittorio Ciani, sculptor: bust of George Clinton, Senate Chamber; Giuseppe Fagnani, painter: portrait of Henry Clay, Speaker's Lobby; W. Iardella, sculptor: carved medallions in Rotunda; Arthur Lorenzani, carver: three relief portraits over doors of remodeled House Chamber Gallery; Giuseppe Martegani, sculptor: bust of Garibaldi, lobby of Old Law Library entrance, first floor, Senate Wing; Louis Milione, carver: design representing "Patriotism," East doorway, Senate Chamber remodeled; Edward M. Ratti, carver: eight relief portraits over Gallery doors, remodeled House Chamber; Antonio Salviati: mosaic portraits, Garfield and Lincoln, Senate Wing, Gallery floor; Gaetano Trentanove, sculptor: statue of James Marquette, Wisconsin, for Statuary Hall in House Connection; Giuseppe Valaperti, sculptor: Eagle on the Frieze, Statuary Hall; Francis Vincenti, sculptor: bust of Beeshekee, Chippewa Indian Chief, Senate Wing.

While the list of the Italian artists who worked in and on the Capitol is a long one (the names here given do not exhaust the enumeration), many native artists also contributed their genius and talents.

From the early days of the republic, Italian artists were eagerly sought after to embellish exteriors and interiors of state capitols, libraries, municipal buildings, and other public structures. In the wake of the Civil War, Italian sculptors were much in demand to enliven public squares with military heroes astride stone horses and naval heroes pacing marble decks.

Italians were recognized not only as persons of superlative artistic talents but of cultural, scientific, and literary accomplishment. Many Americans wished to learn the musical language of this supremely enlightened people. In 1747 Italian was being taught in a private school in New York. In 1753 the University of Pennsylvania (then known as the College of Philadelphia) advertised for an instructor to teach Italian, French, and German. We have already noted that Carlo Bellini, chosen as Secretary for Foreign Affairs for Virginia, instructed students of the College of William and Mary in his native tongue. Italian books attained a respectable circulation. Educated people knew that forty per cent of the English vocabulary had its genesis in Latin, the mother of the Italian language.

The captivation of Italian speech was such that when actors and actresses from Italy appeared on the American stage, they were applauded as enthusiastically by the non-Italian-speaking audiences as by those who listened to their native idiom. Tommaso Salvini, a giant of a man, performed in Shakespearean roles in Italian and was cheered at every performance. Of great bulk and majestic poise, he made one of the most effective Macbeths in the history of the stage.* Drama critics rated Ernesto Rossi, who also performed in Italian, as one of the most appealing, convincing, and poignant Hamlets of all time.

Although Eleanora Duse belonged to a later era, of which I shall treat in a subsequent part of the book, she played to standing room audiences in her various tours of the United States, always speaking in Italian.

With a study of the Italian language, acknowledged by all linguists as melodious in sound, structure, and rhythm, there went naturally a consuming interest in music itself. Philip Tragetta, musician and composer born in Venice, and friend of Presidents Madison and Monroe, established a conservatory of music in Boston in 1803, and then in 1838 inaugurated a program of concerts in Philadelphia in another conservatory founded by him.†

Italians, and, to a certain extent, the French and the Germans also, brought high-grade music to America while the colonies and the new republic were still struggling for economic and political survival. Nevertheless the Americans were eager for the comfort and encouragement of song and aria. As early as 1760, Italians were performing publicly on the violin and pianoforte and Italian vocalists were lifting their voices in classic melody for the audible enlightenment and spiritual exaltation of young America. The exhilarating *Barber of Seville* by Gioacchino Rossini was sung in its entirety by an Italian company in New York in 1825.

In 1832 Lorenzo Da Ponte, famous as libretto author of Mozart's *Don Giovanni,* brought an opera company from Italy which enjoyed great success in New York. Before long, operas were being performed regularly in permanent opera houses owned, managed, and directed by Italians, with Italian singers and musicians.

Thomas Jefferson, alert to anything and everything that could improve the growing nation of which he was president, conceived the

---

* In 1880, while on tour, Salvini visited the House of Representatives in Washington. The Speaker and all members rose and applauded in homage to him.
† Congressional Record, May 5, 1955, A3068.

idea of a military band which would stir pride in American democratic ideals and accomplishments. Knowing the worth of Italian musicians (he and his wife had studied music under the noted teacher Francis Alberti), Jefferson instructed his representative in Italy to recruit bandsmen. In September 1805 fourteen of them arrived at the Washington Navy Yard aboard the U.S. frigate *Chesapeake*. These Italian musicians became the nucleus of what was to become the most famous musical organization in the land, the United States Marine Band. During the course of its glorious career this band has had six Italian conductors: Gaetano Carusi, Venerando Pulizzi, Antonio Pons, Joseph Lucchesi, Francis Scala, and Francisco Fanciulli.

As already indicated, the Italians in America, up to and including the period of the Civil War and even for a number of years following the war, prompted universal esteem. Prior to the Civil War only a few "Monday Pioneers" disturbed the innately friendly climate of the nation. Monday Pioneers were those who arrived in America on Monday, and then called those who arrived on Tuesday "foreigners."

A change in attitude toward Italians began to manifest itself in the 1870s. Although Ellis Island, the United States Immigration Station in New York Bay, did not begin to function as such until 1892 (Castle Garden being its predecessor) I will use the term Ellis Island Era to designate that sorrowful and unjust period when, immigration from Italy being unrestricted and at flood tide, certain strata of non-Italian society in America disparaged, exploited and oppressed the Italian.

In *A Nation of Immigrants** President John F. Kennedy spoke feelingly of the hard conditions and hostility faced by immigrants in the Ellis Island Era:

> One New York newspaper had these intemperate words for the newly arrived Italians:

> The floodgates are open. The bars are down. The sally-ports are unguarded. The dam is washed away. The sewer is choked . . . the scum of immigration is viscerating upon our shores. The horde of $9.60 steerage slime is being siphoned upon us from Continental mud tanks.

However, from the days of Christopher Columbus to the days of Abraham Lincoln, Italians were not evaluated according to the

* Harper & Row, New York, 1964. Originally published by Anti-Defamation League of B'Nai B'rith.

amount of money they paid for their passage across the ocean. "A man's a man for a' that!" The Italians were wanted and they were highly regarded for what they were—a sincere, able, industrious, sober, and religious people, imbued with idealism and motivated by wholesome desires and honest aspirations. They displayed marked ability as architects, construction engineers, chemists. They could not be excelled as stonemasons and in many of the crafts. They entered into business as merchants, hotel and restaurant owners, and importers.*

They ranked high in all the professions. In the law there were Italian practitioners of note, one of them, Charles Antonio Rapallo, achieving in 1870 the highest judicial office in the state of New York —Justice of the Court of Appeals. In the clergy, the Italian priest Father Louis Pise was elected Chaplain of the United States Senate in 1832, the moving senator being the illustrious Henry Clay. Father Samuel Mazzuchelli opened with prayers the first session of the Territorial Legislature of Wisconsin in 1836, and was then elected chaplain.

In the field of education, Father Giovanni, S.J., who was born in Bergamo, Italy, became the first president in 1812 of Georgetown College, which developed into Georgetown University (my alma mater). In addition to his administrative work at the college, Father Giovanni taught science. In 1855 Father Anthony Maraschi, with a group of Jesuits, founded the College of St. Ignatius, which later became the University of San Francisco. In 1887 Father Joseph Cataldo, with another group of Jesuits, founded Gonzaga University of Spokane, Washington. In 1865 Eugene Carusi was one of the founders of the National University of Law in Washington, D. C. (another alma mater of mine), and served as its chancellor from 1906 to 1924.

It would be an act of supererogation to enumerate the trades, callings, and occupations of Italians in the United States from colo-

---

* John Marshall's account book for 1785, when he was a member of the Virginia Assembly meeting in Richmond, showed an entry of six pounds, six shillings, to "My Club at Farmicola's." Farmicola was a Neapolitan who owned and operated this popular hotel and tavern, where "Generals, Colonels, Captains, Senators, Assemblymen, Judges, Doctors and Clerks of every weight and calibre and every hue of dress, sat together about the fire, drinking, smoking, singing and talking ribaldry."

nial days to the Ellis Island Era. It is enough to say that they participated in every endeavor that went into the making of the modern counterpart of what Rome was when, in the words of Dr. Solomon B. Freehof, "order and civilization were impressed upon a lawless world from the seven hills by the banks of the Tiber."

Even before the American Revolution, the colonies were importing Italian products. Musical instruments, sheet music, olive oil, vermicelli, and art wares arrived from Italy, usually through England, although some ships crossed the ocean directly from the Mediterranean. In 1772 two enterprising Italians, Anthony Vitalli and Pasquale Lenzi, made and sold Italian sausage in Philadelphia.

It was considered a mark of distinction and refined elegance to have studied in Italy. A Professor and Mrs. Bridenbaugh, writing of this period, remarked:

> When these graduates from the Grand Tour returned to their native shores, they furnished their homes with Italian antiquities and filled their gardens with neoclassic statuary, sought to elevate the taste of the less fortunate townsmen and in general set themselves up as connoisseurs and critics.*

Benjamin Franklin carried on considerable correspondence with Italian scientists and exchanged letters with the illustrious political philosopher Gaetano Filangieri. The American Philosophical Society from time to time elected Italian scholars to their group.

There was perhaps more serious reading in America prior to the Civil War era than later. The people knew history—past and contemporary—and saw Italy marching down the centuries heralding the forces of enlightenment destined to give man greater learning, improved health, increased comfort and safety, and expanded opportunity for happiness.

They knew that without banks there could be no stability to the world of commerce and they knew that the world's first bank took form in Genoa in the 1400s. They knew also that the Italians invented credit banking and double-entry bookkeeping, without which the edifice of business would fall apart like a deck of cards in mid-air.

They knew that in the early commercial history of England the Italian bankers lived on a street which they named Lombardy Street

---

* *Rebels and Gentlemen*, by C. and J. Bridenbaugh, 1942, quoted by G. Schiavo in *Four Centuries of Italian-American History*.

after their homeland of Lombardy. That street was now the financial center of the British Empire.

They knew that the great Italian scholar Charles Joseph Botta had written in 1812 a four-volume history of the American Revolutionary War which was generally accepted as the best work extant on this subject so dear to their hearts. John Adams had praised it highly, the second President of the United States having declared: "It is indeed the most classical and methodical, the most particular and circumstantial, the most entertaining and interesting narration of the American war, that I have seen." Thomas Jefferson was no less effusive in his praise, and stated that once he started reading the work he could not put it down. "He [Botta] has had the faculty of . . . enlivening the whole with the constant glow of his holy enthusiasm for the liberty and independence of nations." President Madison was no less reserved in his approval of the work.

The American people knew that the music of the sweetest and most nostalgic melody in all songdom, *Home Sweet Home*, was derived from an Italian love song which John Howard Payne heard while roaming through the pastoral delights of scenic Sicily.

The American people knew that Italy was not only a land of economists, scientists, and scholars, but a land which had a special appeal for romantic hearts, intense humanitarians, and brilliant brains. The three most romantic poets of the age, Percy Bysshe Shelley, Lord Byron, and John Keats had forsaken their ancestral homes to live in the country which Byron apostrophized with:

> Italia! O Italia! thou who hast
> The fatal gift of beauty.

Robert Browning and Elizabeth Barrett Browning, equally illustrious poets, had left England to dwell amid the glories and beauties of Italy.

Gabriel Rossetti and his sister, Christina Rossetti, two of England's most cherished poets of the nineteenth century, were Italian in origin, and this fact seemed to enhance their fame and charm among English-speaking people.

America knew that one of her most beloved poets, Henry Wadsworth Longfellow, whose poetry was a never-emptying jug of rhythm and beauty, had studied in Italy, spoke Italian like a Roman, and had translated for Americans that "medieval miracle of song," the

Divine Comedy of Dante Alighieri. There was a Dante Club at Harvard University.

America knew that it was an Italian, Marco Polo, who had fascinated the peoples of the western world with the first authoritative account of the riches, mysteries, trades, and customs of China and the whole Asiatic world.

Men and women of genius from many parts of the world paid their tribute to Italy by taking up residence there for short or long periods of time. Edward Gibbon got the inspiration for his *The Decline and Fall of the Roman Empire* while musing among the very ruins he was to rehabilitate and reanimate in his magnificent and monumental work. Washington Irving, who wrote perhaps the most authoritative and classic biography of Christopher Columbus, visited Italy many times.

Wolfgang Goethe, after an extended sojourn in Rome, said: "How shall I leave the only place in all the world which can become a paradise for me? I find here the fulfillment of all my desires and dreams." Friedrich Nietzsche, the harsh philosopher from the same country, mellowed during his days in Italy. Richard Wagner composed music in Italy. The famous Russian novelists Nikolai Gogol, Ivan Turgenev, Maxim Gorky, and Feodor Dostoevsky wrote much of their intriguing prose in Italy.

The French George Sand, who dressed in male clothes and a man's name, penned some strong feministic literature while sojourning on the Italian peninsula. So did the English George Eliot, another woman wearing a man's name.

Margaret Fuller, one of the most brilliant and scholarly of women, and a friend of Ralph Waldo Emerson, early manifested an ardent sympathy for the Italian patriot Mazzini and his plans for a united Italy. In 1848 she arrived in Italy and, in Rome, fell in love with and married Giovanni Angelo Ossoli, a soldier in the army of Garibaldi defending Rome. During the battles and the long siege, she directed two Italian hospitals.

Florence Nightingale, renowned English nurse, hospital reformer and humanitarian, was born in the city of Florence, Italy, which gave her her name. Her heroic work in the Crimean War reduced the mortality rate of the sick and wounded soldiers from forty-two to two percent. Longfellow immortalized her in verse as "The Lady with the

Lamp," alluding to the rounds she made at night of the sick and wounded.

Harriet Beecher Stowe, author of *Uncle Tom's Cabin*, and Julia Ward Howe, who turned the song of "John Brown's Body" into "The Battle Hymn of the Republic," both visited in Italy. William Gladstone, the celebrated English premier, made frequent trips to Italy, was grounded in its literature, and spoke the language fluently.

Hans Christian Andersen of Denmark created some of his delightful fairy tales while traveling through Italy, which he regarded as a fairyland in itself. His fellow countryman Bertel Thorvaldsen derived inspiration for his sculptural masterpieces by studying art in Italy. John Ruskin, celebrated English art critic, loved to roam in Italy, as did his illustrious countrymen William M. Thackeray and Samuel Taylor Coleridge. Norway paid her obeisance to Italy through her famous playwright Henrik Ibsen. Hungary was represented in Rome's foreign colony by the poet of the piano, Franz Liszt.

Our own inimitable Mark Twain wrote no inconsiderable Americana while residing in Florence, Italy. Nathaniel Hawthorne created *The Marble Faun* and Henry James his *Daisy Miller* in Rome. Thomas Gray, Thomas Macaulay, and Sir Walter Scott, whose names are immortal in literature, drank from the fountains of wisdom, romance, and poetic symmetry in Italy. John Milton found inspiration in Italy.

William Shakespeare, the most powerful writer ever to trace poetic drama across paper, laid the plots of his immortal plays—*Julius Caesar, Romeo and Juliet, Merchant of Venice, Othello, Taming of the Shrew, Coriolanus, Two Gentlemen of Verona, Titus Andronicus* —in Italy. For his plays whose plots were laid in ancient Rome, he drew heavily on Plutarch, the Roman historian, who, with his gifted pen, re-created more than anyone else the glory, grandeur, majesty, drama, and romance that were Rome.

Shakespeare stands supreme as the greatest dramatist of all times. If he drew so lavishly from Italy in portraying the dignity, nobility, and achievement of man, it was because he saw in Italy a land of achievement, dignity, and nobility. The non-Italians of the pre-Civil War period in America did not go to the trouble of making this rational deduction. There was no need to, because there was no prejudice against Italians, there was no necessity to argue in their favor. The Italians were what they were. They hailed from a land whose astronomers, scientists, philosophers, academicians had given order, understanding, and comprehension to the vast universe.

Americans and the rest of the world knew what they owed to Italy, which gave to them the Gregorian Calendar by which their lives were regulated and the events of the year planned. It was the Gregorian Calendar which divided time neatly and accurately into months, weeks, and days, assuring calendar uniformity to a universe which might otherwise seem chronologically chaotic. Up until the reign of Julius Caesar, the civil equinox differed from the astronomical by three months so that winter came too early and autumn smothered summer before it had a chance to don its gay floral apparel. Caesar abolished the use of the lunar year and regulated the civil year entirely by the sun, establishing the twelve-month year with the varying months so that the seasons would arrive at appropriate intervals.

Scientific as this calculation was, it seems that somewhere along the line a nut or screw in the chronological machinery loosened, so that each year the equinox was receding 11 minutes 14 seconds and that every 128 years a day fell out of existence. Luigi Lilio Ghiraldi, a physician of Verona, went over the whole complicated time machine, located the slipping screws, tightened them and recommended to Pope Gregory XIII a correction of the calendar. To catch up on what had been lost, ten days were dropped after October 4, 1582, and the length of the year was marked out to 365 days, 5 hours, 49 minutes, and 12 seconds. England, apparently still smarting under Pope Clement VII's excommunication of Henry VIII, refused to accept the calendar change until it found itself stumbling in a historiographical and horological mire. It required an act of Parliament in 1752 to put England and its colonies into step.

The working out of time units with infinite exactitude required, of course, astronomical perception combined with mathematical genius. Italy was not lacking in that type of intellectual prodigality. One of the greatest astronomers and mathematicians of all time was Galileo Galilei. At the age of nineteen, while attending Mass in the Cathedral of Pisa, he noted that the huge bronze lamp suspended from the ceiling never remained still. With an unerring eye he measured the swing of its oscillations and observed that they were uniform in rhythm and time. He experimented in his home with other swinging objects and came to the scientific conclusion that a swaying object can become an infallible instrument for measuring time. He wrote a thesis on the isochronism of the pendulum and in that moment there was born that sturdy sentinel of existence, so dear to the memories of our childhood, the hallway clock.

At the age of twenty-two Galileo invented the hydrostatic balance which measures the specific gravity of solids. He invented the thermometer. He invented the proportional compasses. He was the first to prove that the path of any projectile is not a horizontally direct line, but a parabola. He proved by demonstration from the Tower of Pisa that falling objects all descend with the same speed and that the rapidity or retardation of their fall is due only to the influence of air currents and not to the weight of the objects.

He disproved the popular notion that natural light is stationary and that it appears simultaneously everywhere, affected only by shade and not by distance. He was the first to clearly grasp the idea of force as a mechanical agent, and in this branch of science he paved the way for Sir Isaac Newton and the law of gravitation.

In pre-Galilean times the sky was a mystery and stars had angular points. The Milky Way was a blurred celestial highway. Galileo revealed that stars were spheroids and that the Milky Way was a succession of individual stars. He accomplished this revelation through his invention which was called "Galileo's Tube," a development of the elementary Dutch telescope. With this long ocular hand he tore away the veil from the mysterious skies and manifested to all mankind, greater beauties than had ever been beheld before in the firmament. Man now saw for the first time the satellites of Jupiter, the hills and valleys of the moon and the spots on the sun. He proved the rotation of the sun on its axis and demonstrated the accuracy of the Copernican system as opposed to the Ptolemaic theory.

Galileo's scientific conclusions based on investigation and repeated experimentation led him into difficulties with the reigning establishments in Church and State. Undeterred by opposition and undismayed by masked warning, he wrote his famous work *Dialogo dei due massimi sistemi del mondo* which has earned the eulogy that "it would be difficult to find in any language a book in which animation and elegance of style are so happily combined with strength and clearness of scientific exposition." He was summoned before the dreaded Inquisition in Rome which charged him with heresy for refuting the accepted doctrine that the earth was stationary. In the face of threatened torture Galileo sank to his knees and recanted, but beneath his breath he murmured *"Eppure si muove"* ("But it moves just the same"). Modern writers claim that Galileo never made the utterance but I am satisfied that this venerable and courageous man, with all the dignity which goes with an awareness of one's worth, did defy error to the end.

On the four hundredth anniversary of Galileo's birth, February 15, 1964, the New York *Times* editorially declared that Galileo, "probably more than any other man, created modern science."

Galileo's amanuensis, Evangelista Torricelli, was inspired into an inventive rapture of his own. Conceiving the idea that atmosphere had weight and measurable pressure he put his thesis into practical application and invented the barometer, whose warning signs of coming storms and other natural violences has saved countless lives on land and sea.

5 MONA LISA AND CAPILLARIES

As continents, rivers, bays, countries, and states often bear the names of their discoverers, explorers, or benefactors, many parts of the anatomy of man have acquired the names of the physicians and surgeons who conducted experiments and made studies aimed at repairing those organs or their functions following disease, breakdown, or injury. The large number of Italian names identifying body locations and functions vividly illustrates the part Italians have played in relieving man of the torture of pain, by restoring to him bodily soundness. Thus, on any large chart of the human body, one can see the pons Varoli in the brain, named after Dr. Varoli; the Eustachian Canal named after Dr. Eustachio, the organ of Corti in the ear and the rods of Corti in the retina named after Dr. Corti, the Fallopian tubes named after Dr. Fallopio; and so on: the fissure of Rolando, the canal of Vidi, the duct of Botallo, the Scarpa's triangle and fascia, the cartilages of Santorini, the ducts of Rivini, the spaces of Fontana, the sinus of Valsalva, the band of Giacomini, the corpuscles of Paccini, the crescents of Gianuzzi, the nerve of Lancisi, the foramen of Thebesio, the aqueduct of Cotugni, etc., etc.

Dr. Marcello Malpighi, who was a professor at the University of Bologna from 1660 to 1691, was so renowned in medicine that his name has become an adjective: Malpighian, which refers to his numerous treatises, discoveries, and types of treatments. Webster's dictionary lists the following Malpighian terms: Malpighian body, Malpighian capsule, Malpighian corpuscle, Malpighian layer, Malpighian pyramid, Malpighian tubes or vessels, and Malpighian tuft.

And then there is the word galvanism, which means the therapeutic application of electricity to the body. Galvanism is a word built on the name of Luigi Galvani who invented the metallic arc and announced his theory of animal electricity in 1791. Galvanism has evolved into many word derivatives (fifteen are listed by Webster's), and there have been not a few critics who have galvanized themselves into vituperative utterance against Italy and Italians, not realizing they were unconsciously paying tribute to the great Italian Galvani.

Many Italian doctors were practicing medicine in America during the Columbus-Lincoln span, and patients manifested complete confidence in them because they knew that the science of medicine was an old one in Italy. The first great school of medicine in Europe saw light in Salerno in the 800s. For centuries the book *Regimen Sanitatis Salernitatum* (*Rule of Health of the University of Salerno*) had been pointing the way to good health through exercise, proper food, fresh air, cleanliness, and water consumption.* The first man to describe concussion of the brain was Lanfranchi of Milan (birth year unknown, died in 1315). His book on head injuries became a classic in surgery.

Another book, *Adversaria Anatomica*, by Giovanni Battista Morgagni, of the School of Medicine, University of Bologna, was accepted on this side of the ocean as a fundamental text in the study of anatomy. In 1761 this same Morgagni published his *De sedibus et causis morborum* (*On the Sites and Causes of Disease*), thereby creating the science of pathology. He led the way in demonstrating the absolute necessity for basing diagnosis, prognosis, and treatment on a comprehensive knowledge of anatomical conditions.

Dr. Oliver Wendell Holmes, who was familiar with the works of the Italian trail-blazers in medicine, said of medical classics in general:

> These books were very dear to me as they stood upon my shelves. A twig from one of my nerves ran to every one of them.

Dr. Max Neuberger of Vienna, in his *History of Medicine*, saw in the universities of Salerno, Bologna, and Pavia the first laboratories:

* *What Civilization Owes to Italy*, by James J. Walsh, Stratford Company, 1930.

The Italian anatomists initiated at the end of the fifteenth century the most famous period in the history of the art of dissection and became the teachers to the physicians of the world.

The great William Harvey of England, who was the first to acquaint the world (1628) with the nature of the travels of the blood through the body as it gains impetus and momentum from the great pump of the heart, studied medicine at the University of Padua under the famed Fabricius da Aquapendente, for whom an anatomical theater was constructed. Harvey's discovery of the circulation of the blood and his profound thesis on the subject established him a giant in the temple of medicine. Only in one phase was "his demonstration of the circulation incomplete." The Encyclopaedia Britannica states that "Harvey did not see the capillary channels by which the blood passes from the arteries to the veins." The Britannica then goes on to say that "this gap in the circulation was supplied thirty years later by the great anatomist Marcello Malpighi, who described the capillary circulation four years after Harvey's death."

The Britannica says further of Malpighi that he was "one of the first to apply the microscope to the study of animal and vegetable structure; and his discoveries were so important that he may be considered to be the founder of microscopic anatomy." Ever since philosophers began to inquire and quest into the mysteries of the world and the human body particularly, they stood puzzled over the phenomenon of breathing. Where did the air go after it entered the nose and mouth, and what happened to it? Even after this branch of learning was taken over by scientists and doctors the enigma about air and lungs continued. Malpighi experimented on dogs, tortoises, and frogs, and in 1661 published his book *De pulmonibus* (*On the Lungs*), and revealed with anatomical precision for the first time the true conception of the respiratory apparatus.

In addition Malpighi was the first to "attempt the finer anatomy of the brain," describing the "distribution of gray matter and of the fibre-tracts in the cord, with their extensions to the cerebrum and cerebellum with great accuracy." On top of all this, Malpighi was a celebrated botanist and a work of his on the anatomy of plants was published by the Royal Society of England.

It is with no lessening of admiration for Dr. William Harvey and his monumental discovery that one cites *The Story of Medicine* by Dr. Victor Robinson of Temple University wherein he states that

Italian anatomists were "on the trail" of the blood in the 1500s. Harvey's teacher Aquapendente taught Harvey that the venal valves are always directed toward the heart and that "Andrea Cesalpino (1524–1603) not only visualized the pulmonary and systematic circulation, but actually used the term 'circulation of the blood' (sanguinis circulationi)."

Leonardo da Vinci was the first person in recorded history to draw with scientific precision the human skeleton. There are still in existence two thousand plates by da Vinci of dissections made by him in his studies on this subject. To reproduce the human form faithfully in sculpture or painting, the artist must have almost as extensive a knowledge of anatomy as that possessed by surgeons. The viewer of a canvas portrait assumes he is looking only at the exterior features of the person depicted. This is true if the person responsible for the portrait was merely a *painter*. If, however, he was an *artist*, he began with a portraiture of the invisible, and then, as he built into form and palpable manifestation, he worked into the anatomy of his subject. In smiling, one smiles not alone with lips but with eyes, facial muscles, and the underlying fasciae all the way through to the smallest capillaries. Da Vinci knew these capillaries. The most enthusiastic admirer of da Vinci's masterpiece "Mona Lisa" cannot see those capillaries, but it took da Vinci four years to limn in the thousand physiological finenesses which produced the enigmatic fascination of that artistic masterpiece.

In January 1963 the "Mona Lisa" was brought to America and exhibited in the National Gallery of Art in Washington and in New York's Metropolitan Museum of Art. The Metropolitan, incidentally, owes its great success to General Luigi Palma di Cesnola, whose heroic exploits in the Civil War we have already mentioned. It was he, becoming its director in 1879, who developed it from a "grandiose paper project" into the gigantic world-famous institution of art it is today. On display at the Metropolitan for twenty-five days, "Mona Lisa" was viewed and admired by 1,077,521 persons.

In the whole world of ecclesiastical art no painting is so well known as Leonardo's "The Last Supper." Leonardo here re-creates the scene when Christ has said: "Yea, it is so, one there is among you, who will betray me." If an earthquake had riven the room into two and fragmentized the table before them, the Apostles could not have been more astonished or shocked. Each one denies that it could be he who

would commit so devastatingly unforgivable a crime. Without knowing the exact words spoken by the Disciples in their vehement exon-
eration from so monstrous an indictment, we can almost hear the
voices as we look at Leonardo's work. "It cannot be I!" "It is not I,
oh Lord!" "How could it be conceived that anyone among us, who
are your loyal followers, could conjure up so all-enveloping a universal
disaster?" "No!" "No!" "No!"

Leonardo da Vinci was probably the most talented human being
who ever lived. He was truly a genius and although one might strive
for a more forceful expression to describe this man, there is no other
term to define an individual who is endowed with a capacity to accomplish far above and beyond the capacity possessed by other mor-
tals of the earth. Leonardo was pre-eminent in so many fields of
endeavor, and his works were so vast in quality and quantity, that
one stands mutely helpless before the mere cataloging of them. In
September 1963 the IBM Gallery in New York exhibited numerous
models of inventions made from Leonardo's notebooks. He was born
in 1452, forty years before the discovery of the New World, but his
whole life, in a manner of speaking, could be regarded as the discovery
of another new world. The year 1963 saw the publication of a gigantic
volume on his works. The book measures 15" × 11" × 2½" and contains 518 pages, with several thousand sketches (in addition to re-
productions of his immortal paintings) covering every possible field
in the whole world of intellectual, scientific, and artistic creation.
One leafs through the pages with a growing admiration that leaves
one quite exhausted at the end.

Perhaps da Vinci came into the world ahead of his time. It has
been said he "awoke too early in the darkness, while all the others
were still asleep." Man apparently was not ready to translate into
steel, aluminum, brass, and wood the perfect designs he drew of machines and devices which have been built only during comparatively
recent times. One notes almost with incredulity, or as if dealing in
fantasy, that it was nearly five centuries ago that da Vinci conceived
such inventions as the parachute, helicopter, airplane, air-condition-
ing machine, hydraulic pump, printing press, military tank, scaling
ladder, grinding mill, and excavating machine.

Of his drawings the Encyclopaedia Britannica says: "These are
among the greatest treasures ever given to the world by the human
spirit, expressing itself in pen and pencil." They cover an infinite

variety of subjects such as catapults, diving suits, hygroscopes, fire-arms, boring machines, inclinometer, dredges, bombards, pumps, musical instruments, machine guns, rolling mills, mirrors, screw-cutting machines, and ships.

As a vital student of nature, Leonardo knew the laws of the growth and structure of plants, the properties and powers of water, the phenomena of storms and lightning, of river action and of mountain structure. He was at home in music, architecture, engineering, philosophy, cosmology, optics, astronomy, sculpture, mathematics, and city planning. He built fortifications and canals. He contributed to the construction of the beautiful Cathedral of Milan. When the pestilence of 1484–85 decimated much of Milan it was Leonardo who recommended a breaking up of the city plan and reconstruction of it on sanitary principles. He planned vast engineering works for improving the irrigation and waterways of the Lomellina and adjacent regions of the Lombard plain.

One must not believe that with all his artistic and scientific preoccupations, Leonardo was a recluse toiling morosely in the shades of his incomparable genius. It is to be regretted that the only universally exhibited portrait of him is the one in which a beard covers so much of his face. We do not see the handsome countenance beneath, which sparkled with love of life.

When the Duke of Milan was planning a celebration worthy of his wealthy and renowned dukedom he summoned Leonardo as impresario for the event. Leonardo accepted with alacrity and brought along his harp, for he was one of the most accomplished harpists in Italy. In addition he "led the dance and the tourney, improvised songs and planned the fetes and festivals where strange animals turned into birds and gigantic flowers opened, disclosing beautiful girls."

The natural genius of da Vinci was, one might paradoxically say, supernatural and yet his acquisition of knowledge had to come through the processes of education: books, schooling, instruction. In this regard it was mankind's good fortune that his birth occurred in Italy, which, in the fifteenth century, led Christendom in educational facilities. Dr. William Harvey said of Italy that she was the "alma mater studiorum for the world." The undisputed masters in their respective fields—Guy de Chalic, French surgeon; Nicholas of Cusa and Regiomontanus, German mathematicians; Vesalius, Flemish anatomist; Copernicus, Polish astronomer; Linacre and Caius, English physicians—all studied in Italy. Thomas Becket, martyred Archbishop of Canterbury, hero of the fine play bearing his name, was a student at the University of Bologna. On his return to England, one of his teachers, Vacarius, accompanied him and lectured on Roman Law at Oxford.

When the institutions of learning and culture in the Roman Empire disappeared before the barbarian invasions like cities vanishing beneath the lava of a volcanic eruption, a darkness settled over the civilized world. But in this night of a society thrust back into semi-primitive existence, not all was hopelessly black. The monasteries, and particularly those of the Benedictine Order, lighted candles which formed intellectual oases. These grew brighter with the passing centuries until at last they forced a dawn which soon changed into the open daylight of restored Latin scholarship.

The monks preserved the classic lore of Rome and Greece by gathering libraries and copying manuscripts. When in 1450 John Gutenberg in Mainz, Germany, invented movable-type printing, Italy at once began to feed the knowledge-starved world by printing in book form the precious manuscripts that had been saved from the barbarian flood. By 1500 Venice alone had 417 printers.

The University of Salerno was the first institution of learning to organize higher education into four departments: Curriculum, Coordination of teachers and students of different departments, Examinations, and Conferring of degrees.

The University of Bologna began with a law school headed by the great medieval authority on Roman Law, the Italian jurist Irnerius, invariably referred to as the Lucerna Iuris (the Legal Lamp). In this law school, the foundation of responsibility to order was laid down in the massive blocks of the Roman Law destined to support the legal pillars of civilization. The Roman Law was carried to America by the Spanish and French conquerors, colonizers and teachers, and formed much of the legal system in the American colonies, continuing to be authoritative, even after the Revolutionary War, in Louisiana, Florida, and other territories still under Spanish-French domination and influence.

Many of the University of Bologna teachers were women. It is reported that one of them in the fourteenth century, Novella d'Andrea, was so attractive that in order to keep the students' minds on their studies, it was found expedient for her to lecture from behind a little curtain!

Although the English colonies were naturally bound by the English Common Law, the American people regarded with abhorrence some of the harsh and even brutal aspects of that legal system which listed, for example, some two hundred offenses punishable by hanging. The common law also permitted torture and such grotesque penalties as the pillory and the ducking stool. Although the more savage aspects of the English common law were never enforced in the colonies, the Americans nevertheless turned with hopeful anticipation to the reforms advocated by the great Italian lawyer of Milan, Cesare Bonesana Beccaria. His book *Of Crimes and Penalties* (published in 1764) vigorously condemned the barbarities of criminal law and called for the abolition of the death penalty, torture, and confiscation of property. He made the point that to the extent that punishment deters crime, it is not the harshness of the penalty but the certainty of it which is most effective, and recommended that punishment, upon conviction, be prompt, moderate, and certain. In this same field Beccaria was followed by Cesare Lombroso, and still later by Enrico Ferri, founder of the Positive School of Criminology, who was my preceptor at the University of Rome. The influence of these three Italian criminologists on ameliorating the rigors of the English common law and in inaugurating a more humane and enlightened approach to the problem of the criminal has been immense.

Sons of wealthy Americans who went abroad to study, invariably included Italy in their scholastic itinerary because they knew that whether or not they attended a formal institution of learning they found in Italy itself a vast university roofed only by the sky. For here had lived, tutored, and meditated some of the greatest scholars of all time. Here they had spoken and committed to parchment or the printed page the wisdom of centuries, to guide, instruct, and uplift mankind. One of these scholars, perhaps the greatest, was St. Thomas Aquinas, who demonstrated that Reason supports Faith, that Logic enthrones the Scriptures, and that the most learned of men must be the most religious of men. It was said that the intellect of this scholar, who later was canonized, was so vast that "it needed to be measured in parallels of latitude and meridians of longitude."

It was in Italy that Dante Alighieri pursued his melancholy pere-grinations into imaginative heavens and hells, opening to the mind of man his own potentialities for good when guided by love which leads to the all-embracing yearning for the Infinite. In point of dra-matic fire and poetic splendor, Dante's works rank next only to those of Shakespeare.

Francesco Petrarch, credited with Dante (and Boccaccio) as being a co-architect of the Italian language, immortalized constant love in sonnets, madrigals, and songs which he addressed to the lovely Laura, who seems to have been the only person in the world not to have been impressed by them. This coldness of Laura, if such it was, in no way lessens the warmth or detracts from the beauty of his poem: *Rhymes on the Life and Death of Madonna Laura.*

Giovanni Boccaccio, the third triumvir of Italian language archi-tects, is credited with being the first master of Italian prose. His fame rests mostly on his *Decameron,* but he wrote other works, distin-guished in diction, narrative, and exposition, and not classified as "indelicate."

In Italy lived and sang Ludovico Ariosto who wrote in 1516 the imposing epic *Orlando Furioso.*

And then there was Niccolò Machiavelli, author of *The Prince,* a book generally known to educated people in the Columbus-Lincoln era who had anything to do with public and political life. As secretary to the ruling council of Florence and as traveling ambassador, visiting all the foreign courts of Europe, Machiavelli acquired an encyclopedic knowledge of governmental intrigue and high power politics. He was willing to sacrifice some individual liberty for a ruling power which could achieve independence of Italy from foreign domination. In achieving what he regarded as an ideal objective, he was willing to employ the means required. These means often omitted moral values. He had one aim and that was to build the state. He decried the use of mercenaries for national defense and advocated armies obtained by conscription. The blueprint he drew for a strong national unified state became a pattern for the ambitious who sought personal aggrandize-ment and power, wholly unrelated to the welfare of the people. His advocacy of shrewdness and intrigue was in keeping with the practi-calities of the day. In a later era his work has been appraised in the light of other standards so that it has become synonymous with the concept of foxy maneuvering. As one surveys the political history of the last one hundred years, one wonders whether the world has not been more Machiavellian than Machiavelli. Machiavelli was read widely not only because of *The Prince* but also because of other learned and historical works. He is regarded by many as possibly the greatest prose writer of the Renaissance.

Another Italian classicist, who scarcely needs biographical delineation, was Torquato Tasso, who was born in Sorrento in what is known as Siren Land. Smiling and flowering at the summit of grandiose cliffs against which the seas dance, Sorrento is a mecca of loveliness to which many of those who have felt its charm always return in happy obeisance to its inviting song *Torna a Sorrento*. During several months of the war, as military governor of the Sorrentine peninsula, I maintained my headquarters in Sorrento's main piazza, graced in its center by the statue of Tasso. Tasso's epic poem *Jerusalem Liberated* earned for him the commendation of Pope Clement VIII who invited him to Rome to be crowned as poet laureate. He died just before the crowning.

Vittorio Alfieri, tragic dramatist and poet, was enthusiastically admired in America for his five odes to the American revolution and succeeding independence. Giacomo Leopardi, whose life span was only thirty-nine years, is regarded as one of the most universal of poets Italy has produced.

There were but few Americans with any literary appreciation living in the nineteenth century who did not know of Alessandro Francesco Tommaso Antonio Manzoni. His romantic, historical novel *I Promessi Sposi* (*The Betrothed*) published in 1825–26, was a classic which inspired tears, laughter, and pulsating hearts in a score of languages. Another gifted writer was Edmondo de Amicis, whose book *Cuore* (*Heart*) was a lyrical apostrophe to childhood and all its tender associations, adventures, and dreams.

6 *QUO VADIS, DOMINE?*

Ralph Waldo Emerson said:

> An institution is the lengthened shadow of one man . . . and all history resolves itself very easily into the biography of a few stout and earnest persons.

More of those stout and earnest persons lived and wrought in Italy than in any other territory of similar size since man began to record substantial deeds on stone, parchment, paper, and marble. A baby was born and he was named Julius Caesar, no more extraordinary a name in itself than John Smith in Latin. Yet, because his skull contained a brilliant brain, his hand grasped a keen sword, his fingers closed over a trenchant pen, and his tongue uttered words of invincible command, his name denotes an age and an empire. He extended the borders of Italy until they encompassed nearly all of the then known world. He was assassinated on the Ides of March 44 B.C., but his name continued to rule, the successive rulers of Rome calling themselves Caesars, even after the blood strain had ceased. Nationalities other than Italian accepted the word Caesar as symbolic of the highest sovereign power. The Germans rendered the word as kaiser, and the Russians spelled it tsar.

Marc Antony, Cicero, Scipio were all men of Italy who wrote their names in titanic letters on the mountain ranges of history. The Roman emperors Augustus and Hadrian ruled so well that their names have become synonymous with wise and humane government; the emperors Caligula and Nero ruled so perniciously and cruelly that their names are bywords for bad government.

Gibbon's monumental work *The Decline and Fall of the Roman Empire* portrays the colossal figures who had built the greatness of Rome and describes those who in colossal failure brought it to ruin. The mighty stream of Christianity formed in Rome. It was to this city that Peter came to build the Church of Christ on the rock of faith. Encountering fierce opposition and persecution, he finally reluctantly decided to abandon the ramparts. Leaving Rome via the Appian Way, he beheld a vision. It was the Master advancing toward Rome. *"Quo vadis, Domine?"* the astonished disciple asked. The Master replied that He was on His way to Rome to be crucified anew since Peter was abandoning the mission he had embraced amid the heights of Judea. Peter made the sign of the Cross and returned to the city which was to become Eternal, returned to take up again the spiritual masonry of laying stone upon stone to build the Church of Rome. As he was completing his labors, he was seized and crucified head downward.

Not all Romans opposed Christianity. The centurion who stood guard at Golgotha and witnessed the Crucifixion exclaimed: "Indeed this was the Son of God."* Saint Luke, who wrote the Third Gospel and attended upon Paul as a physician, was a Roman citizen, because Julius Caesar had decreed that all physicians in Rome were *ipso facto* Roman citizens. Saint Paul was also a Roman citizen. The Master, appearing before him in a vision, addressed him:

"Be of good heart: as thou hast given testimony of me in Jerusalem, so now it is needful thou shouldst give it in Rome also."

Even Vergil prophesied the coming of Christ. "Behold the last age of the Cumaean prediction has come," said this great Roman classic poet, "there is renewed a long series of generations, behold the Virgin returns, the reign of Saturn recommences, behold a new progeny is sent down from the highest heaven."

In A.D. 312 Emperor Constantine found himself confronted with a revolt led by Maxentius. Preparing for a head-on collision with the rebellious forces at the Milvian Bridge in Rome, he beheld in the sky

* Matthew 8:10–12.

the figure of the cross beneath which he read the words: *In hoc signo vinces.** He caused a standard to be made in this form and, with this at the head of his army, galloped into battle and into triumphant victory. From the imperial throne he declared Christianity as the religion of Rome.

About two and a half centuries later, Gregory, the Prefect of Rome, shocked at beholding youths from England being sold in the market place as slaves, resolved to convert England from paganism. He had actually set out on this bold enterprise when Pope Pelagius II died and Gregory was chosen his successor. Gregory entrusted the English mission to Saint Augustine. Gregory the Great, as he is known in history, was worthy of his title. Although not employing the title, he effectually became Emperor in the west as well as Pope. He demanded respect for civil law, he reorganized the whole papal administration, revised the church music from which emerged the famous Gregorian chant, and brought about the universal recognition of the ecclesiastical supremacy of Rome.

Several centuries later Germany resisted this supremacy and its emperor, Henry VII, boasted that he would bend the power of the Church to that of the State. Gregory VII, who was then wearing the tiara at St. Peter's, reacted vigorously. He ordered Henry (in January 1077) to don penitential garb and appear before him for chastisement at Canossa, where the Pope was then sojourning. At Canossa, Gregory commanded Henry to stand barefoot and bareheaded in the snow in the courtyard of a ruined castle for four days as penance for his pretensions. This episode gave to language the excellent phrase, "going to Canossa," meaning contrite submission to authority.

To list and tell of the saintly figures of the Church who were Italian by birth or performed their pious works in Italy would take this book beyond its intended scope, but one cannot omit mentioning several who are revered as universal benefactors in the Catholic and non-Catholic world. Pope Gregory XIV was a figure greatly admired by the Abolitionists in America because in 1591 he commanded, under pain of excommunication for those who disobeyed, that all Indian slaves in the Philippines be freed. Saint Francis of Assisi is celebrated as much in lay history as in the annals of the Church because he demonstrated by his life and his deeds that goodness is

---

* Encyclopedia Americana, title Constantine I.

not to be worn in sackcloth and to be devoid of mirth and laughter. On the contrary, Francis preached the gospel of spiritual and physical health through a merry heart.

My father's name was Antonio and we worshiped at the shrine of St. Anthony of Padua, whose intervention is entreated in the finding of lost articles. Saint Anthony was one of the greatest orators of the ages and often preached to audiences of thousands who gathered to listen to his fiery eloquence, as the result of which "family feuds that had lasted for generations were appeased under his pleading, the poor were taken care of, injustices were corrected, restitutions made and scandals repaired."

Nor did Saint Anthony limit his efforts in behalf of a better world to preaching. He was perhaps the first to effectuate a reform which did not reach its ultimate fulfillment in England until the nineteenth century. He prevailed upon the ruling body of Padua to abolish the hideous penalty of imprisonment for debt.

The patron saint of Italy is Saint Catherine of Siena, celebrated and eternally remembered because of her "cheerful piety and eloquence."

In lay history it might be difficult to find a person who was more devoted to the Church, more dedicated to religious office, more observant of all forms and ceremony in the Christian rituals than the discoverer of America. The initiation of each voyage, the making of each landfall, the beginning and ending of each day saw Columbus on his knees in prayer. Brave beyond words of appraisement, daring without limit or reserve, as audacious in battling the elements and the storm as in contesting the hostility, untruth, and ignorance of the day, he yet was humble in his faith and placed himself resolutely into the hands of the Infinite.

Living that faith while undertaking the most history-laden voyage since the beginning of time, he must rank as Italy's greatest contribution to America. And, in the listing of secular events which have monumentally changed the course of history for the improvement of the human race by broadening the base of existence to allow for a fuller life, more extensive enjoyment of liberty, and ever-augmenting happiness, the discovery of America on October 12, 1492, must head that wondrous enumeration.

One of the most astonishing surprises of my life was to learn that San Salvador, where Columbus' epochal and earth-expanding enterprise achieved dramatic fulfillment, is comparatively unknown to the traveling public. When in 1957 I could make the pilgrimage, I learned that the only way to reach San Salvador, an island approximately fourteen miles long and six miles wide located some two hundred miles southeast of Nassau, was to fly to Nassau and from there proceed to my destination by small airplane which twice a week shuttled to several of the Bahama Islands.

I carried with me a large American flag and an equally imposing standard of the City of Pittsburgh which I intended to plant temporarily at San Salvador and then present on my return to Mayor David L. Lawrence of Pittsburgh (later governor of Pennsylvania). And so, on a beautiful September morning in a tiny one-engined mosquito plane, I set off from Nassau with the pilot, a priest, Father Nicholas, and my flags for the glory-fringed birthplace of America— San Salvador.

For two hours we soared over a brilliantly blue sea which mirrored the coloration of the sky above. Gradually I began to feel an acceleration of pulse and then I became aware that my heart was pounding faster than the engine of our plane, for in the distance I could make out a long terrestrial arm greeting us. It was a bit of earth extending into the trackless sea with the same boldness it had projected itself into the dawn of that memorable October 12. I felt myself with the storm-tossed mariners of 1492 who for seventy-one days had expected to be swallowed up by the mysteries of the deep, and I imagined myself hearing the voice of Rodrigo, a sailor aboard the *Pinta*, crying: "Land! Land!"

It is my belief that persons of mighty intellect and supreme spirituality always leave something of their personality on the ground they have trod. Thus, there on that luminous shore of San Salvador, I could feel a sensation of closeness to, and affinity with, Christopher Columbus. Father Nicholas blessed the flags and then in a chapel close by, he celebrated the formal Mass of Thanksgiving.

I explored the island even as Columbus and his crew of eighty-eight must have explored it in 1492. I found it lush with vegetation, and rich in scenic delights. It sparkled with lakes, was honeysweet with the woods and flowers, and vocal with the song of birds. In their warbling I seemed to hear an echoing of the question that kept recurring in my mind: Why is it that this glorious birthplace is seemingly forgotten by the nations whose roots are sunk deep in America?

No bronze statue records this fabulous event, no memorial obelisk rises to the azure heavens, no marble tableau re-creates the scene that startled the natives in the dawn of that mystically enchanting autumnal day in 1492.

Columbus was not only a discoverer, but also an explorer, a colonizer, and a founder of nations. On his three succeeding voyages he carried with him carpenters, masons, artisans, agriculturists, seeds, plants, and implements with which to build the foundation of a new civilization. Yet he gained no personal reward. In the whole span of his life Columbus never knew comfort or ease. For eighteen years he had plodded through Europe like a mendicant seeking means and ships with which to make his epochal discoveries, and for fourteen years he had plowed the heavy seas in leaky ships, subsisting on nothing more substantial or palatable than salt pork, hardtack, and dried peas. He lived and voyaged over unknown waters, he fought his way through jungles and hostile tribes, he was without medicines, doctors, adequate sleeping facilities or shelter. During many nights of perilous passage he kept the watch in sleepless vigil and bone-chilling exposure.

It was inevitable that at last his vigorous frame could stand no more, and sighing, he gave up the ghost. He died on May 20, 1506, and, in fulfillment of his dying request, his body, forty years later, was transported to Santo Domingo, one of the islands discovered on his first voyage.

And there I visited him after I had departed from San Salvador. In the impressive Cathedral of Santo Domingo, the oldest in America, the remains of this great man rest. I knelt at his tomb in memory of this unparalleled figure who gave to mankind a new world which is named for someone else, who brought riches to others and received in recompense iron chains, and in whose discovered lands posterity has greatly lengthened the span of life, which for him was brief. He was dead at fifty-three.

7 ARCHITECTURE, SCULPTURE, PAINTING, AND MUSIC

What Italy gave to the world she gave particularly to America because America as a new and growing nation was all hunger, thirst, and eagerness for instruction, guidance, and inspiration. When we have related the Italian accomplishments and achievements known to America in the Columbus–Lincoln period we may wonder why a people so civilized, artistic, scientific, literary, and philosophical—so rich a benefactor to the mind, heart, eye, and ear of the new world —could have been treated so ignobly and lamentably during the Ellis Island Era.

The great educator Nicholas Murray Butler, president of Columbia University, said:

> The place of Italy in civilization is best shown by trying to subtract that place from world history. . . . Take away her scientific accomplishments, her statesmanship, her leadership of the world for many years and what have you left? The world looks badly decapitated. . . . You can subtract Italian culture from civilization only by destroying that civilization.

Lord Macaulay, the great English historian, wrote:

> Italian civilization, nearly 3,000 years old, has never faded out. The nights which have descended on Italy have been nights of Arctic

summer, the dawn always reappearing before the reflection of the preceding sunset has faded from the horizon.

There is scarcely a country in the world which, if it once felt the tramp of the Roman legions, did not also at the same time hear the scraping of Roman trowels, the blows of Roman hammers, the digging of Roman shovels, the creaking of Roman ropes lifting massive blocks of stone and marble into place to produce aqueducts, monuments, and amphitheaters which are still the wonder of the modern world. Charles Dickens tells how the Romans

> had made great military roads; they had built forts; they had taught them [the British] how to dress and arm themselves much better than they had ever known how to do before; they had refined the whole British way of living. . . . When laborers are digging up the ground to make foundations for houses or churches, they light on rusty money that once belonged to the Romans. Fragments of plates from which they ate, of goblets from which they drank, and of pavement on which they trod, are discovered among the earth that is broken by the plough, or the dust that is crumbled by the gardener's spade. Wells that the Romans sunk still yield waters; roads that the Romans made form part of our highways.

Whether it be in England, France, Germany, North Africa, or the Middle East, one constantly comes upon sturdy Roman architecture which has withstood the violences of war, earthquakes, invasions, and the erosions of the centuries. Ancient viaducts, stadia, and amphitheaters are constantly being uncovered, the dirt and the dust of some twenty centuries being wiped away, and put to use again. The most famous of the outdoor centuries-laden structures is, of course, the Colosseum in Rome which, oval-shaped, 617 feet long and 512 feet wide, had an audience capacity of some 50,000. Its triple row of eighty arches, with three orders of three quarter columns, decorate the exterior, and above these a fourth series of pilasters crowns the elevation, which rises to the height of 187 feet. How were these mighty rocks and the three hundred tons of iron staples which joined them, lifted into place with the nicety and precision of a jeweler's gem fitted into a brooch? How was the gleaming marble which originally plated the entire amphitheater hauled from the quarries a hundred miles away, when there were no railroads, no cranes, no steam lifts? The only answer is the engineering genius of this mighty race of people, the Romans.

What was the engineering genius which wrought the Pantheon, declared by experts to be the most mathematically perfect piece of architecture extant, which, although built two thousand years ago, preserves its perfect stateliness as if dedicated yesterday? Standing 142½ feet high, with the diameter of the rotunda 142½ feet and walls 20 feet thick, it is so "subtly designed that although the walls are half-domed and half vertical inside, it looks as if the dome began right at the floor." It is now the Westminster Abbey of Italy, holding the mortal remains of kings, poets, and artists, among them the incomparable Raphael.

Perhaps the most phenomenal aspect of the ancient Roman structures is that although the population of Rome at the time could not have exceeded a million and the population of the whole world was only one-tenth of what it is today, the structures were built on titanic lines which would make them huge, even according to today's standards. The Castel Sant'Angelo on the Tiber would dwarf any memorial in America or any part of Europe, yet it was built as a tomb for Emperor Hadrian and his family in A.D. 135–139. It was a vast cylindrical tower of solid masonry 210 feet in diameter, ornamented with columns and statues resting on a terrace 150 feet high, the tomb itself being topped by a mountain of cypresses, surmounted by an altar bearing the huge Quadriga of Hadrian. In 590 Pope Gregory the Great beheld an angel sheathing his sword above Hadrian's mausoleum and interpreted it as a sign that the plague which had been scourging the city had ceased. Thus Hadrian's Tomb became Castel Sant'Angelo, a colossal eye-filling pile which instantly chains the excited attention of every viewer of the Tiber.

Rome abounded with stupendous triumphal arches, many of which still stand today, each one looming magnificently against the eternal sky. One can still visit the Roman Forum, the Trajan Forum, and the Forum of Augustus in which he can easily visualize intellectual giants striding and speaking in tones of thunder. And then there are the Temple of Venus and Rome, the Pyramid of Caius Cestius, the Tomb of Caecilia Metella, the Column of Marcus Aurelius, the Baths of Caracalla, the Diocletian Baths, all gold and amber from the brush-strokes of time.

Nor did the monumental measurements of the Eternal City diminish with the passing of ancient Rome. The largest ecclesiastical edifice in the world is Saint Peter's Church. Bramante described it as the Pantheon piled on the Basilica of Constantine. It was 120 years in construction, its many architects including the masterful Bramante, Michelangelo, Maderna and Bernini. It measures some 750 feet in length, 450 feet in width, covers four acres of ground and ascends into the sky 438 feet. Although vast enough to hold 60,000 persons, it is so perfectly proportioned that no one feels lost amid the great spaces. The statues, holy figures, and altars are all fashioned to harmonize with the stupendous size of the edifice. Thus, it is not until one gets immediately adjacent to a sculptured cherub that he becomes aware that the infant is fifteen feet high. It is not until he examines at close quarters the mosaic picture of an Apostle that he discovers that the pen with which the Apostle is writing is six feet long. The paintings and mosaics are overwhelming in their beauty and symmetry.

The crowning glory of St. Peter's is indeed its crown, the dome. An object of veneration by the faithful and of awe by the whole world, this great mass of iron and marble is so exquisitely balanced, so finely wrought, so delicately formed that it seems to float in the air. The world has paid tribute to Michelangelo by reproducing his architectural and engineering masterpiece over national and state capitols, cathedrals, churches, art galleries, and libraries.

The setting of St. Peter's Church is perhaps as architecturally resplendent as the church itself. St. Peter's Square, with its towering obelisk, its dazzling fountains which spray an iridescent mist over the entire esplanade, and its stupendous colonnade, must rank as the most beautiful piazza in the world. The Bernini Colonnade, which has been described as the "grandest Doric peristyle since the Parthenon," marches majestically in four rows of 71 travertine columns each, producing a prodigious ellipse which can embrace a quarter of a million people. Browning said of the colonnade that it holds its "arms wide open to embrace the entry of the human race."

The columns circle with such engineering precision that a person standing in the middle of the plaza can see only one row. To further overwhelm pilgrim and tourist, 100 statues of saints stand guard on the colonnade.

Italy is a country of piazzas—spacious, sun-bathed, and fountain-drenched. In piazzas the people meet for conversation, a cup of coffee, a glass of wine, a snatch of song, and banishment of solitude, for the Italian ever yearns for companionship. The piazza is the soul and the spirit of the city or *paese* it adorns. No one can visit the spectacularly enchanting Piazza San Marco in Venice and not feel exalted, not only for the moment but in every later recollection of it. Of prodigious dimensions, measuring 575 feet in length and 230 feet in width, and bordering, as it does, the great expanse of the Grand Canal, it seems, in the midst of such artistic exquisiteness, to be a continuing undulation of the lagoon's multicolored reflecting waters. Every piazza on the Italian peninsula has its own quaint and characteristic charm and they all form part of the classic landscape of this land of marble splendor.

Architecture is to Italy what grandness is to the Alps. The Cathedral of Milan, the Duomo in Florence, the Palazzo di Giustizia in Rome, the Palazzo Pubblico of Siena, the Towers of the Porta Soprana in Genoa, the Sforzesco Castle in Milan, the Ducal Palace in Genoa, the Roman Arena in Verona, the castles of Naples and Bari, the ancient temples of Sicily—they are only a few leaves in the forest of monumental sublimities that is Italy.

No one can stand by the Cathedral of Milan and not conclude that he has beheld, not a classic, not a masterpiece of architecture, but a sheer miracle in marble. Five hundred feet long, 180 feet wide, and reaching heavenward to a height of 400 feet, it yet dominates the metropolitan skyline with all the delicacy and exquisite refinement of ivory-wrought enlacement. One hundred and fifty spires surmount the gleaming edifice, each one carved, fretted, and so artistically designed that it seems to stand alone. Multicolored sunlight falls into the vast nave through enormous windows painted with biblical scenes. No matter where one turns, one looks up at mosaics made up of hundreds of thousands of particles of tinted stone or glass so perfectly joined that the result is that of a finished painting. Statues of noble proportions and countenance occupy every niche and perch, of which there are hundreds, but this is only the beginning of this empire of statuary. The roof with its countless steeples seems an open-air pipe organ, with figures numbering thousands adorning and ornamenting every possible angle of view. A visitor to Italy, standing open-mouthed before this vast harmony of heart-stopping artistic and architectural beauty, using words from the German philosopher Schelling, pronounced in another connection, declared it to be "frozen music."

In Pisa one finds another exquisitely wrought cathedral, although on a modified scale. It is one of the three man-made wonders serenely welcoming its visitors in what the Pisans call the Meadow of Miracles. The second miracle is the Baptistery, a jewel as round as a wedding ring, with an amazing echo which reproduces the faintest whisper. And then there is the Miracle which defies the law of gravitation.

So much has been said and written about the pending feature of the Tower of Pisa that its beauty as Romanesque art has been almost entirely overlooked. Even if the Tower were wholly erect, it would excite immediate admiration. Reaching into the azure heights 180 feet, with eight galleries, each one girt with dozens of perfectly engineered columns of gleaming immaculate marble, it is surmounted by a carillon of bells in its uppermost turret. The tower first showed signs of leaning in 1174. At that time only three galleries had been completed and the architect, Bonanno Pisano, feared to go higher. Construction was suspended for nearly a century and then Giovanni di Simone, who called himself "The Omnipotent," reasoned that if he built the further galleries at a compensating angle, all would go well. When di Simone began his work the tower leaned ten inches from the perpendicular. When he finished his "straightening" process, the tower was nearly ten feet out of line! In 1300 the third architect, Tommaso di Andrea, added the belfry with its 22,000 pounds of melodious bells, but in 1934 the bells had to be silenced because their vibrations seemed to accelerate the tilt. Several years later a highly skilled engineer drained water from the soil at the base and injected with pressure 900 tons of concrete. This seemed to arrest the inclination, but during World War II, artillery bombardment in the area set the tower in motion again. It now departs fourteen feet from the vertical and it is estimated that the tilt is increasing about one inch every sixteen years. There are experts who predict that the tower will fall during the next two or three decades. Others predict it will last for centuries. Naturally I prefer the latter prophecy because it would make me sad to read that this beautiful, venerable tower of marble had crashed and left a void against the blue Italian sky.

Italian architecture has inspired and continues to inspire builders throughout the world. America and many other nations have paid generous tribute to Italy by copying many of her historical edifices and monuments. To begin with, as has already been stated, the Capitol of the United States, and that of nearly every other state capitol, is surmounted by a dome generally resembling the form of St. Peter's. Thomas Jefferson, as architect for the capitol of Virginia, was influenced by the outlines of the Maison Carrée, the Roman temple at Nîmes. In building his own charming residence, the famous Monticello (meaning little hill in Italian), he derived inspiration and guidance from the "Four Books" by Andrea Palladio, sixteenth-century architect. He also drew from Roman examples in doing the University of Virginia campus. The Library, for instance, derives from the Pantheon. So do the Law Library at Columbia University and the chapel at Syracuse University. It was eminently fitting that the Jefferson Memorial itself in Washington should be patterned after the Pantheon, since he regarded it as the most beautiful round building ever constructed.

The Union Station in Washington is Roman style and its chief feature of design is derived from the Arch of Constantine. The Pennsylvania Railroad station in New York, which has tragically fallen beneath the attack of commercialism and jackhammers was a monument which could take its place in any panorama of ancient Roman grandeur. Eighty-four imposing Doric columns surrounded its vaulted concourse of classical splendor modeled after the Baths of Caracalla.

The Public Library in Boston includes a courtyard modeled after the Palazzo Della Cancelleria in Rome. The Fenway Court also in Boston is built in Italian style around an open court, and the Old South Church is "Italian Gothic."

The famous National Academy of Design in New York is Venetian Gothic in style. The City Hall of San Francisco has a central pavilion in the form of a Roman temple.

The church of the Sacred Heart, Washington, D. C., is derived from early Romanesque peculiar to northern Italy. The majority of homes along New York's upper Fifth Avenue are, properly speaking, Italian *palazzi*, and if they had been constructed during the Renaissance, they would undoubtedly have been so named. The Congressional Library at Washington is Italian Renaissance architecture.

Closely akin to architecture is sculpture which, in its massive form, is more monumental than ornamental. Grandiose triumphal arches and massive tombs require the services of surveyor and architect, but they cannot be complete without the sculptor's chisel.

In the world of sculpture it can scarcely be disputed that Italy has reigned supreme. While it is true that much of the ancient Roman sculpture was copied from the Greek art, the Romans themselves, even in the copying, developed a genre which soon became distinctive and exclusively Roman.

Sculpture is more than beauty; it goes beyond the concept of esthetics. Where it represents the human form it imparts encouragement to man in the durability of man. Every excavation which unearths ancient statuary enlightens and enheartens the race because it lends further assurance of long life and immortality, for which every living person has a welcoming hand whether or not he consciously extends the hand. As impressed as one may be by a visit to the national House of Representatives or the Senate, he derives perhaps a greater assurance of permanence in our democratic institutions when he steps into Statuary Hall, formerly the House of Representatives, where he may look upon the imperishable George Washingtons, Thomas Jeffersons, Daniel Websters, Henry Clays, Robert Fultons, Samuel Houstons, Roger Williamses and Ethan Allens, who in their deathless permanence assure perpetuity to the principles of the Declaration of Independence, the Constitution, and the Bill of Rights.

Moses was the original and supreme lawgiver. The laws chiseled in stone by the Divine Sculptor are affirmation that man can, through law, go on surviving, despite iniquity and disaster, despite evil and catastrophe. One senses *that* security of law when he looks at Michelangelo's "Moses" in the church of San Pietro in Vincoli in Rome. The viewer may feel as he approaches this stupendous bearded figure an increasing solidity in the very ground beneath his feet; he may also sense an additional dimension of immutable well-being, confident he is breathing the air of a universe controlled by law, not one which is the helpless prey of mere chance.

When Michelangelo completed this immortal piece of perfection he stood before it in meditation, somehow expecting something. The statue seemed so much alive that he expected it to talk. When the lips did not move, Michelangelo brought his hammer down hard on Moses' knee and commanded: "Speak!" A slight laceration in the marble at this point lends credibility to the legend.

As Leonardo da Vinci stands peerless as the universal genius, Michelangelo must reign supreme as the superb master in sculpture and painting, plus superlative talents in architecture, engineering, and poetry. Michelangelo's genius was first given authoritative recognition by Lorenzo the Magnificent, the uncrowned ruler of Florence. Although many coals of fire have been heaped upon Lorenzo as a tyrant in government, he has earned his place in the history of benefactors for his encouragement of all the arts, and particularly sculpture. He saw in Michelangelo, as a lad of fifteen, a promising youth who would startle the world and he gave him a place in his palace and garden of sculpture, supplying him with teachers who, in but a short time, were to receive instruction from their youthful pupil.

Michelangelo's "Pietà," which was brought to the New York World's Fair in 1964, is now probably the most well-known and admired piece of statuary in existence. For sanctity of subject, purity and beauty of form, delicacy of execution, and supreme appeal to reverence and pity, the Pietà, in my estimation, has no equal in the whole white universe of immaculate marble. Michelangelo finished this unparalleled work at twenty-two, but in genius there is no immaturity.

When Francis Cardinal Spellman persuaded Pope Pius XII to permit the Pietà to be shipped to New York for exhibition at the World's Fair, the art universe recoiled aghast. If it should break on the long voyage, who could ever repair it? If the ship on which it was to be transported should sink, what could ever replace it? Pius XII, followed by Pope John XXIII, believed that the religious comfort and exaltation the statuary would bring to millions who would otherwise never have the opportunity to see this hallowed masterpiece, would justify the risk of travel. Every precaution, however, was taken to insure safety. It was packed in a foam plastic material known as dylite polystyrene and then tightly bound in a case prepared for special buoyancy so that if the ship on which it was to sail should sink, the case would float and, by an attached self-activating wireless device, rescuers would be summoned to save this matchless paragon of art, impossible of reproduction. It was insured for $26,000,000, although, had it not successfully accomplished the journey, even that fortune could never have compensated for its loss.

And while it was on display in the Vatican pavilion at the World's Fair, there was never an end to the long lines of reverent humanity filing by to admire and be blessed by the sanctified presence of the Pietà.

Like Leonardo da Vinci, Michelangelo knew anatomy exhaustively. No surgeon at the operating table could have been more aware of the tissues, muscles, and bones with which he had to contend than Michelangelo was aware as he sculpted. He never worked from a clay model but fell directly upon the raw material, and in doing so, felt not that he was creating a statue but that he was liberating an imprisoned figure. And as he wrought, no one could approach him because of the flying chips.

Michelangelo's figures all speak of titanic resoluteness and determination to get on with God's work. He never allowed the conceit of others to thwart him, nor would he descend to petty argument. After Michelangelo completed his work on "David," one of the civic leaders (Gonfaloniere Soderini) of Florence criticized the nose as being too large. Without a word Michelangelo ascended the scaffolding with a mallet, chisel, and a handful of marble dust. Making a great show of chiseling about David's face, without touching it at all, Michelangelo let marble dust fall from his hand in little clouds. Much gratified, Soderini said: "That's fine! You've now given life to the statue."

Michelangelo knew his power and he recognized the genius of others. Upon beholding the bronze doors (East Portal) of the Baptistery in Florence, with Lorenzo Ghiberti's bronze sculpture of dramatic episodes from the Bible, Michelangelo spontaneously cried: "These doors are worthy of the gates of Paradise!"

He was the towering glory of the Renaissance, but preceding him were those who, without Michelangelo, might themselves have stood at the pinnacle of artistic fame. Filippo Brunelleschi has been called the father of Renaissance architecture. His dome for the cathedral of Florence was an inspiration for Michelangelo himself and holds fast the eye in fascination for its soul-lifting grace, plus sturdy structural composition.

Donatello di Betto Bardi, another giant in the gigantic days of the Renaissance, is regarded as the founder of modern sculpture. He executed the first equestrian statue in bronze, the "Gattamelata," since ancient times. Supremely adept at working on huge figures, he was equally masterful in working with fragile little figures in bronze and exquisite terra-cotta busts.

Vying for laurels in this same arena of artistic versatility was the famous Benvenuto Cellini who could produce the large "Perseus with the Head of Medusa" in the Loggia dei Lanzi in Florence and then execute with elegant finesse and daintiness the tiniest figures and tableaux in gold and silver. As an artist Cellini looms as large as his "Perseus," but as a member of society he unfortunately approaches the size of some of his salt and pepper shakers. His famous *Autobiography* reveals him as more literary than loyal, more mendacious than moral, more philanderer than philosopher.

In this same incredible period of the Renaissance one meets the celebrated Leopardi, Verrocchio, Giovanni da Bologna, Mino da Fiesole, Benedetto da Maiano, Baccio Bandinelli, Giacomo della Porta, the three della Robbias, and the two Rossellinis, not to mention Leonardo da Vinci.

As if to emphasize to the world the prodigality of talent in Italy, many of her artists like Michelangelo and da Vinci carved out their fame in more than one medium. Giotto di Bondone was sculptor, painter, and architect. In 1334 he designed the world-famous, beautiful Campanile of the cathedral of Santa Maria del Fiore in Florence. His sculpture matched the thrilling quality of his architecture and as a painter he brought animation and vividness to walls and life to ceilings, such as they had never known since antiquity.

Giotto was a Florentine as were Fra Angelico, Fra Filippo Lippi, Domenico Ghirlandaio, Michelangelo, Leonardo da Vinci, Tommaso Masaccio, Paolo Uccello, Sandro Botticelli, and others of that miraculous group of painters whose brushes were wands creating wonders.

An American millionaire, whose name is mercifully kept secret, offered the suggestion that soil from the Florentine region be brought to America to "grow artists on it." More than soil is required to grow genius. There must be, in addition, climate, environment, tutors, a slight attribute such as natural talent, and then a proper selection of ancestors. Each city in which art flourished, and that was true in nearly every city in Italy, produced enough masterpieces to supply the nation rather than merely a circumscribed urban area. The products of Italian painters have enriched the world. Americans of extreme wealth and American art galleries have purchased originals or authenticated copies to beautify and inspire generations.

The person who is not moved by a great painting can only be one who does not understand or appreciate the divine art of living. Every

act we perform, every object we perceive, every individual we encounter, is a painting, but we cannot linger with it. It appears for
the instant and then departs. It is followed by another painting, but
this quickly also goes the way of its predecessors. The continuity is
so rapid that we are not aware that we are moving through a universal
art gallery of time. Thus, when we stop to admire a painting—it may
be only a bowl of fruit—we speak of its coloring and its naturalness,
and the closer it resembles what is ours to see merely for the looking,
the more attention it compels and the more awe it inspires.

If we could capture a minute and hold it for an hour, what an
exciting spectacle and dramatic phenomenon it would be! Of course,
this cannot be done, but the next best thing is to capture a scene, a
living image, and lo! the tenderness of the Christ child, the vastness
of the sea, the bowl of fruit, the smile of Mona Lisa are ours for eternity. We are holding fast to the passing of time. When we look at a
worthy canvas we are peering through the eyes of immortality.

On the ceiling of the Sistine Chapel in the Vatican, one sees not
only immortality but Genesis. Nothing can convince one of the
stupendousness of this work unless he sees it, and, even then, he
walks away paradoxically incredulous. It is almost beyond human
capacity to thoroughly grasp what was here accomplished by one
man. For four years Michelangelo painted from a scaffold forty-five
feet above the pavement, lying on his back with a candle attached to
the peak of his cap which dropped wax, mixed with colors, into his
face, as he re-created the creation of the world. The vaulted space
which covers 10,000 square feet abounds with 343 Biblical figures,
which vividly relate the overmastering story of the beginning of the
world, the Fall of Man, Noah's Flood, and the purification of man
through eternal life.

Behind the altar the wall animatedly bursts with Michelangelo's
dramatic masterpiece, "The Last Judgment," one of the largest frescoes
in the world and probably one of the most powerful paintings in the
history of art. Measuring 66 feet in height and 33 feet in width, it
leaves the viewer helpless as he studies the myriads of figures ranging
before the Redeemer, in their varying attitudes of fear, foreboding,
or ecstasy as they hear the verdict of eternal Judgment. Heaven,
Purgatory, and Hell loom before them. While engaged in executing
this colossal work, a Vatican official named Biagio impeded and an-
noyed Michelangelo with constant interruptions. Michelangelo re-

taliated by painting Biagio as Minos, the guide to Hell. The doomed man rushed to Pope Paul III to protest, but the pontiff, not without a sense of humor, replied: "My dear Biagio, if Michelangelo had placed you in Purgatory, I could do something for you, but in Hell no one can save you, not even the Pope!"

At the age of seventy, Michelangelo penned his beautiful sonnets, to the Roman lady Vittoria Colonna, the only known love interest in his long life, which extended to his ninetieth year. One day, the aging artist and the Roman lady were discovered sitting in the dim twilight of a deserted church "talking soft and low." It is good to know that this superlative genius of a man who, throughout his whole life, had to battle opposition, envy, ignorance, and sloth, as he strove to make the world more beautiful and man more self-dignified, did find one moment when he rested and talked soft and low to an understanding heart and a loving soul.

While Leonardo and Michelangelo lived, there came into this world the third member of the peerless Renaissance triumvirate, Raphael—slender, tall, with long golden hair, and "the face of an angel," as described by Pope Julius. Never did one paint with more facility and grace, never did one bring to the canvas such sweetness of expression and grace of attitude as did Raphael. He painted over one hundred Madonnas, each one an overpowering revelation of beauty, serenity, and exaltation. Today they are literally priceless. One, "The Alba Madonna," costing more than a million dollars, was acquired from the former imperial gallery in Leningrad, and presented by Andrew Mellon, former Secretary of the Treasury, to the National Gallery of Art in Washington.

Raphael's "La Disputa" and the "School of Athens" would in themselves have made him an immortal among artists but these are only two frescoes of the hundreds which flowered from his never-ceasing brushstrokes. The walls, ceilings, and corridors of the Vatican speak to you of drama, history, and indescribable beauty through the matchless paintings and tapestries of Raphael. Their vivid imagery takes you into the realm of the impossible, even though the finished creations are before your eyes.

I shall never forget the time I looked upon his painting "The Entombment" which depicts Christ being carried from the Cross to the tomb. The limp body of the Saviour, the invasions of the purple hues of death, the agony of the women helplessly looking on, contrasted with the stalwart figures carrying the body, brought to my eyes and to those of all other beholders, tears which no one attempted to suppress.

At the age of thirty-five Raphael realized that there was a great joy of love on earth, apart from what he created in the heaven of art, and he asked for the hand of Maria di Bibbiena, beautiful niece of Cardinal Bibbiena. The Pope assented to the union but asked Raphael to postpone the wedding until he could complete the many projects which awaited his masterful hand. But as Raphael worked feverishly, Maria died. One year later Raphael joined her in the Pantheon. For a year Michelangelo wore mourning on his sleeve for the young and beautiful artist who could have been a model for one of his own artistic creations.

In addition to these three incomparable masters, and of such dazzling genius that they cast their own classic shadows, are Titian, Tintoretto, Paolo Veronese, Giorgione Gentile, Giovanni Bellini, and Sandro Botticelli. Titian, whose name was Tiziano Vecellio, plunged into his life's work early, as if, like Raphael, he had not long to live. In his teens he was painting pictures with colored juices extracted from flower petals. He really had no reason to hurry his career since he lived to ninety-nine, all the time pouring gorgeous tints and hues onto his canvases in the long series of masterpieces we now call Titians. His "Assumption of the Virgin," depicting the Virgin Mary being welcomed by God in Heaven, is a painting that, once seen, remains with one like a personal experience.

Botticelli's fame is equally enduring. His spectacular "The Birth of Venus" and "Spring," together with his "Adoration of the Magi," "The Last Communion of St. Jerome," and "The Temptation of Christ," are all characterized by his graceful, flowing lines and poetic atmosphere.

No one could ever do justice to the Italian painters* in a short chapter, but before leaving the subject one must at least mention Benozzo Gozzoli, whose figures are supreme animation; Andrea del Castagno, many of whose characters portray the need in life for in-

---

* On the façade of the Art Institute of Chicago appear the names of fifteen of the world's greatest geniuses in art: Donatello, Memling, Botticelli, da Vinci, Dürer, Michelangelo, Raphael, Titian, Andrea del Sarto, Correggio, Holbein, Veronese, Tintoretto, Rubens, and Velázquez. Two are German, two Flemish, one Spanish, ten are Italian.

cessant action and, if necessary, combat; Michelangelo Caravaggio, whose amazing portrayals in light and shadow have few equals in any nation or period of time; and Antonio Allegri da Correggio, of whom it has been said that his work combined some of the best qualities of Raphael, Leonardo da Vinci, and Michelangelo.

One of the reasons why Italy down through the centuries has suffered repeated invasions is that the invaders coveted her works of art. While it would be difficult to carry away the Colosseum, it was no trouble for looters to seize canvases, after ripping away the frames, roll them up like carpets and transport them back to their home countries. Of all the art thieves, none surpassed in criminality the Nazi Hermann Goering, whose agents filled with Italian masterpieces many railroad trains traveling north and through the Gothard Pass. Fortunately the treasures he stole and concealed in German palaces, warehouses, and even salt mines were located after the war and brought back to Italy.

It will be recalled how the Cathedral of Milan, with its architectural and sculptural riches, was referred to as "frozen music." Considering that the whole Italian peninsula is a vast hinterland of marble, bronze, and stone monuments and figures, one might say that Italy itself is a land of visual music. It is also a vast concert hall of audible music. In many ways, Italy is the cradle of modern music.

We have seen in our discussion on anatomy that many parts of the human body have been named after Italians. In music the whole anatomical language is Italian. No matter in what country music is played or sung, the musical terms are almost always Italian. *Da capo, allegro, oratorio, opera, libretto, adagio, largo, soprano, contralto, basso, crescendo, diminuendo, andante, finale, forte, fortissimo, piano, pianissimo, staccato, con brio, marcato* are all Italian words. And they have become so much a part of English literature that they function as metaphorical phrases.

The history of music in Italy combines with the history of its people and the history of the Church as well, because from earliest times music formed part of the Christian ceremonial. The four authentic scales which were the bases of the medieval system are attributed to St. Ambrose who, as Bishop of Milan, proclaimed in the fourth century antiphonal singing in all the churches in his diocese. In the eleventh century Father Guido d'Arezzo developed a system of recording musical tone which led to formalized composition. Dante's friend Pietro Casella is the earliest known composer of madrigals, in the late thirteenth century.

By the sixteenth century, church music had acquired polyphonic displays which Pope Pius IV believed incongruous in the sacred atmosphere in which it was played and sung. He directed Giovanni Pierluigi, who is known in history as Palestrina, to reform and chasten church music. His work in this field was so successfully noteworthy that he became known as the greatest composer of his age. The great German composer Richard Wagner found Palestrina's masses and motets "a spiritual revelation."

Jacopo Peri was the first opera composer, his work *Dafne* being sung in Florence in 1597. Claudio Monteverdi is regarded as the creator of modern musical drama, bringing into play as he did with his work *Orfeo* in 1607 a much larger orchestra than had previously been employed. Giacomo Carissimi and Alessandro Stradella were others who so guided and refined the art of music that already in the seventeenth century the world recognized Italy as the home of the greatest musicians. At the end of that century Alessandro Scarlatti stood forth as the leader of opera in composition and teaching.

In addition to recording music on paper and giving it ear by voice and instrument, Italians produced the musical instruments themselves. Even in the Middle Ages the organ in Italy had reached a high state of development. In its present conformation the violin is an Italian invention, and never were better violins made than those which came into being in Cremona under the masterful hands of the Amati, Guarneri, and Stradivari families. Antonio Stradivari, to be forever celebrated under the latinized version of his name, Stradivarius, died in 1737 at the age of ninety-three. Since more than a thousand instruments, including violins, violas, and cellos, came from his gifted hands, it is probably certain that a number of Stradivariuses enlivened American parlors when chamber music was the height of fashion up to the middle of the nineteenth century.

The most celebrated, and almost legendary, figure who worked aural magic with a Guarnerius was Niccolò Paganini, whose virtuosity was so dazzlingly and pyrotechnically brilliant that it was said he had sold his soul to the devil who invisibly stood by his side at all concerts to supply the fire that never came from any other violin before or, we presume, since.

Of the Italian composers who wrote and were performed prior to the middle of the nineteenth century it is enough to name Arcangelo Corelli, Gaetano Donizetti, Vincenzo Bellini, Maria Luigi Cherubini, Antonio Vivaldi, and then, of course, Gioacchino Antonio Rossini, whose *Barber of Seville, Semiramide,* and *William Tell* can still turn a concert hall, a bandstand, or an operatic stage into a melodic bonfire.

One of the most popular composers of opera of all time is Giuseppe Verdi, with his *Rigoletto, Il Trovatore, La Traviata, Aïda, Otello,* and *Falstaff.* To dwell on his fame would be as superfluous as painting the mountains.

And it would be to gild gold to expatiate on the genius of Pietro Mascagni, whose *Cavalleria Rusticana* is perennially popular, and Giacomo Puccini, with his *La Bohème, Tosca,* and *Madama Butterfly.*

Colonel Giuseppe Maria Francesco Vigo, whose assistance to General George Rogers Clark, as scout, spy, and banker contributed immeasurably to the winning of the Northwest Territory.

COURTESY, INDIANA DEPARTMENT OF CONSERVATION.

Giuseppe Garibaldi. One of the greatest soldiers in the entire history of man's struggle for freedom and independence. President Lincoln offered him a major general's commission in the Union Army.

COURTESY, CULVER PICTURES.

The Garibaldi Guard being reviewed by President Lincoln and General Winfield Scott, July 4, 1861. COURTESY, THE ILLUSTRATED LONDON NEWS.

Between 1820 and 1963, over five million Italians entered the United States at various ports. Here we see a typical Italian immigrant family at Ellis Island. COURTESY, GEORGE EASTMAN HOUSE.

Constantino Brumidi
"The Michelangelo of the Capitol of the United States"
COURTESY, LIBRARY OF CONGRESS.

Car of History sculpted by Carlo Franzoni.
Originally in House of Representatives, now
in Statuary Hall, U. S. Capitol.
COURTESY, LIBRARY OF CONGRESS.

Saint Frances Xavier Cabrini. First and only
United States citizen canonized a Saint. Founder
of Missionary Sisters of the Sacred Heart.
COURTESY, THE PITTSBURGH CATHOLIC.

Guglielmo Marconi, inventor of wireless telegraphy. Here he is shown
with Pope Pius XI on occasion of world's first radio communication by
ultra short-wave, Vatican Palace, February 11, 1933.

COURTESY, UNITED PRESS INTERNATIONAL.

8 THE WESTWARD "GULF STREAM"

After discovering the New World, Christopher Columbus, as we have seen, immediately set about to colonize it, and every succeeding ship sailing to Columbia-land teemed with restless colonizers, forest-levelers, tillers of soil, and builders. Obstructions intruded. The natives resisted, and nature fought with storms, wildernesses, unharnessed waters, and periodically crippling climate.

To those who feared neither hardship nor danger, the new lands offered the prospect of gold and rich lands and, what was even more precious to many voyagers, political freedom and religious liberty. By 1770 those who had answered the call, plus those who were descendants of the early colonists, numbered three million, all working and building in the bustling settlements, ambitious villages, and rapidly growing towns and cities of the curving Atlantic seaboard. Much indeed had been accomplished since John Smith unfurled the banner of James I in 1607 and since the Pilgrims, minus the blessings of the same James, had disembarked at Plymouth in 1620. Politically, the three million people formed thirteen colonies owing allegiance to King George III, but they were offended by his attitude. They particularly resented his impeding the flow of further manpower desperately needed to develop the colonies' natural resources.

Accordingly they petitioned the King to allow more ships to raise sails and head for hospitable America. The King resented their presumption in daring to tell him what he should do. He drastically curtailed their representation in government, increased the already unbearable taxes and quartered soldiers among them. The colonies raised the flag of revolt. Thomas Jefferson, in classic language told the King why. One of the reasons he spelled out was that King George III

has endeavored to prevent the population of these States; for that purpose obstructing the Laws of Naturalization of Foreigners; refusing to pass others to encourage migrations hither, and raising the conditions for the new Appropriations of lands.

Having once thrown off the monarchial yoke, the Americans cried across the seas to their kinsmen near and far to join them. Many responded to the cry and the land prospered, but still not enough harkened. Increasingly more hands were needed to wield the ax in the wilderness and the hammer and saw in the towns. There were yet vast and numerous virgin forests offering their timber, there were still immense flatlands begging for the company of fruit trees and stalks of corn, wheat, and maize. There were enormous tracts of land available for factories which were crying to be born if the new country was to compete in progress with the other countries of the world.

As late as 1841 America was still asking her overseas cousins to leave the ancient world and begin afresh in the new. President John Tyler, in his message to Congress on June 1, 1841, emphasized the invitation:

"We hold out to the people of other countries an invitation to come and settle among us as members of our rapidly growing family, and for the blessings which we offer them we require of them to look upon our country as their country and to unite with us in the great task of preserving our institutions and thereby perpetuating our liberties."

As early as 1795 George Washington had called upon all Americans, in his Thanksgiving Day Proclamation of that year, "humbly and fervently to beseech the kind author of these blessings . . . to render this country more and more a safe and propitious asylum for the unfortunate of other countries." Thomas Jefferson also pleaded the case for the oppressed of other lands: "Shall we refuse to the unhappy fugitives from distress that hospitality which the savages of the wilderness extended to our fathers arriving in this land? Shall oppressed humanity find no asylum on this globe?"*

In 1856 the Democratic Party platform proclaimed America to be "The Asylum of the Oppressed." By 1860 the United States, from a narrow strip of colonies forming an irregular arch on the Atlantic coast, had become an empire spanning the continent from Atlantic to Pacific. Its area covered 2,022,387 square miles or 1,294,327,680 acres. On a per capita basis each man, woman and child, would be entitled to 61.38 acres.

While, of course, some of this acreage would not be available for agricultural, industrial, or residential purposes, it was still clear that if the United States was to take its place in the array of nations as a power that could defend its interests and accomplish the maximum well-being of its people, its population had to be augmented. It was obvious that the normal birthrate could not supply enough people to cultivate the untilled land, extract the enormous mineral deposits from the earth, extend the railroads, construct new ports, and erect factories and mills.

President Abraham Lincoln, with his far-seeing eyes, perceived the need and called for the establishing of a "system for the encouragement of immigration." Congress agreed and in 1864 placed on the statute books "An Act to Encourage Immigration." This encouragement speedily traveled to Europeans via personal letters, newspaper articles, guidebooks, pamphlets, and maps. American western states installed information agencies abroad to disseminate attractive physical facts on the opportunities for economic independence in the New World. American railroads expended large sums of money advertising the felicities of the Promised Land.

The urging acted like huge rams battering down the dikes and dams holding rivers at stationary levels, and a new stream poured into the ocean of human affairs. It swept from East to West bearing countless ships laden with those who responded to the call of America for immigrants, more immigrants, and still more immigrants. From 1861 to 1870, 2,350,000 crossed the Atlantic and hurried down the gang-

* In 1778 Jefferson wrote to Richard Henry Lee: "Immigrants from Mediterranean regions are of more value than those of Northern countries—they bring with them a skill in agriculture and other arts better adapted to our climate." (Padover-Jefferson, p. 105m).

planks into New York, Boston, Baltimore, Philadelphia, New Orleans, and other American ports to take places in the army of builders of America. From 1871 to 1880 nearly three million more avid constructors arrived. In the following decade the westwardly-pouring "Gulf Stream" bore vessels carrying an additional 5,250,000 workers to these shores. From 1890 to 1900, 4,000,000 incoming passengers arrived, and then, during the first decade of the twentieth century, the incoming figures swelled to 8,795,000.

The America-bound travelers hailed from every country and clime in Europe. Italy, only three-fourths the size of California, filled more ships than any other nation except Germany. Counting those who sailed in that fleet-laden period of immigration and their offspring —now an integral part of every state in the union—the Italians in the United States presently number over 21,000,000. The Reverend Theodore E. McGarrick, sociologist and Dean of the Catholic University in Washington, stated in an address delivered on June 10, 1963, that, based on census statistics,

> "the young of Italian stock is the largest among all the foreign stock populations in the United States, counting for more than 13 per cent of the total, and being a full half percentage point above the Germans, who rank second. More than one out of every eight persons of foreign birth or parentage in this country is of Italian stock."

The tide of Italian immigration reached flood level subsequent to that of the Irish and the German, since Italy, as previously stated, did not become a wholly united country until 1870 when Rome was proclaimed its capital. At the highest level, however, of the European dam-burst, the Italian inundation reached a higher crest than that of any other nationality. From 1880 to 1900, 550,000 Italians entered the United States; from 1900 to 1910, the ingress from Italy was twenty-five percent greater than that of any other nation in any ten-year period, for a total of 2,045,877. In a single year 300,000 Italians disembarked at Ellis Island. Like the tributaries of a mighty river, rising from many sources, the swelling stream of Italians coursed, gushed, and swept into the sea, ferrying its individuality across the ocean in the westward-sweeping immigrant "Gulf Stream."

The Italian mountaineer hurried down from his mountain top, the peasant quitted his field, the shoemaker thrust aside his last, the blacksmith closed his shop, the mason dusted his apron, the fisherman folded his nets, the carpenter, bricklayer, and plumber downed their tools—they were going to America, the America of Columbus, of Amerigo Vespucci, of John Cabot, of Philip Mazzei, the America of their fellow townsmen who had just returned after working in New Jersey, Delaware, Pennsylvania, and New York. These prospective immigrants ignored the fables that gold was to be had for stooping on the streets of New York, that fortunes were to be made in a week. They discounted the stories of riches and opulence awaiting all pilgrims. It was enough that they would have the opportunity to work and that they would be free to fashion their own destiny. They believed in America, the America of George Washington, Thomas Jefferson, Abraham Lincoln—and Giuseppe Garibaldi.

Moreover, they had faith in themselves as Italians. No matter how poor the village in which they lived, no matter if its streets were unpaved and modern conveniences lacking, there was always a road somewhere close by, a road in good repair, a road that traversed the centuries back to the era of the Romans, the master road builders of the world. Roads over which had moved the power, the culture, the progress of Latin civilization. The villagers knew that as these roads traveled back to the days of majestic, invincible, and enlightened Rome, these same roads would lead them also into the future of dignity and freedom from want.

These were the roads the immigrants followed on their way to the seaports to board the vessel that would transport them over the route traversed by their original countryman Cristoforo Colombo and his sons and their descendants. Every immigrant carried with him two pieces of baggage. One bulged with clothing and food (cheese, salami, bread) so that he might make a neat appearance in America and maintain life until he obtained remunerative work. The other bag was equally large but not bulky, it was not even visible to others. It was crammed full with the heritage of his culture, the traditions of his land and his religious devotion. The first bag was often depleted of its contents before the Italian got a job or even after he obtained an ill-paying one. But the second bag sustained him and supplied him with the courage and fortitude to go on regardless of deprivation, hardship, and rebuff.

However, despite the brightness of his hopes and the confidence of faith in his destiny, the departing *paisano* felt a melancholy shadow clinging to him. He was leaving Italy. Here he had drunk deep of the sweetest drinks of life, his carefree, childhood days; here he had climbed mountains, swum rivers, explored caves. Here he had grown into youth. Here he had danced at *festas* with pretty *signorine,* here he had known friendships and comradeships he thought would last forever. Now he was leaving these companions, the green meadows in which he had pastured sheep, and Italy's blue skies. America he wanted, America he needed, but Italy was in his bones, his blood, his memories. He could take these memories with him, yes, but the sweetest of recollections can hurt. The more fragrant the rose of memory, the sharper the inevitable thorn cuts into the flesh of reality, as one realizes that the petals have fallen, never again to be reassembled.

Antonio is leaving father, mother, brothers, sisters, bosom friends. They are all in the *piazza* bidding him fond farewell. There is the attempt at jollity, there is forced laughter, and then someone lifts his voice in song, a gay song, but the merriest notes are wet with tears. The mule cart that is to take Antonio to the railroad station has arrived. There are kisses and embraces. "*Mamma! Papà!*" "*Figlio mio! Scrivi presto!*" "*Arrivederci! Addio! Caro!*" Antonio climbs into the cart, and as it starts away he waves his arm, and keeps waving it until the mass of stone which is his *paese* has turned into a mountain of stone in his breast.

He is at the railroad station and he boards the train. Something within him is keeping time with the melancholy rhythm of the swaying cars and the screeching locomotive. At last he arrives in the famous, fabulous city of Naples where the masts of ships in its spectacular semicircular harbor form a veritable forest. He is at the dock, a tag has been tied to the lapel of his coat, he moves with hundreds of others similarly tagged, and, like the flocks of sheep he had shepherded in the *campagna,* they are all herded into the hold of a mighty vessel almost as large as his own *paese.*

Antonio is on his way to America. On the dock he had purchased a paperbound book which in bold letters on the cover "guaranteed" to teach the reader English by the time the ship arrived in New York. Antonio smiled. He saw the catch. The book said it would "teach," it didn't say that the reader could *learn* English in sixteen days, the scheduled duration of the voyage. Antonio enjoyed reading. He had attended the village school until he was fourteen and when he had tended sheep he always carried in his pocket Manzoni's *I Promessi Sposi.* When he worked in the wheatfields or among the beds of let-

tuce, cauliflower, tomatoes, peppers, and beets, he lay on the ground
during the rest periods and devoured the history book his school-
teacher had given him. He had kept up a close relationship with the
professore, who acquainted him with what was happening in the
world. And now he was on the way to the newest world of all.

Antonio had no idea where he would eventually take root in the
new continent. An Italian who came from the United States and
referred to himself as a *padrone*, had visited him in his *paese* and offered to advance one-half of the passage money, provided Antonio
would agree to pay it back *con un premio* (with a bonus) after he had
started to work at the job the *padrone* would get for him. It seemed
a fair enough agreement and Antonio accepted.

Sixteen days after the ship had weighed anchor in Naples, it sailed
into New York Bay, which had been discovered by da Verrazano, as
Antonio had been told by the *professore*. Though large, the ship still
didn't seem big enough to have contained the small army which
poured ashore with him at Castle Garden, the immigration depot.
After a brief examination and questioning, the doors of quarantine
swung open and Antonio, eyes blinking, stepped out to the streets of
New York—in America! Trembling with excitement he moved along
with the other immigrants, all bound for the office of the *padrone*,
who now appeared in person, the very man who had talked to him
in Antonio's *paese*. The *padrone* called names from many sheets of
paper, the voyagers responding "*Presente!*" as their own names were
reached. There were some two hundred in Antonio's group and, after
the roll call, they were taken to a large building where they lined up
for bread and coarse soup, and were then assigned to bunks in the
same building.

The next morning the *padrone* announced that jobs had been
found for all of them, on a *ferrovia* (railroad) that was being built
some fifty miles out of New York. The hours would be from six in the
morning until six in the evening, and the wages one dollar a day,
from which would be deducted the cost of maintenance and, at intervals, a certain other amount until the *padrone* had been reim-
bursed (with interest) for the sums he had expended.

At four the next morning they were routed from their bunks, and,
as they hurried to wagons standing outside the doors, they gulped
a glass of black coffee. They were on the way to their first job in
America, the initial job for most immigrants from Italy, the job that

was the very foundation of American industrial progress. It was the letter "A" in the alphabet of construction, and the alpha in the book of progress—"picka shov," as the Italians called it.

The prospect of swinging a pick all day long did not daunt Antonio. There was something satisfying and even enheartening about the work. Planting his feet firmly on the ground, raising the pick above his head and bringing it down zestfully, imparted a deep satisfaction. He felt he was digging for that dollar which was to be paid him, the pick was a sledge with which he was breaking the chain which bound him to the *padrone,* he was digging to make himself a part of America.

After several hours of pick-wielding, the men about Antonio loudly complained: the work was backbreaking, monotonous, muscle-tearing. But Antonio smiled beneath his mustache. His pick rose and fell, the clods flew upward like birds on the wing, the excavation deepened and the ditch lengthened. Pride rose with the bulging biceps of the twenty-year-old youth. He wasn't lacerating the earth, he wasn't shoveling dirt, he wasn't producing calluses—he was building *a railroad!* In America!

At six o'clock the whistle blew and the sweating immigrants dropped their tools as if they were hot pokers. Wagons clattered up, the exhausted workers clambered aboard, the horses that seemed even more tired than the laborers dragged their burden behind them to a row of shanties, the home of the ditchdiggers. Here they seized pump handles; water splashed into basins, soon turning black from the mud and grime washed from the faces of the toilers, who were now herded into a long shanty for boiled beans, white bacon, and bread. Coffee, with condensed milk from a can, helped to wash down the coarse meal, made palatable because of desperate hunger and exhaustion. At nine o'clock everybody had thrown himself on to his cot, some not even undressing.

Antonio went back into the dining shanty, and, by an oil lamp, read more from the book guaranteed to teach English in an ocean's crossing. There was really no need for English on this job. The *padrone* talked Italian. The foremen, although not Italians, were eloquent pointers and signalers, and easily made themselves understood by extravagant gestures and even more extravagant profanity. But Antonio was thinking ahead. He wanted to learn English fast; it would enable him more quickly to understand America, the fever of which was raging in his veins, despite the aches sprouting in his back.

It has been said that the mind of a man toiling at a job, whose movements are simple and endlessly repeated, washes to a blank, his faculty of imagination erodes, and he degenerates into an automaton. But not with Antonio, whose thoughts kept time with his flashing pick and whose imagination accompanied every deft thrust of his shovel. He could see himself excavating for the treasure of progress, shoveling away all grumbling and self-pity. He was building a railroad, not only for America, but for Italians who were still to come from Italy, and particularly for Maddalena, the dark-eyed, slender, beautiful *signorina* with whom he had danced at the *festa* of San'Antonio in his *paese*. He would soon be twenty-one and happily he anticipated man's responsibilities and joys—work, marriage, and the raising of a family. But he had to earn more wages. A year later he climbed out of the ditches, having paid back what he owed the *padrone*, and he descended into a coal mine in Pennsylvania. Here he was his own boss and the amount of money he earned depended on the number of cars he could fill with the coal dug out of the earth with his pick and dynamite.

After a year in the mine he had, by the strictest economizing, saved enough to buy a steamship ticket for Maddalena, whom he had been courting by mail, and when she arrived, they were married. What more could Antonio wish for? He had health, a job, a felicitous companion and a bond with his mother country which would never sever. He beheld in Maddalena the personification of Italy with its sentiment, poetry, and culture of the ages. He was reading and studying all the time, becoming more and more American. He played no cards, frequented no saloons; he was making American history his own. He wanted his children to be devoted to America and all that America meant, but he felt they would achieve this devotion all the more ardently if they were imbued with the spirit of the Italians whose genius had advantaged the whole world. Maddalena could at home impart to them that love for the old country while the children at school would learn to respect, obey, and love America. In this dual love, he saw the ideal of life, the supreme good of living.

One day the mine in which Antonio worked exploded, and the roof caved in. Five days passed before he could be rescued. In the meanwhile twenty-five of his fellow workers had been killed, either by the initial blast or by the after-damp. Maddalena pleaded with Antonio never to go into the mine again. "Take any job," she entreated. "I will help. I'll take in boarders if necessary. We'll manage, but I don't want to see you again going down into that cavern of death." And so Antonio went back to the railroad, went back to digging again, to laying track again, but at least the roof was safe. His wage was now $1.50 a day. With his own hands he built a house on the banks of the railroad overlooking the Ohio River. It wasn't much of a house architecturally. In fact, it wasn't much more than a shack, but in Maddalena's entranced eyes it was a castle with shining turrets, sky-piercing spires—it was home. And into this home came their first child—a little miracle, Annina.

Raphael could never have painted a prettier angel than Annina, no song could lift the heart higher than did her smile, no sunshine could be brighter than her presence. Now she was actually saying words and walking on her own. It was all so wonderful that Antonio and Maddalena could never explain why it was they had been so blessed with happiness in their little castle on the Ohio. But suddenly the turrets of the castle collapsed, the windows no more glistened gold in the sun, the boards with which Antonio had built the castle became boards again, and he was living with Maddalena in a shack. Annina went into a dimpled sleep and waked no more.

The young parents prayed for guidance in this new land. What had they done wrong? Grief beggared their lives for a year, but in their despair they applied themselves even more industriously. Maddalena took in roomers. She cooked and served the food which they purchased, she laundered their clothes, and packed their lunches, and for this they paid $3 a month. Antonio's wages had been increased to $1.75 a day so that when Annina's little brother Giovanni arrived, they could dismiss the boarders.

In another year's time Giovanni was followed by Raffaelo and still a year later by Antonetta. Two years passed and then Roberto arrived. Antonio had planted a large garden in the land bordering his house and he grew enough vegetables to provide for his family and still sell a few baskets of lettuce and tomatoes to others to augment his wages. Every week or two he purchased a barrel of broken *pasta* at a *pasta* warehouse. This was made up of odds and ends of *spaghetti, maccheroni, linguine*—every type of *pasta* manufactured—that had been broken and thus was not salable to the general trade. Antonio and Maddalena could not help being glad for the careless workers who broke the *pasta*, because with a couple of dollars they acquired food for almost two weeks. And now with fresh tomatoes they could make sauce for the *pasta*. Before, they had used only a little bit of olive oil fried with a little hot pepper.

The children's clothing was comfortable in the summer because it was well ventilated, but in the winter the patched garments could not keep out the freezing weather. They possessed no overcoats and when they returned home, their bodies almost blue from exposure, the coloration did not change easily because there was only one kitchen stove to warm them. Nor was it a picnic to wash one's face outdoors in a basin on a horizontal plank nailed to a fence, the water being poured from a bucket that often had a covering of ice which had to be broken in order to get the water flowing.

Though the children's garments left much to be desired, they were getting the best clothing in the world for their minds. They were being dressed with education in the free schools of America. It was only a little country school they attended but the teacher seemed to know everything and the children brought home books that excited even Antonio and Maddalena, who dreamed of the day their offspring would take their places with dignity and respect in the life of America, earning wages that would supply them with good clothing, nourishing food, and warmth no matter how wintry the winds of life might blow.

When the United States went to war with Spain, Giovanni joined Teddy Roosevelt's Rough Riders, fought in Cuba and came back in a blue uniform with yellow stripes and a sombrero pinned up at the side, a dashing hero to his two sisters and three brothers. And as the first three sons reached working age, they got jobs on a railroad section gang, toiling close to their dad. The fourth one, Francesco, worked in a steel mill by day and went to school at night, steering his life by a star which pointed to a lawyer's career. The other daughter, Rosina, became a telegraphist. Antonio and Maddalena offered prayers of thanksgiving for the opportunities of America to live in self-dependence, self-respect, and with a continuing perspective of further improvement and increased happiness. They now had a more substantial home, shaded by a slight mortgage and five fine mulberry trees, the saplings of which had come from Antonio's *paese*.

When America declared war on Germany, two of the brothers sailed away to the battlefields of France. One did not return, and the mulberry trees spread their melancholy shade for young Raffaelo resting in eternal peace and glory in Flanders Field. Maddalena, with a sob in her throat, placed a golden star in the window. Antonio hung in the next window the American flag. He knew now he was truly an American because the blood of his boy was in the red stripes.

Fifteen years later, Francesco, who had become a successful lawyer, was elected judge. On the day he was to be installed in office, Antonio and Maddalena sat in the courtroom, trembling in their ecstasy. It was true and yet it could not be true. The forlorn immigrants who had landed in America many years ago had had many dreams, but even in the rosiest clouds of hope and promise they could not visualize a shining judicial robe for one of their own children. At the moment that Francesco took the oath, Antonio lifted to his lips the folds of an American flag at his side and kissed the nation's ensign, murmuring at the time some words. That night at home, Francesco said to his father: "Papa, I saw you kiss the flag at the swearing-in ceremony and I know you spoke some words because I saw your lips move. What did you say?" Antonio lowered the large-bowl pipe at which he had been puffing, and as creamy clouds of smoke ascended to the ceiling, he replied: "My boy, I said: 'Thank God for a country where even the son of an Italian immigrant coal miner and railroad section hand can become a judge.'"

9 THE ELLIS ISLAND ERA

America indeed offered to its new citizens and their children opportunities which probably would never have been theirs in the old country. At the same time many of the immigrants had here to face adversities and indignities deeply wounding to their sensitive natures. With a perversity that is difficult to understand in an enlightened country, large numbers of people in America forgot that they themselves had once been immigrants, as they looked with jaundiced eye at those who had succeeded them on the Atlantic ferry.

The Monday pioneers scoffed at Tuesday's arrivals. Only fifty-nine years after the signing of the Declaration of Independence, which declared "all men are created equal," there sprang up, like a toadstool after a dark rain, a so-called "Native American movement" which called for the expulsion of the so-called "Irish Papists." This fugacious growth disappeared, but its polluted soil was quickly occupied by the "Know-Nothing Party," also aimed primarily at Irish immigrants who had come here when offered jobs by the builders of railroads, canals, and factories.

The Know-Nothing Party characterized immigrants as "paupers and immigrants," and demanded a drastic curtailment in citizenship privileges to "foreigners." It proclaimed "America for Americans," defining Americans as those who were descended from at least two generations of American ancestors, with no trace of Roman Catholicism in that genealogy. It is sad to relate that this political toadstool flourished at least eleven years and that under its tenebrous umbrella five state governors were elected, several state legislatures were controlled, and, in 1856, it had acquired enough political strength to nominate former President Millard Fillmore as its candidate for the presidency. It is pleasant, however, to relate that although Fillmore's White House incumbency had not been entirely a failure, the voters of the country retired him to private life when he became the Know-Nothing candidate (he carried only one state), and, in doing so, informed him and the world that no party, guided by so narrow-minded an outlook and so bigoted a view of America's destiny, could expect to put a man in the White House.

Still the Know-Nothing Party brand of intolerance did not accompany Millard Fillmore into the shades of innocuous desuetude. In 1877 its cast-off but yet serviceable mantle, reinforced with yellow patches of religious bigotry, was snatched up by the American Protestant Association, which, by 1896, had acquired a million members, demanding that America's doors be locked tight to Roman Catholic immigrants. They accused the Catholics in America with planning to destroy Protestants and, in "self-defense," the Toledo council of the organization stocked several hundred Winchester rifles. Almost in comic opera style this arms-gathering operation of the A.P.A. marched out on the stage of public knowledge when the A.P.A. failed to pay for the rifles, and the arms dealers sued for their money!

But there was no *opera bouffe* about the Ku Klux Klan which followed the A.P.A. in the murky swamps of intolerance, blasphemously burning crosses and desecrating American flags in the name of Americanism.

Not all those who have practiced intolerance in America have been members of organizations such as those mentioned. Individuals whose persons were never contaminated by a Klansman's gown, and in whose minds never ran the prejudices, hatreds, and idiocies of the Know-Nothing Party, nevertheless have used the same arguments that had been advanced in white sheets shimmering in the light of flaming crosses. These individuals seriously maintained, and there are some even today who will contend, that America would have been a better country if it had barred all immigration after the Revolutionary War.

Since 1820, when the United States Government began to keep

immigration records, to the present time, over 42,000,000 immigrants have entered the United States. The survivors of those immigrants, plus their descendants, make up today a total population that far exceeds in number the descendants of the original colonists. Thus, immigration deriders should not speak too glibly about an immigration-less America. Had the ports of the United States been closed to all foreigners following Washington's defeat of Cornwallis, the United States would have remained a long, lean country occupying the eastern border of a Balkanized North America, with the rest of the continent flying the flags of France, Spain, England, and Russia. Nor could there have been an expansion of territory to the west which could have been held against invaders. Had there been no immigration to the United States in what I have termed the Ellis Island Era, it can even be questioned that the United States could have won in so comparatively brief a time, if at all, the two world wars into which she was forced.

Had there been no post-Civil War immigration, would the United States have achieved and held the industrial and commercial supremacy in the world which it has now maintained for three-fourths of a century? No economy can possibly prosper without customers. Who have been the most numerous customers in the United States but the immigrants and their proliferating families? As President Kennedy well put it:

It was no accident that the period of greatest immigration coincided with the period of greatest economic expansion. Nor is it any accident today that those states with the highest proportion of first and second generation Americans also show the highest per capita income, the highest proportion of telephones, radios, and TV sets, the highest salaries for teachers and the greatest amount of capital invested in productive enterprise.

But in 1887 a supposedly intellectual person, H. H. Boyensen, wrote in the *Forum:*

Every steamship unloading upon our shores its motley herd of Germans, Bohemians, Hungarians, Poles, and Italians, re-enforces the ranks of this party of destruction and prepares the way for a new revolution, or attempt at revolution.

The party referred to was the Knights of Labor, the first national labor union in the United States. Its program included advocacy of an eight-hour day, a Bureau of Labor in the Federal Government, and abolition of child labor. Boyensen charged further that the immigrants were finding their places among the subverters of social order because:

> all the lower strata of society, and particularly the immigrated portion of it, are, at present, hungry, not necessarily for food, but for all the good things of life which are beyond their reach.

It is even more shocking to read that this intemperate language was more or less echoed by the erudite Henry Cabot Lodge, historian, member of Congress and United States senator for thirty years. This valiant knight-errant of the *status quo*, whose keen-edged political sword did more than that of any other to kill American participation in the League of Nations, which, with our support, might well have averted World War II, proclaimed in the *North American Review* of January 1891 that:

> The condition of a large mass of the laboring population in the city of New York is enough to alarm every thinking man; and this dreadful condition of things is intensified every day by the steady inflow of immigration.

Even while the United States was moving into the first rank among all nations in manufacturing prowess, principally because of the manpower and vast consumer potential of its post-Civil War population, Henry Cabot Lodge was condemning immigration from southern Europe, arguing that Mediterranean immigration involved "nothing less than the possibility of a great and perilous change in the very fabric of our race." Where have we heard such a cry since? It was Adolf Hitler who proclaimed the perfect Nordic race, but even he was not the first one to propound that ethnic pretension. Kaiser Wilhelm II had already declared it, and persons were not lacking on this side of the ocean to ape that mustachioed megalomaniac.

In 1916 Madison Grant, flaunting the imposing designations of Chairman of the New York Zoological Society, Trustee of the American Museum of Natural History, and Councilor of the American Geographical Society, brought out a book with the ominous title of *The Passing of the Great Race*. Didactically he asserted that the Nordics are the supermen of the earth and that races drawn from the "lowest stratum of the Mediterranean basin and the Balkans," were "human flotsam and the whole tone of American life, social, moral, and political has been lowered and vulgarized by them." He said that blue, gray, and green eyes are a revealing sign of the superior Nordic race and that "dark colored eyes are all but universal among wild mammals and entirely so among the primates, man's nearest relatives. It may be taken as an absolute certainty that all the original races of man had dark eyes."

Who has the idea that Hitler was the first man to plan to do away with the incurable and the unfit? Listen to Madison Grant:

> Mistaken regard for what are believed to be divine laws and a senti-mental belief in the sanctity of human life tend to prevent both the elimination of defective infants and the sterilization of such adults as are themselves of no value to the community. *The laws of nature require the obliteration of the unfit* and human life is valuable only when it is of use to the community or race.

Madison Grant frowns on democracy. He thinks that the people of America have too much to say. "*Vox populi*, so far from being *Vox Dei*, thus becomes an unending wail for rights and never a chant for duty."

Henry Fairfield Osborn, Research Professor of Zoology, Columbia University, wrote a preface to this book in which he spoke of the "superior force and stability of heredity," as against that of "environment." Posing the hypothetical question as to what was the "greatest danger" which confronted the American Republic today (1916), he replied that it was "the gradual dying out among our people of those hereditary traits through which the principles of our religious, political, and social foundations were laid down and their insidious replacement by traits of less noble character." The "less noble character" was, of course, according to both Osborn and Madison Grant, to be found in the immigrant from southern Europe. In 1917 Osborn wrote further that America had to "chiefly depend" for leadership, courage, and loyalty and "devotion to an ideal," on the "Anglo-Saxon branch of the Nordic race." He conceded that "many members of other races" were doing their part "but in no other human stock which has come to this country is there displayed the unanimity of heart, mind, and action which is now being displayed by the descendants of the blue-eyed, fair-haired peoples of the north of Europe."

It might be pointed out here that by 1917, the year Osborn was slandering the southern Europeans, the Italians had already sacrificed over 300,000 lives in World War I, a common cause, in which America, battling for the democracy and humanity of the world, was being crucially threatened by the blue-eyed, fair-haired teutonic militarists from the north of Europe! Even the most listless leafing through Nazi history books would disclose that Hitler vehemently proclaimed the same ideas so arrogantly expressed by the zoological professor Osborn and the zoological society chairman, Madison Grant. The latter unqualifiedly condemned the principle of equality under law and grimly warned America that:

> The days of the Civil War and the provincial sentimentalism which governed or misgoverned our public opinion are past, and this generation must completely repudiate the proud boast of our fathers that they acknowledged no distinction in "race, creed, or color," or else the native American must turn the page of history and write: "FINIS AMERICAE."

If one would impatiently dismiss Madison Grant with the conclusion that his frothings were those of one who could never gain an audience in America, let him be reminded that his book had seven printings and went through four editions. As late as 1930 we find him returning to the scolding platform of doom in a book entitled *The Alien in Our Midst,* wherein he unqualifiedly condemns the constitutional amendments which freed the Negro and provided for popular election of senators and woman suffrage. He also asserted that aliens "from Eastern and Southern Europe were drawn from the lowest social strata of their homeland and mistake the liberty they find in America, and the easy-going tolerance of the native American, for an invitation to license and crime."

He said that during World War I, "in all the industrialized states, the replacement of the native American went on rapidly," and he found to his horror that "Vermont was full of French-Canadians; that farming lands along the Connecticut River had been taken up by the Poles; that Boston was overrun by the Irish; that New Haven had become almost an Italian city; that Rhode Island was swamped by aliens, and that Detroit and Chicago were to all intent foreign cities."

He was particularly incensed over the fact that New England had become "hysterical over slavery and *Uncle Tom's Cabin.*"

Was Madison Grant an inconsequential figure? One of America's successful authors, Kenneth L. Roberts, urged in his book *Why Europe Leaves Home* that: "Every American who has at heart the future of America and of the race that made it a great nation owes it to himself and to his children to get and read carefully *The Passing of the Great Race* by Madison Grant."

Picking up Grant's trumpet, Roberts proclaimed the virtues of the Nordic race and blasted the "worthlessness" and the "futility" of "the good-for-nothing mongrels" of what he regarded as the inferior races:

> The American nation was founded and developed by the Nordic race, but if a few more million members of the Alpine, Mediterranean, and Semitic races are poured among us, the result must inevitably be a hybrid race of people as worthless and futile as the good-for-nothing mongrels of Central America and Southeastern Europe.

Roberts described the Mediterraneans as "the small, swarthy, black-haired, long-skulled people which form the bulk of the population in Southern Italy, Greece, Spain, and the north coast of Africa."

In 1930 John E. Edgerton, President of the National Association of Manufacturers, joined Roberts and Grant in slandering future citizens of the United States:

> I ask you to call the roll of the armies of gunmen in our cities, of the worst criminals in our jails and penitentiaries, of the anarchists, communists, foreign-language newspapers, and other lists of disturbers containing unpronounceable or exchanged names. Then go back to the time when the foreign tides began to sweep into our country and measure the distance that we have retreated in those years from the moral and political standards which we then commonly recognized and accepted.

In his book *America's Race Heritage*, published in 1922, Clinton Stoddard Burr asked: "Why do we still allow the dregs of Southern and Eastern European nations to swarm into our community by the thousands every day?"* He said that the Northwest European arrivals were assimilable but not the Mediterranean peoples:

* In his interesting book, *Sons of Italy*, Antonio Mangano relates the following. An anti-immigrationist complained to an immigrationist: "These dagoes are an ignorant lot." "Yes," was the reply, "but they are of the same race as Tasso, Dante, Verdi, Garibaldi, and Cavour." "Oh, come now, they aren't Tassos or Garibaldis." "No, neither are you George Washington or Lincoln!"

The average arrival born in northwest Europe will in general be absorbed within the homogeneous American stock, whereas the average person of American birth, but of Slavic, Italian, or Polish-Jewish ancestry, is unlikely to be absorbed into the American stock.

Burr did not stop with the mere slandering of the Mediterranean immigrants. He advocated that each one of them should be "catalogued, photographed, finger-printed and placed under the supervision of the government." Also, that they should be allowed to enter only under indenture, that is, a sort of refined serfdom. Then, Burr magnanimously offered that, "at the completion of his indenture period, the laborer from Southern and Eastern Europe could be sent back to the land of his fathers."

Of course the Ku Klux Klan, through their Imperial Wizard, H. W. Evans, added their meed of racial hatred:

Ominous statistics proclaim the persistent development of a parasite mass within our domain—our political system is clogged with foreign bodies which stubbornly refuse to be absorbed, and means must be found to meet the menace. We have taken unto ourselves a Trojan horse crowded with ignorance, illiteracy, and envy.

These and other statements were the type of individual opinions expressed by persons in public life who irresponsibly made the world believe that they were expressing the sentiments of the American people. And this is the withering propaganda the Italian immigrant encountered when, his heart aflame with anticipatory joy, he entered through the outer gate which had been opened by his countryman, Christopher Columbus, only to find the inner economic, social, and political doors slamming in his face. Even before he could prove his worth, pass his tests, and be tried accordingly, an officious jury had declared him inferior and unwanted.

They who slammed the doors indicted and summarily convicted a people which for two thousand years had held high the torch of civilization—of culture, science, literature, art, and philosophy. They libeled a people that had constructed a bridge over which millennia of history passed and brought man safely into the realm of law, order, responsibility, freedom, and opportunity—America.

In the 1920s Senator Thomas Heflin of Alabama never mentioned immigrants without calling them "that horde of foreigners." He never extolled the honesty, loyalty, stability, and Americanism of the millions of foreign-born Americans, with their descendants, but he did hold forth at length on the tiny fraction of immigrants who ran afoul of the law, a percentage which did not exceed that of the native-born. His tongue lashed out at "kidnapers and murderers with their wild vagaries, their guns, dirks, and bombs," as if any decent person would protect such criminals, and he endeavored to paint a picture which suggested that every immigrant ship coming into our harbors was manned by "kidnapers and murderers," and carried cargoes of guns, dirks, and bombs. Never was there so distorted a view of European immigrants as that found in the demagogic jungle of Senator Heflin's harangues.

Some of the antipathy the Italian immigrant had to encounter was, of course, based on misunderstanding, and a deliberate closing of eyes and ears to truth. The Italians, for instance, were accused of being asocial because they lived in all-Italian communities. But where else could they live? They were in a strange world far from the only world they had known. Sentimental by nature and poetic by instinct, the immigrant took refuge from the harshness of his surroundings by going back in memory to the little village in which he had known only good will and camaraderie. He recalled fondly the friendly creek which babbled by his home, the fresh and clean vineyards he had tended, the church *festas* with their music, singing and dancing in the public square. In the old country, no matter where he went, he knew everybody. Here, outside his immediate associates in work and domicile, he knew nobody. Despite the density of population in Italy, the *paisano* had enjoyed more elbow room there than here where he lived in a shanty or in two or three rooms with a dozen persons, and where the whole Italian neighborhood was surrounded by a Chinese Wall of ostracism, higher and more unscalable than the mountain ranges in Italy which, lofty as they were, were not forbidding and belligerently aloof. There the air was pure and not streaked with the dust of churning streets, the smoke of mills, the soot and fumes of coal camps.

And so, the Italian immigrants stayed together, a little bewildered, a little uneasy, but still hopeful for the best, imparting mutual encouragement, relating to one another their experiences and adventures of the day, resolving and preparing to make themselves worthy citizens of this great land, in spite of those who ignorantly, prejudicially, and often selfishly refused to understand them and offer the kind word they needed so much.

Since the only jobs available to the mass of Italian immigrants were those which required physical exertion, they returned to their lodgings in the evenings wholly fatigued after some twelve hours of unremitting labor. Once they had washed up and eaten their supper, they had no will but to rest and prepare for the next day's exhausting toil. Because of this community-living and lack of participation in the entertainment and pastimes of non-immigrants, the Italians were called clannish and their communities were characterized "Little Italys," "Woptowns," "Dago Hills," and "Macaroni Hollows."

As Southerners during the post-Civil War days never referred to a Northerner except to call him a "damn yankee," the Italians, during the Ellis Island Era, were called dagoes, ginneys (or guineas), wops, spaghetti and garlic eaters. Since spaghetti and meatballs has now become a popular American dish, the term "spaghetti-eater" can no longer be regarded as a term of reproach. There are few kitchens in the land today which are not on occasion redolent with the pungent aroma of garlic and the piquant fragrance of oregano. And surely no visit to seashores or other resorts would be complete without the consumption of several slices of aromatic, mouth-watering *pizza*.* *Pizza* is now part of the English language, as are the phrases *mamma mia!*, *paisano, compare,* and *isabox!* Nor could the language do without the phrases *Roman candles, chicken cacciatora, fresco, cupola, arena, gusto, millinery* (taken from merchants of hats in Milan), *Machiavellian, confetti, regatta, lava, profile, Madonna, Venetian blinds, influenza, vista, incognito, jeans* (from Genoa), *stanza, soda, motto, cameo, umbrella, canto, sotto voce, macaroni.*

However, in the latter years of the nineteenth and the early years of the twentieth centuries, the words dagoes, wops, and ginneys were epithets applied to Italians in a disparaging and not merely a descriptive sense. Hence, I reacted quite unsympathetically when, in my school days, the bully of our town, Tom Baden, called me a dago in the very presence of Penelope Worthington, in whose eyes I had already been considerably reduced in social standing because she fig-

* Dickson Preston, Scripps-Howard staff writer, reporting on the Democratic National Convention at Atlantic City, August 28, 1964, said that President Johnson's birthday cake was decorated with a "spray of bluebonnets imported by Macy's department store from Italy."

ured I was a "foreigner." I winced like one receiving a lash and then remarked with quiet determination, "Tom, don't you ever call me that again." I wanted to retain *some* status with Penelope.

"What will you do if I call you a dago again?" he taunted, emphasizing dago.

"I'll beat you up," I replied, gritting my teeth. I was rather small and slender for thirteen, and he was large and robust for fourteen. He laughed derisively. Several days later we were eating our lunches in the schoolyard. Tom's lunch, which was packed in a neat, ornamental metal box with a handle, consisted of fresh ham sandwiches made with snow-white bread, a cut of apple pie, an apple, orange, a fancy bottle filled with coffee and milk, and a piece of candy. My lunch was wrapped in an Italian newspaper and consisted of one large fried pepper-and-egg sandwich, made with dark Italian bread. Tom called it a dago lunch. I said nothing until I had swallowed the last crumb of the savory, olive-oil-soaked bread, and then I asked him to please never use the word dago again. "How can you eat such a foreign-looking mess, dago?" he taunted.

I walked over toward him. He put out his foot and tripped me. I struck at him and his fist shot out and hit me squarely in the forehead. I staggered back and Tom guffawed. In that moment Penelope appeared on the scene. I swung mightily with my right fist, but it was only a feint. Tom dodged to avoid it, and my left fist landed squarely on the point of his chin. In that instant I thought my hand had broken, and I could feel every bone in my body vibrating. Nevertheless I thrilled to the impact. Two thousand years of Italian vindication had gone into that blow. As Tom wobbled, I now brought my right fist into play and hit him on the side of his head. His nose began to bleed.

"I'll kill you for this, Mike, you damn dago!" he screamed and lunged. His body weight against mine unbalanced me and I fell, but before hitting the ground I got my left foot behind his ankle and he toppled with me. We struggled on the ground, punching and kicking. Suddenly he was on top of me directing straight thrusts and uppercuts. In reaching up to stay his punching bag arm, I got his right ear in my hand and twisted it like one winding a clock. He yelped and screeched and lost his advantage. I now was astride him and, getting a perfect hold on his ear, I started winding the clock again.

"Ouch! Ouch!" he shrieked. "Stop, Mike, you damn d—"

"What were you about to say?" I asked sweetly as I wound the clock some more.

"Mike! Stop! Please stop! I'll apologize—and I promise—I'll never use that word again!"

I got up and lifted him to his feet. I wiped the blood and dirt from his face and said: "I'm awfully sorry I had to do this." Although my whole body was aching, I felt happy and proud that I had been vindicated and I looked around for Penelope to receive her congratulations, but she was nowhere to be seen.

The next morning as we entered the schoolhouse together I said to him: "Good morning, Tom." He smiled, all cordiality, and replied: "Good morning, Michael." That afternoon the school principal summoned us into his office and gave us both a good thrashing with the rattan for fighting in the schoolyard.

10 CLIMBING THE LADDER

Many used the belittling term dago because by so doing they thought they experienced an elevation in status for themselves. It has ever been thus. One of the least difficult ways for mediocre characters to assume importance is to disparage others. The person who lacks ability and moral stature to rise on his own merits thinks he can look over the heads of rivals by pushing them down. However, no small portion of those who spoke disrespectfully of, and to, Italians, did so for selfishly economic reasons. The less weight given the Italian on the social economic scales, the less wages railroad companies, coal operators, and other industrialists would have to pay for his services. The more the immigrant could be portrayed as a person lacking in normal reactions and sensibilities, the less he had to be assured in the way of human comforts and even decencies. Vast industrial and commercial projects were pending: railroads and highways cried to be built, reservoirs demanded construction, rivers needed to be dammed and diked, buildings waited to step out of blueprints, subways longed for light, tunnels yearned to be pushed through hills and mountains. Since all this was occurring before the general use of steam shovels, cranes, and bulldozers, the tremendous earth-cutting work had to be accomplished by manpower.

The Italian immigrants were a strong and healthy people. Most of them had lived outdoors in the old country. They possessed strong backs and powerful muscles; they manifested stamina. But if the employers were to give them credit for this physical potential, they would have to pay them a reasonable wage. Since the world was still reasoning with the mind of the medievalists that the man who did not have to dirty his hands in labor was superior to those who bent their backs in toil, it was easy and profitable to characterize the immigrant as an inferior person. Thus, the greedy industrialist—this did not apply to all of them—found it advantageous to bay with the ignorant and name-call the immigrants dagoes, wops, ginneys, bohunks, hunkies, spicks, etc. Since the immigrants could not fight back with language, they had to swallow the derogatory epithets and accept the miserable wages, and the treatment that accompanied them.

Many of the employers hired the Italian immigrants through the *padrone,* who, speaking Italian and English, knew where to round up newly-arrived workers, and got a commission on every pair of brawny arms he could recruit. Antonio Mangano in his *Sons of Italy* relates the story of an immigrant who, with fifty other Italians, was employed in this manner. Each of the men first had to pay the *padrone* six dollars *bossatura,* fee for the boss. They were herded aboard a train for Lake Erie, where they were lodged in six dilapidated boxcars. They slept on "beds of boards placed across two boxes," under old coats and horse blankets. Rousted out of bed at three in the morning they set out on a two-hour journey to their job of tearing up old rails.

In a few seconds the sweat was rolling in streams. The rails were heavy and the men worked with might and main all the forenoon. There was no let-up, no mercy. From shortly after five until twelve, about seven hours, the men labored without rest. "The beasts," said the *padrone,* "must not be given a rest, otherwise they will step over me." As the men silently appealed to him for mercy, I was filled with pity, and often during the day, tempted to beg the *padrone* to let them rest. But how could I approach a raging maniac? He was what the railroads wanted. . . . After seven hours of the hardest labor the younger men had sausages and bread; the older men were satisfied with bread alone. Yet, with coffee in the morning and bread at noon, these men worked for ten hours every day under the blistering sun or in pouring rain. . . . Stopping work at four, the men returned to their ramshackled cars to cook, eat, and sleep.*

For this the men got ten dollars a week, but they didn't even receive all of this:

> The money was all sent to the boss, who first took out of it whatever the men owed him for food. If a man tries to save more, by buying little food, the *padrone* charges him a certain sum just the same. I kept a list of the boss's prices and the store prices at one city in Ohio, and always the boss's were 200 or 300 percent higher. Sometimes the men would buy what they had to of the boss, throw it away, and go into the city to buy.

> If one of the men wished a letter written to his family in Italy, it cost him twenty-five cents, the stamp ten cents, and the envelope five cents. So the men didn't send many letters.

When one of the gang was asked why they didn't complain he replied there was no one to complain to. They knew no English and if they complained to the *padrone*, they would be discharged. "He can get plenty more, and those fellows far from home or friends don't know where to look for other work."

When immigrants could find no employment in the city where they landed or anywhere close by, they became wanderers in distant states, working on railroad tracks, reservoirs, river dams, highway construction, canal beds, in stone quarries, on docks, in fisheries, and in lumber camps, accomplishing the strenuous herculean labor which the Monday pioneers avoided, but which was indispensable in the physical development of the nation. The immigrants' backs became the ladder up which Progress climbed to prosperity, but then having reached it, scorned "the base degrees by which (it) did ascend."

Bleached by the sun, bowed by heavy toil, gaunt from inadequate food, discomfited by ingratitude, their immigrant blood was still transfused into the giant of American industry, without which it might well have faltered. The Monday morning pioneers looked down their noses at the immigrants of the late nineteenth and early twentieth centuries, the Madison Grants and Kenneth Robertses snarled at them, the Know-Nothings expostulated, and the Ku Klux Klan

---

* Mangano footnotes this account with "The Wop in the Track Gang" by Domenick Ciolli, in *The Immigrants in America Review*, July 1916.

reddened the skies with the fires of their hatred, but it was, nonetheless, this vast producing and consuming population of immigrants who made possible the greatest industrial expansion in the history of the nation.

While there was nothing spectacular, romantic, or engaging in digging and building with one's hands, the America of today could never have been possible without that work. Nor was it without physical danger. Not a few mountain cliffs on the continent mark spots where Italian pick-and-shovel men disappeared over rocky edges while working on projects destined to extend the highways which now interlace America. In the depths of the earth, extracting with perilous explosives the minerals which are America's greatest wealth, many a premature or delayed explosion carried away life or limb of brawny miners who hailed from Italy. In the structural conquest of the air, as steel beams wedded to brick and concrete rose to high and higher altitudes, not infrequently an Italian hod-carrier or mortar mixer lost his footing and fell to the pavement beneath, a martyr to America's progress. It was an era of concrete: concrete walls, concrete foundations, concrete buildings, concrete viaducts, sewers, pavements. Concrete mixers churned throughout the land and into the revolving operation went not only water, cement, and broken stone, but also Italian sweat and blood.

In time the Italians entered the factories, furnaces, and mills, whose foundations they or their immigrant predecessors had manually excavated. There were no workmen's compensation laws in those days so that a crushed hand or an amputated leg brought no financial crutch to the crippled workman, unless it could be shown that the employer had violated some law. Antonio Mangano told of an immigrant's daughter, Filomena Manelli, who worked in a factory where, in violation of a statute, no protective guard covered the rapidly whirling wheels. Pretty Filomena's hair got caught in one of these unprotected wheels and before the machine could be stopped she had suffered severe head injury and disfigurement. She was taken to a hospital and the accident reported to the police.

The next day two policemen went to the factory with Filomena's father, and there they found every wheel in the factory protected by the prescribed safety guard. "I don't understand," Filomena's father said bewilderedly, "I've been here myself and saw the wheels without guards." The next day the riddle was solved. The girl who had worked next to Filomena visited her in the hospital and told her that the employer had installed the wheel guards immediately after the accident. "He scared the girls and said he'd fire them if they told on him." She shrugged her shoulders helplessly. "You know how hard it is to get work—what can the girls do?"

Being out of a job in the Ellis Island Era was not like it is today when one almost immediately obtains public assistance. Then, unemployment meant destitution or the personal humiliation of receiving a slice or two of bread wrapped in the crepe paper of a semi-mendicancy.

Those who hired Italians on the assumption that they possessed no skill beyond that of performing manual labor not only committed an injustice against the immigrant but also unwittingly deprived themselves of profitable returns which could be theirs. A little inquiry would have revealed to them that the employees they were treating so shabbily were persons endowed with profound intelligence, acute perceptions, and occupational abilities. A little questioning would have opened their eyes to the trades and callings in which the Italians were proficient and the particular crafts in which they excelled over all others. For instance, it would be difficult to find better skilled stonemasons than the Italians. They have such a steady hand and precise eye that, with a single blow, or possibly two, of hammer or trowel alone, to say nothing of hammer and chisel, they can fashion a stone or brick into the most irregular shape so that it will fit perfectly into the irregular hole or gap that is to receive it.

In railway engineering the Italians have demonstrated an aptitude of supreme scientific skill, as may be witnessed in the three grand passageways of the Mont Cenis, Saint Gotthard, and Simplon tunnels, perennial monuments of "Southern Latin" engineers and constructors.

To list the fields in which Italian artisans and craftsmen have demonstrated top-ranking proficiency would be to enumerate nearly all the occupations and trades in the whole gamut of man's utilitarian projection. But the Italian immigrant had no way of proclaiming his particular adeptness unless he was given an opportunity to show it. Consequently, thousands of talented hands and fingers capable of fashioning into final detailed form the most ponderous piece of stone, wood, clay, or machinery, were wrapped around a pick, shovel, or the handles of a wheelbarrow.

Pascal D'Angelo, Italian immigrant, sweated at pick and shovel work when his soul cried for expression in meter and verse. In the story of his life as a laborer, *Son of Italy,* he soliloquized plaintively:

> Everywhere was toil—endless, continuous toil, in the flooding blaze of the sun, or in the splashing rain—toil. In Hillsdale, Poughkeepsie, Spring Valley, New York; Falling Waters, West Virginia; Westwood, Ramsey, New Jersey; Williamsport, Maryland, where the winding Potomac flows; Utica, New York; White Lake, Otter Lake, Tappan, Staatsburg, Oneonta, Glens Falls, and many other places where we could find work, always as a pick and shovel man. . . . If I bring you to all the above-mentioned places you will never be able to understand all the work I was compelled to do, while I labored there. You cannot feel from the cold roads and steel tracks all the pains, the heartaches, and the anger I felt at the brutality of enforced labor. Yet we had to live. We laborers have to live. We sell our lives, our youth, our health—and what do we get for it? A meager living.

The foremen tyrannized, the work brutalized, the wages of approximately $1.50 a day scarcely brought edible food to his lips and decent clothes to his back. D'Angelo could stand no more:

> Why I am nothing more than a dog. A dog. But a dog is silent and slinks away when whipped, while I am filled with the urge to cry out, to cry out disconnected words, expressions of pain—anything—to cry out! . . . For a long time I paced the soft green in front of our shanty. Then I entered. The men inside were grumbling mournfully to one another, barely visible in the gloom. I had resigned myself to my fate. I was a poor laborer—a dago, a wop or some such creature —in the eyes of America. Well, what could I do? Nothing.

In the mills and factories the Italians were paid a few more pennies than they received as laborers, but they missed the outdoor life to which they had always been accustomed. Still, there were wives to be brought over from the old country, there was still the family world to build anew. And so they drudged in furnaces, refineries, cotton and woolen mills, coal and iron ore mines, printeries, boilerworks, barrel factories, porcelain and enamel works, lamp shops, waterways, paint factories, railroad yards, stockyards, and marble quarries, where they invariably got the jobs that required the heaviest expenditure of muscular effort, that smeared them with the most grease, dust and dirt, and remunerated the least.

To satisfy the landlord and obtain enough *pasta* for the whole family, the income of the father had to be augmented, so the young sold newspapers, blacked shoes, and carried parcels. The daughters earned a dollar or two by putting together artificial flowers and sewing buttons on garments for concessionaires. In sorrowful abandonment of the sacred Italian tradition that the wife-mother was the lady of the house and remained at home, many Italian women bent over "sweatshop" work in factories, in cellars and attics. In thirty-five percent of the Italian homes, the wives took in boarders.

When it came to tasks that were wholly beyond the ken of other nationalities, the Italians could demand their worth. Thus, in carving stone and granite, they received as much as ten dollars a day. But it was work that took a terrible toll of the carver's health. The stone dust lodged in his lungs, frequently causing tuberculosis, and there was also the danger of flying stone chips which could inflict serious head or eye injury.

To the average observer at Ellis Island, all immigrants looked alike and, in view of the notions propagated by the anti-immigrants, the observer imagined that everyone coming from the Mediterranean was uneducated and available only for rough manual labor. The slightest knowledge of history would have reminded the observer of the vital part played by Italians in saving education from drowning in the flood of barbarism which had engulfed Europe after the downfall of the Roman Empire. Many of the men hurrying down the gangplank with their battered cardboard suitcases, although no different in outward appearance from the farm laborers, were men of science, doctors, lawyers, teachers, and merchants as well.

Most immigrants liked agricultural work, but it was not easily procurable because this meant traveling to distant places, and railroad fares were expensive. However, with that perseverance which has always been a trait of the Italian people, those who were determined to live al fresco and help Nature produce her generous crops, got to faraway Texas, Louisiana, Wisconsin, and California. Many found their fresh-air meccas in upper New York State, New Jersey, and Connecticut where they worked on truck farms and eventually saved enough to buy little tracts of land for themselves which they worked into business enterprises.

Those who saw the Italian agriculturist in the field could see that with his zeal, eagerness, and application he was bound to get out of the soil the very most that it could possibly yield and even if that particular terrain which engaged his devotion was unproductive, he would caress and cajole something out of it.

But whether it was on a farm, in the city, in a mill town or a coal-mining patch, the immigrant's wife was his constant helpmate and inspiration. Whether she was an Italian mother, an Irish mother, a Hungarian mother, Austrian, Slavic, Polish, Jewish, German, Greek, Scandinavian, Bulgarian, Lithuanian, Croatian, Russian, Czech, Albanian, or Rumanian mother, all America is eternally indebted to her.

Born and reared in a little village which clung to a mountainside or was buried in a deep valley, she married at a tender age the youth with whom she had tilled the fields and brought in the sheaves of wheat. But while the blush of bridehood was still in her cheeks, she was left alone. Her young husband took ship to distant America, to find a new home and seek a broader horizon.

Anxiously she waited while the days and months painfully dragged their course. Finally came the letter with the steamship ticket. She bundled up her belongings and with a kerchief about her head eagerly boarded the ship to join her lifemate in a land of which they had dreamed in the days of their village courtship.

She found her lifemate installed in a shack, a shanty, a railroad car, or a lumber camp, but here was the foundation of a new life, and here, by his side, she prepared for the years ahead.

The country was young, it needed manpower and she gave to America five, six, even seven or more children of her body and of her soul. And then, while her husband strove in the snows and ice of winter or in the blistering heat of summer in ditches, on railroad tracks, highways, in mill or coal mine, she toiled from morn to night at the washboard, at the stove, at the cradle, or with scrubbing brush on the floor.

Now the bloom of young womanhood is gone. Late into the night by a flickering oil lamp she sews, stitches, irons, and patches. She sends her five, six, or seven boys and girls to school, while she wears an old dress and stays at home. Her children must have an education so that they will not be called names like their parents were; so that they may be respected in the community.

And then at last, her offspring grown, as her cup of joy runs over, we see how want, deprivation, and hardship have taken their toll. Her bones ache from a hundred ills, she coughs and the children gather around her bed. She kisses them, and with a smile she is gone.

She is the unsung heroine and pioneer of latter-day America. No statue can be erected high enough, no marble is too precious with which to sculpture a fitting memorial to the immigrant mother. She, who with her breasts nurtured us, with her arms raised us, with her ideals inspired us, with her tears washed us clean, with her devotion saved us, and then on the altar of love and loyalty laid down her worn-out and spent body.

And from her place in Heaven, she sends down her blessings on America for what America has offered to her children in this great land of ever-shining destiny.

May the people of America never forget what they owe to that sweet and blessed soul, the Immigrant Mother of us all.

11 LAW AND ORDER

I do not believe that any American today can look upon the treatment generally accorded the immigrant during the Ellis Island Era and not be astounded. No one, of course, knows better than I that even with this inhospitable treatment went opportunity which would never have been found in Europe. Nevertheless, it can only be a matter of astonishment that, in a land founded on the principles of equality and justice, so much inequality and injustice could have been visited on those who traversed the Atlantic in the nineteenth and twentieth centuries imbued with the same hopes and aspirations as those cherished by immigrants who crossed in earlier decades.

Senator James Reed of Missouri, in a speech in the United States Senate in 1924, stated that thirty-six different languages were spoken in New York before the Revolution. Yet the people were fused together into a fighting army that wrested freedom from a haughty and mighty foe. That polyglot army and citizenry did not dress alike, speak alike, or follow similar domiciliary customs. They were often in tatters, often without food, fuel, and adequate shelter, but they built America. The polyglot immigrants of later years did not dress alike, speak alike or live alike. They also were often in tatters and lacked adequate food, fuel, and shelter, but they carried on the same traditions as the pioneers of the Republic and they pushed forward the economic, political, and cultural frontiers crossed by the original colonists. Why then, were they ridiculed, lampooned, and discriminated against by the Madison Grants, the Heflins, the Kenneth Robertses, and a long line of industrialists?

The winds of xenophobia which whistled across America in the Ellis Island Era can only leave one bewildered as to how they gained momentum, what was their ultimate goal, and what did they achieve —for America. Senator John K. Shields of Tennessee was one of those who whirled the crank of the hurricane machine. He declared that the immigrants of the early 1900s were different from those who arrived in the early history of our country, that they are a "cause of serious alarm," and that they menaced "the purity of the blood, the homogeneity, and the supremacy of the American people and the integrity and perpetuity of our representative form of government." Placing no limit on the cyclone of his dire prophecies, he exclaimed that "if we permit the great American type of citizenship to be diluted, mongrelized, and destroyed, our civilization and free institutions will not survive. No mongrel race has ever achieved greatness in peace or war."

Senator James A. Reed of Missouri refused to accept this prophecy of "mongrelization" of the American people and reminded the Senate that there was a time when the Irish were being slandered as were the southern Europeans of the early 1900s:

"When the Irish first came here they came very largely, the great influx after the famine days. They were poor, they were ragged, they came in the steerage of ships. They were denounced. The highbrows met in indignation in all parts of the country. The gentleman with proscriptive soul was there. He declared the Irish would ruin this country, because, he said, they were ignorant; and they were ignorant, largely ignorant because a tyrannical government had closed their schools and persecuted their schoolmasters and had closed the door of learning in their face. They were poor. Poverty and want had put its white finger upon them and reduced them to a condition of absolute starvation. They came here and herded together. They slept in shanties. Some of them lived in the most impoverished and desperate condition for many years. Yet who is it today who dares in America denounce a man of Irish lineage? They are numbered among our orators, our poets, our statesmen. The sons of those immigrants have taken their place proudly with the rest of the people."

This exchange took place in the United States Senate during the debate on the Immigration Bill of 1924. This legislation proposed not only to restrict immigration but also to make it selective. It provided that the annual quota of immigrants from any given country was to be two percent of the number of foreign-born individuals of that country residing in the United States at the time of the 1890 census. The choice of 1890 as the pivotal year had no historical, cultural, or sociological rationalization to support it. It was chosen because in that year there were less of the southern-European-born than the northern- and western-European-born in the United States. Thus the Act would automatically and drastically decrease immigration from Italy and other Mediterranean countries. R. A. Schermerhorn in his work *These Our People* stated that the Act of 1924 was intended to portray the United States as a "white-Anglo-Saxon-Protestant civilization somehow fighting against hordes of 'foreign' or 'colored' elements which threaten to destroy its pristine purity."

The bill passed Congress and was approved by President Calvin Coolidge. To show how the act worked to squeeze southern Europe out almost entirely, it will be noted that Great Britain was allowed an annual quota of 65,361; Germany, 25,814; Italy, 5645; and Greece, 308. The words of Emma Lazarus on the pedestal of the Statue of Liberty read: "Give me your tired, your poor, your huddled masses yearning to breathe free." Commenting on this beautiful exhortation while he was still in the United States Senate, John F. Kennedy said the quotation, in view of the Quota Immigration Act, should be amended to read:

> "As long as they come from northern Europe, are not too tired or too poor or slightly ill, never stole a loaf of bread, never joined any questionable organization, and can document their activities for the past two years."

Those who participated in the congressional debates on immigration held one of two opposing points of view. One side, which I will call the anti-immigrationists, advocated drastically restricted immigration, to the point practically of closing the doors to southern and eastern Europe. The other side, which was made up of what I will call the immigrationists, believed properly in excluding such persons as would be detrimental to America, such as physical and mental defectives and persons of criminal tendencies, but otherwise allowing the country to accept as many immigrants as could be healthily absorbed. They vigorously contested discrimination against southern and eastern Europe.

Senator David I. Walsh of Massachusetts of the immigrationist group scored those who referred to the southern Europeans as "mongrels, garbage, and riff-raff." He pointed out that the superstructure of the nation's prosperity was built on the back of immigrant labor:

"In 1918, 58 percent of the steel and iron workers were foreign born, 61 percent of our packers' labor, 62 percent of the bituminous miners and wool weavers, 69 percent of the cotton-mill operators, 72 percent of clothing shopmen, and 65 percent of the sugar refiners' help came from abroad."

Senator Reed of Missouri supported Senator Walsh:

"Where did this narrow spirit of proscription come from? It used to be taught that here was a habitation for the oppressed of the earth. We remember that along the lines of Lexington, at Concord, at Valley Forge, at Yorktown, there stood many races of men, speaking many languages. . . . They all had the religion of liberty in their hearts, their divine fires of God Almighty planted in the hearts of men, the divine fires of liberty burning there."

And then addressing himself to the later Americans he said:

"They have stood on the field of every battle that has been fought and they have stood in the arks of peace, in the avocations of civil life, side by side with the man whose grandfather came from the same country only a little while before, and they have made good."

Senator Magnus Johnson of Minnesota told of a mining disaster in his state where forty miners were killed and pointed out that most of them belonged to people from southern Europe:

"That is where we are putting the immigrants when they get here; we are putting them down in the mines, in the hell holes of the earth, where nobody else wants to work; we are putting them to work on the railroad tracks, in the lumber camps, in the worst places that can be found. Why? Because those who think so much of a high standard of living do not like to go into such occupations."

Senator Shields of Tennessee rolled into the Senate a heavy siege gun: a report from James J. Davis, United States Secretary of Labor.

This James J. Davis, a Monday Pioneer hypocrite, if there ever was one, had arrived in America in 1881 and was now prepared to tell the country about the inferiority of the immigrants. He said he had conducted an investigation which revealed to him results which authorized him to classify the present-day immigrants as follows:

Very Superior	153,138
Superior	403,700
High Average	1,016,211
Average	3,702,904
Low Average	2,296,914
Inferior	4,276,537
Very Inferior	2,060,262

On what high bench of Final Judgment did Secretary Davis sit that he could stamp 4,276,573 Americans and prospective Americans as inferior and 2,060,262 as very inferior? The very brazenry of such a wholesale condemnation of over 6,300,000 inhabitants of this country can make us wonder on what basis the Secretary placed himself in the very superior class.

Although Senator Shields continued to fire heavy artillery throughout the debate, it was really Senator Heflin of Alabama who held high his oratorical sword and valiantly charged on the immigrants. He called them an "indiscriminate horde of unfit foreigners," he told of Italians who had kidnaped, and Italians who had murdered, but he never once mentioned who they were, who was kidnaped, who was murdered, and where and when these supposed crimes occurred. He said that the southern Europeans disturbed "the peace and happiness of our people, endangering the lives of our citizens, and constituting a serious menace and danger to free institutions in America."

On the afternoon of April 15, 1924, the Alabama senator held the attention of his colleagues for a couple of hours relating with gestures and vociferous declamation the details of the killing by a half-demented twelve-year-old boy "not long in our country" of another boy. He blamed all the immigrants in the United States, the officers of the government in charge of government, and all those who had a word to say in behalf of the immigrants, for this tragic death. He particularly blamed the Italians. He did so by giving the name of the twelve-year-old immigrant boy and then hypocritically adding: "I am saying nothing against the Italians who are good citizens in this country." The name of the unfortunate immigrant boy was Paul Rapkowskie, which, of course, is not an Italian name.

Senator Johnson of Minnesota, taking the floor to reply to Senator Heflin, said that despite his constant patriotic breast-pounding, the Alabama senator really looked like "an English lord." Heflin beamed and thanked Johnson: "I appreciate the compliment he paid me. He said I looked like an English Lord." Then, pausing, he added, his chest expanding to its widest dimensions: "Well, there is one thing certain about me: You would not mistake me for a foreigner in any quarter of the United States."

Senator Johnson smiled sardonically, and, turning to the senator from Alabama, he asked: "Is not an English lord a foreigner?"

Amid laughter from the gallery and the senators, Heflin made a rapid exit into the cloak room.

When a segment of the population of a country is characterized by educated persons as "riff-raff," as "mongrelized," as constituting a "menace" to the rest of the country, the uneducated people who have less sociological inhibitions, may allow their emotional prejudices and hatreds to take them beyond the limits of proper behavior. Authors, United States senators, and erudite publicists may employ language which convicts and pillories, but it is, after all, only language, and their utterers would vehemently deny that they ever intended that violence should be visited on the victims of their rhetoric. But words can be daggers and once they leave their sheaths, they may be snatched up by the irresponsible, the vicious, and the mobster and used against the innocent, the unsuspecting, and the hapless pawn of circumstance.

One day in 1895 Antonio Agnio was driving a wagon over the streets of New York when he was set upon by a gang of young ruffians for no other apparent reason than to make sport of a "dago." They showered him with stones and decayed vegetables and finally jumped into his wagon beating him in the face. In desperation, Agnio drew a revolver and attempted to drive off his tormentors by shooting at random. One of the aggressors received a slight wound in the leg. Presently ruffians of other regions came charging onto the scene shouting, "Lynch the dago!" The police arrived, ignored the hoodlums, arrested Agnio and threw him into jail where he languished because, being poor, he could not raise the bail fixed by the police magistrate. The New York *Daily Tribune,* in a magnificent editorial entitled "The Dago and the Loafer," called the affair of Agnio, "a rank injustice," stating that it is

> hard that the hand of the law should thus heavily be laid on the poor victim of aggression, that he should be kept from his work, that those who may be dependent on him should be left without sufficient support, while the young hoodlums are left to run at large and annoy other people. It is a notorious fact that many policemen look with good-natured toleration on the New York ruffians' attempts to "have fun with the 'Dago' and the 'Chink.'" Whenever such citizens are involved in trouble with English—or rather Bowery-speaking persons, the police act on the theory that they are to blame. In three cases out of four the fact probably is that they are wantonly baited and maddened beyond what they can and far beyond what they ought to endure. They are unpopular to a certain extent because they work harder and are more thrifty than the loafers who would like to be paid twice as much for doing the same work half as well.

In December 1872 the *Commercial Advertiser* in New York characterized Italians as deficient in "energy and hardihood." The New York *Times* replied in an editorial which should stir the gratitude even today of every American of Italian lineage. The *Times* said that the *Advertiser* was guilty of a "cool ignoring of facts," and then went on to say:

> Since the Latin race is so deficient in energy, it is rather curious that the Suez Canal, a work requiring considerable energy, should have been executed by the indolent and shiftless Latins.
>
> Also, it is equally strange that the same race should have tunneled Mont Cenis in half the time that an Anglo-Saxon people has occupied in the attempt to drive a smaller tunnel under the Hoosac Mountain. The accusation of want of energy and hardihood on the part of the Italians comes with a peculiar grace from a newspaper published in a country discovered by one Italian and named after another. Of course, since the *Commercial* has definitely objected to Italian immigration, it would be of no use to call its attention to the fact—as asserted by the police—that the Italians are the most orderly, in proportion to their numbers, of all foreigners in this city.

These two incidents were trifling in comparison to the dreadful deeds which occurred in New Orleans in 1891, but whether the culmination of a succession of abuses becomes personal tragedy or mere humiliation, either is inexcusable in a land where every individual is entitled, within the limit of the law, to the fullest expression of his personality regardless of national origin, race, creed, color, or religion.

I relate the tragic occurrence of New Orleans with pain and reluctance because it would be more comfortable to believe that so monstrous an event could never have occurred in this land of mine which I love and reverence. I tell it only because I could not feel that I had conscientiously endeavored to tell the story of the Italian in America if I omitted this sad tale, as soul-wrenching as it is to relate it.

On October 15, 1890, David Hennessy, Chief of Police of New Orleans, was mortally wounded by unknown persons. Before dying he said that the men who shot him were "dagoes." He had been conducting an investigation on the city's docks where two rival Italian dockworkers had been feuding. Although the Chief of Police had not identified any of his assailants and had given no description of suspects, his next in command ordered a general arrest of Italians.

It so happened that just at this time a ship from Italy arrived with several hundred immigrants aboard. These voyagers, who of course knew nothing about the Hennessy murder, faced a jeering and menacing mob as they came down the gangplank. "Ship them back!" exclaimed the jeerers. "Let's give 'em what they gave Hennessy!" illogically yelled others to the immigrants who shrank bewilderedly before this inexplicable hostility.

In the dragnet thrown by the police throughout New Orleans several hundred Italians were seized, questioned, and many held incommunicado. Eventually all were released but nineteen. The November grand jury indicted eleven of the nineteen as principals and eight as accessories to the murder of David Hennessy.

During the pendency of the trial, speakers and circulars abused the Italian prisoners, stirring the community into expressions of hatred and hostility against them. In December 1890 the magazine *Popular Science Monthly* carried an article with the inflammatory title "What Shall We Do with the Dago?" The author, Appleton Morgan, answered his question with the declaration that jail was too good for dagoes. Here are his words, fantastic as they may seem: "What have the 'dagoes' to lose by pilfering, assaulting, robbing and murdering? So far as creature comforts are concerned, they live better and work about as much, have warm clothing and better beds, in the meanest jail in the United States than they experienced out of it." And then, pouring more oil on the flames of prejudice against the Italians in prison, Morgan announced that "Local laws seem, therefore, incompetent to deal with this 'dago.' "

The State brought nine of the accused Italians to trial in February 1891. Considerable care was exercised in selecting the jury. 1721 talesmen were questioned before twelve jurors were chosen. In spite of the inflammatory fires being tended by the Italian-haters outside the courthouse, dignity and tranquility prevailed within. The chief defense counsel, Lionel Adams, had been a district attorney, and when he had finished analyzing the evidence the State had to admit it had no case against two of the defendants. The presiding judge, then, on his own initiative, declared that there was no evidence of guilt against still another defendant and acquitted him.

The trial thus proceeded against only six defendants. At the end of ten days, the State having exerted itself to the utmost, the prosecutor harangued the jury for hours, demanding conviction for all of the defendants and shouting that "hanging is too good for them." The judge instructed the jury on their responsibilities under the law and the jury retired for deliberation on their verdict. On March 13, 1891, the jury announced its verdict of acquittal for three of the defendants and declared that they were unable to agree on a verdict for the remaining three. Thus, despite all the propaganda and pressure brought to bear by the State on the processes of law, it was unable to convict a single one of the Italians. Instead of releasing the three defendants who had been acquitted by the jury and the other three exonerated by the judge himself, the judge remanded *all* the defendants back to jail.

The next morning a startling advertisement greeted the New Orleans readers of their newspapers:

MASS MEETING

All good citizens are invited to attend a mass meeting on Saturday, March 14, at 10 o'clock a.m., at Clay Statue, to take steps to remedy the failure of justice in the Hennessy Case. Come prepared for action.

From the moment that the jury's verdict had been announced, angry crowds had begun to form at street corners yelling and chanting revenge against the "dagoes." At ten o'clock they surged into the center of the city, rallying around the statue of Henry Clay—Henry

Clay, the Great Pacificator, the Great Compromiser, the man of law, of reason, of humanity—what irony! A lawyer by the name of William S. Parkerson mounted a platform which had been improvised, and called on the shouting, yelling agitators to take the law into their own hands. As he declaimed, others came running up, seizing clubs and shotguns on the way. Five thousand rioters were presently shrieking, "Death to the dagoes!"

John C. Wickliffe now climbed to the platform and spread out his hands for silence. The audience was indisposed to silence but he yelled he only wanted to inform them on the manner in which their desires could be accomplished. A reasonable but restless quiet ensued and Wickliffe instructed: "Let us proceed in an orderly fashion. I nominate Attorney William S. Parkerson as captain of the execution party, and James D. Houston first lieutenant." The crowd roared its approval. And then, after a modest pause, Wickliffe said he would make himself second lieutenant of the executioners. The mob bellowed approval again, and, brandishing weapons high, marched on the prison in which nineteen Italians were wards of the government and of the law. Six had been wholly exonerated through judicial procedure, there had been a mistrial as to three, and the remaining ten had not been tried at all.

But the five thousand men—purists, nativists, and Nordics—marched. They made only one stop before rendezvous. They paused at a Canal Street gunstore to obtain more rifles and shotguns.

The shrieking firebrands then resumed their dreadful tramp, tramp, tramp, resumed their macabre advance; resumed their death-head charge on the city prison to kill not only Italians but also respect for the jury system, the backbone of American law; respect for decency and justice.

Where was the mayor, the police department, the fire department, the city council? They all knew of this planned assault on law and order, they all had knowledge of this premeditated mass murder. They lifted not a finger to halt this ravishment of law, of civilization, of humanity.

Arrived at the prison the rioters flung themselves at the door with crowbars and large beams and smashed it down. At this point, one of them yelled: "Stop! Let us have some order. All of us can't go in. There'll be disorder and confusion. Let fifty do the job!" Some groaned in protest but the cooler murderers prevailed over the hot-

head murderers and fifty swept into the opened passageway. On the
floor lay two mattresses which seemed to move. They tore away the
top cover. A fourteen-year-old Italian boy whimpered and pleaded
for mercy. In a moment of unexplained pity they spared his life and
rushed on into a gallery where they saw fleeing forms. The warden
had locked up the non-Italian prisoners in their cells for safety but to
the Italians he said: "You'll have to shift for yourselves." One of the
invaders shouted: "There they are!" The cry was taken up by his
frenzied accomplices, and, from them, by the mob outside.

Several of the Italian prisoners ran down a set of stairs and pursued a corridor not knowing where it might lead. Unluckily they had
chosen a dead end and were forced to halt at the termination of the
corridor. Throwing their hands above their heads they implored
mercy. "Give it to them!" one of the ringleaders shrieked. A volley of
shots rang out and the smell of exploded gunpowder permeated the
prison.

From here on I will quote from an account of the horrendous
event as it appeared in a publication entitled *The Annual Register*,
1891.

> Gerachi, who was the last of the fleeing men, received a charge in the
> back of his head and turning a complete somersault, fell on his face.
> He never moved again. Then Monasteri and Caruso fell, the back of
> their heads literally riddled with bullets. Romero, with a cry of
> anguish, turned to his executioners and crouched on his knees with
> his head almost on the ground. In that attitude he was killed. He was
> the only one of the victims who had a hat on his head, and notwith-
> standing the fact that he was riddled with bullets, his hat never left
> its place.

At this point another section of the mob broke into a cell block
where the prisoner Macheca was confined.

> He heard the men coming, and rushed from the cell, but was cor-
> nered in the gallery of the condemned prison. Here a young man in
> the mob hit him on the head with the butt end of a rifle, which
> caused him to drop senseless. It was reported that he was dead; but as
> the crowd was about to leave, someone suggested that, as an extra
> precaution, he should be placed beyond any possibility of recovery, a
> bullet was fired through his brain at point-blank range, and his corpse
> was left where it fell. The mob outside was getting impatient and
> had begun to groan. They demanded that the victims should be

brought out and hanged in sight of all. The streets and squares around the prison were filled with people, among whom were many women and children.

But a still more dreadful act of the tragedy was yet to come. The avengers were not yet satisfied. They got hold of Bagnetto and dragged him out of the building. He had already been fatally wounded, and his dark face was besmeared with blood. As the crowd in the square caught sight of him they uttered a roar of rage. They had heard the shots within the jail but had not seen slaughter. Now was their opportunity. Someone brought a rope, which was noosed and thrown around the man's neck. The other end was cast over the limb of a tree. The dying wretch was swung up, then a fusillade from a score of weapons ended his sufferings.

I will omit the horrible details of the lynching of another one of the Italian prisoners, while men and women from balconies "watched the scene with opera glasses."

When the carnage ended, eleven defenseless Italians had been murdered. Parkerson now mounted the sill of a window in the prison and, amid cheers, shouted to his frenzied co-criminals that since the law had failed, he and his associates had to take "the law into our own hands." He said that lynch law was a "terrible thing" but:

"The responsibility for this day's tragedy rests not with its immediate participants, but with the infamous jury who acquitted the murderers. The people demanded that these murderers should be punished with death. We have executed their will. Now the affair must end here. If you have confidence in me you will disperse and return to your homes, resting assured that if there are any other matters to be attended to they will receive attention."

The assassins and the avid onlookers cheered Parkerson lustily, took him on their shoulders and bore him to his home in triumphant procession. He then again asked them to "disperse quietly," and presumably they did, but the outrage they had perpetrated will never disperse quietly from the history of what man can do to man, in his aggressive and vulgar assertion of "superiority."

We will recall that Osborn, in his introduction to Grant's *The Passing of the Great Race,* said that the greatest danger which confronted America was that it might be dominated by persons of a "less noble character."

How did the noble characters of New Orleans react to what had been done in their citadel of law and order? Resolutions endorsing the action of the lynchers were adopted by the Cotton Exchange, the Sugar Exchange, the Stock Exchange, and the Board of Trade, all of whose members were undoubtedly of a high noble strain.

The New York *Herald* on March 14, 1891, reporting what had happened in New Orleans, ended its story with the following:

Dr. Luigi Raversi, a well-known Italian journalist, editor of *Il Progresso Italo-Americano*, a daily Italian newspaper published in this city, expressed himself in this wise concerning the lynching:

"It is a horrible crime, a massacre of innocents, unworthy of civilized and republican America, a lasting disgrace to a Christian and progressive people. It is a crime a thousand times worse than the unsolved murder of Chief Hennessy because Hennessy was an armed free man and able to defend himself, but the poor acquitted prisoners were unarmed, and fell victims like helpless lambs under the knife of butchers. Remember that these men had been proclaimed to all the world innocent by an American jury, and further, that the persons of these men, who were in the prison under the aegis of the law, should have been sacred. And remember that these men were no longer under the accusation of murder, but that they were free men; that they had been declared innocent. When we look upon the occurrence in the light of these facts the lynching becomes a crime against civilization of the deepest dye."

The New Orleans massacre horrified America as well as Europe. Italy withdrew her diplomatic representative and the United States Government eventually paid an indemnity to the widows and orphans of the victims of the mob. In the May 1891 issue of the *North American Review*, Henry Cabot Lodge expressed himself on the affair. He said that the people of the United States were "startled and shocked," but that it would be unjust to condemn the mob unreservedly because there may have been in the killing a kind of "wild justice." Here are his words:

To visit on the heads of the mob all our reprobation, and to find in its act alone matter of anxiety and regret, would not only be unjust, but would show a very slight apprehension of the gravity and meaning of this event. Such acts as the killing of these eleven Italians do not spring from nothing without reason or provocation. The mob would have been impossible if there had not been a large body of public opinion behind it, and if it had not been recognized that it was not mere riot, but rather that revenge which Lord Bacon says is a kind of wild justice.

Mr. Lodge's remarks will remain for all time as a stain on the record of a man whose middle name was derived from the Italian who discovered that part of the world which gave Henry Cabot Lodge birth.

While Mr. Lodge was defending the New Orleans mob, another person, this one with humanity and charity in her heart, prepared to go to New Orleans not only to offer comfort and solace to the families of the deceased victims, but also to set up, as she had done in many parts of the western world, a convent, chapel, and orphanage for the Italian poor of the city, for the oppressed and the maltreated.

When she arrived, she found, as Pietro Di Donato related in *Immigrant Saint*:

> The Italians still vividly bore the raw stigmata of the atrocity inflicted upon them the year before—the lynching of the eleven immigrants. With towering indignation she heard the particulars of the slaughter from the tearful widows, children, and friends of the murdered men, and she firmly resolved to uplift the Italians of New Orleans.

She came with her nuns, the Missionary Sisters of the Sacred Heart. They located a dilapidated tenement house on St. Philips Street, rebuilt portions of it, scrubbed and painted it, and turned it into a House of God to which the New Orleans immigrants could repair for spiritual guidance and secular encouragement. In this city, which had seemed so cold despite its tropical climate, she initiated works of mercy. She learned of an Italian immigrant who, forty years before, had lost his eyesight in an industrial accident but had received no financial assistance from the industry involved and was reduced to street beggary. She was able to obtain his admittance to a home for the blind, and for weeks she visited him each day to prepare him for his first Holy Communion.

What she accomplished in New Orleans she repeated in various cities, working among the neglected, ostracized Italians of the United States. She established churches, orphanages, and hospitals. Born in Italy she came to America because she had learned of the indignities to which some of her co-nationals were subjected. She became a

United States citizen. Although a semi-invalid she insisted on working incessantly—ministering to the sick and the disabled, helping the poor, the persecuted, the unemployed. Her worn-out body found surcease on December 22, 1917. On July 7, 1946, in Saint Peter's Church in Rome, she became the first United States citizen to be canonized —Saint Frances Xavier Cabrini.

12 DIGGING THE SUBWAYS

Italians who had trades and callings managed with planning and thrift to save enough money to open their own tailor shops, barbershops, shoemaker shops, grocery stores, delicatessens. They were peculiarly adept in merchandising fruits and vegetables and, with a little capital, they could go into business by buying pushcarts and vending their wares on the streets or directly to the housewives in their homes. Many became importers and vendors of Italian wines, cheeses, salamis, and *pasta*. Italians instinctively revere the greatness and nobility of men who have made history, so that many, artistically inclined, made up miniature plaster-of-Paris busts of such immortals as George Washington, Giuseppe Garibaldi, Benjamin Franklin, and Abraham Lincoln and sold them on the streets.

Those who loved music and needed its cleansing and refreshing power every day but whose youth was behind them and whose fingers were no longer agile enough to extract the magic of harmonious sound from the violin, pianoforte, clarinet, or mandolin, purchased on credit little barrel organs. These music wagons phenomenally reproduced reasonable, auditory facsimiles of great operas and rousing marches, and their patriarchal owners rolled them over the streets of New York, Boston, Philadelphia, and other large cities, making a humble living from the pennies and nickels which fell into the little hat often proffered by a trained monkey who wore a green jacket and who always thanked the donor with his extravagant gestures of gratitude and appreciation.

The Italians added color and picturesqueness to the American scene. They vended statuettes, they gave you classical music whether you liked it or not, and sketched pictures of you if you stopped on the sidewalks to watch the embyro artists in their smocks, and then handed the sketches to you for a gratuity.

In many of the larger cities, but particularly in New York and Brooklyn, there were large urban areas where the visitor could easily believe he had miraculously been transported to Italy itself. Here, if he wished, he could buy Italian newspapers, books, and magazines, Italian foods of every kind, Italian plants and flowers, Italian provincial costumes. He could relax in Italian puppet shows and Italian motion picture houses. The streets were gay with flags, flowers, and ribbons in honor of a saint's day. Italian music and song poured from dozens of music shops where one could purchase the latest Caruso records.

One could not only buy a Caruso record but also hear the celebrated tenor in person at the Metropolitan Opera House. There were, of course, magnificent voices before Caruso's and many sang after him, but never again perhaps will the human voice pour forth the golden streams of lyric beauty which issued from the lips of this operatic immortal. To have heard Caruso in his prime—and he was in his prime from the day in 1898 when he electrified the audience at Milan's Teatro Lirico to his last appearance in 1920 at the Metropolitan —is a distinction which music lovers of today wear as an accolade. He was one of the few persons who in his own lifetime—and it was a short one (he died at forty-eight)—became a legend. He was beloved on three continents, not only because of his heavenly gifts but also because of his sweet disposition, charitable nature, and love of humanity. His widow, when his voice was stilled forever, paid him a most singular and touching tribute: "He was a very good man, and he could also sing."

Other celebrated singers thrilling their audiences at the Metropolitan during this era were Antonio Scotti, Pasquale Amato, Giovanni Martinelli, Giuseppe de Luca, Beniamino Gigli, and Titta Ruffo. Nor were the ladies hiding their beauty and angel voices. Among those who captured the hearts of America in this golden era of song and sheer grace of face and form were the lovely Lina Cavalieri, Luisa Tetrazzini, Claudia Muzio, and Amelita Galli-Curci. Earlier, there had been Adelina Patti, one of the great nineteenth-century coloratura sopranos.

The assistant conductor at the Metropolitan when it opened in 1883 was the Italian Cleofante Campanini, and the conductor from 1894 to 1902 was Luigi Mancinelli. The most famous, of course, was Arturo Toscanini, of whom we will speak later, but there were other celebrated ones: Gaetano Merola, Gennaro Papi, Ettore Panizza, Vincenzo Bellezza.

The Metropolitan also had its complement of distinguished impresarios, the most talented of them perhaps being Giulio Gatti-Casazza who was general director from 1908 to 1935.

It was during the latter part of the Ellis Island Era that Rudolph Valentino, Italian actor, achieved cinematic heights in the *Four Horsemen of the Apocalypse* and became the favorite of moviegoers, especially women, through the country.

It was in this epoch also that Amadeo Pietro Giannini, son of an immigrant from Genoa, opened his Bank of Italy in San Francisco. When the earthquake of 1906 rocked and leveled most of the city, Giannini loaded two million dollars into a wagon and traveled throughout the stricken city, paying out to depositors what they needed in immediate cash, and lending money to those who were in dire distress. When people would say that they could offer no security, Giannini would look at them and reply: "Your face is sufficient security for me."

One fellow-Italian seeking a loan said that he could offer only his hands for security. Giannini scanned them and remarked: "Those calluses show you are a hard-working man. We will need you to rebuild the city." He turned to his assistant and said: "Mark up this man for one thousand dollars."

It was this type of friendly relationship with the people that made Giannini one of the most respected men in the banking world. Later he changed the name of his bank to the Bank of America, a fiscal institution whose magnitude today is not surpassed or even equaled in the entire world. No person of any business knowledge at all could say he did not know of A. P. Giannini.

Also during this period many Italians became successful contractors and erected not only large buildings but also often whole towns in themselves. They launched numerous construction programs in the country. It was a delight for some of these contractors, proud of their ancestry, to place in the pay envelopes of their workers, as part of their wages, a few bright, shining American silver dollars designed by a fellow Italian, Anthony deFrancisci.

It is a paradox beyond compare that despite this continuing and ever-augmenting manifestation of what Italians were contributing to the building, progress, might, and culture of America, the Italian still was not accepted as an American. Notwithstanding the work which the Italian immigrant had performed in assuring transportation, security, safety, comfort, and well-being to the non-Italian, the latter, in too many instances, was still reluctant to accord him the recognition and appreciation he merited. The Italian shoemaker paved the streets with leather for him, the Italian barber trimmed his hair and cleansed him of his beard, the Italian stonemason constructed the sturdy granite bridges over which the non-Italian walked and rode, the Italian excavated deeply into the earth to anchor the foundations and the steel columns from which gleaming buildings of glass and steel went soaring into the skies, the Italian dug the subway through which the urbanite rocketed behind his newspaper, but when it came to giving the Italian his just due, he was, after all, only a wop. He was still unassimilable, he still belonged to an inferior race, he was still delaying the uniformization of our population, he was still uneducated, he was still not American. The doors of America should have been closed to him and immigration should have been limited to populations from northern and western Europe.

The Monday Pioneers who scorned the immigrant did not appreciate that they might never have gotten away from their own backbreaking and poorly-paid work, so as to go on to more remunerative and attractive employment, had it not been for the immigrants who took over the more strenuous and lesser-paid jobs. They did not stop to reflect on how much of America has shown respect for Italy. Not only is the capital of our nation enshrined in a district named after Columbus, but scores of cities, counties, and communities bear the name of Columbus and Columbia. Ten American towns have adopted the name of Rome, sixteen are named Monticello. Scattered throughout the country there are Veronas, Milans, Piedmonts, Napleses, Venices, Parmas, Comos, Turins, Sorrentos, Modenas, Etnas

—all bespeaking the admiration and affection which the American people have felt toward Italy and Italy's history. Why then should there have been in the Ellis Island Era such a stupid attitude toward Italians?

Why did so many non-Italians picture Italians always as dark, swarthy, and living in intellectual darkness even when, in illuminating their own homes, they threw on a switch which flooded the rooms with light from bulbs on which is stamped the number of "volts"—a term derived from the name of one of the great physicists of all time, Alessandro Volta? Volta invented the voltaic pile, declared by many scientists to have been a greater invention than the steam engine. His scientific achievements were such that in 1801 Napoleon invited him to Paris to demonstrate his experiments and ordered a medal struck in the Italian's honor. A manufacturer of bulbs computed for me the estimated number of bulbs in the United States in 1964. He came up with the figure of one billion. If all these, each one bearing the name of the Italian inventor, were lighted in one continuous stream, the resulting incandescence might well crisscross the continent. The resulting illumination might also wipe out for all time the dark thoughts of those who have regarded Italians as inferior in the world of science.

Italians have not only contributed greatly to America's industrial, commercial, scientific, and cultural progress, but also suffered in her losses, setbacks, and tragedies—mine cave-ins, tenement fires, railroad wrecks, factory explosions, storms and floods. In 1914 one of the saddest chapters in labor history was written in blood in Ludlow, Colorado, when state militiamen fired on striking coal miners and set fire to their tent colony. Among those burned to death were one Italian woman and seven Italian children ranging in age from three months to six years. Three Italian coal miners were shot to death.

It is not true, as asserted by the Heflins, Shieldses, and Madison Grants, that the Italians did not assimilate with the rest of the American population. They assimilated in blood at Ludlow, they assimilated in blood at Guilford Court House, Gettysburg, and Belleau Woods. They assimilated in the mud and dirt, in the gravel pits, in the canal silt and wherever sweat was needed as mortar to hold together the bricks and stone blocks in the building of ever-progressive America.

If there still exist some slight variations among the various nationalities with regard to customs, habits, cuisine, ceremony, music, those differences do not affect assimilated Americanization. On the contrary they make for a more interesting, colorful, and picturesque nation.

I trust that the day will never come when we will not have St. Patrick's Day parades, Columbus Day banquets, Pulaski Day celebrations, and festive ceremonies eulogizing the greats of other nations. Should that day ever arrive, a great charm will have disappeared from America. It is the very fact that we are a nation of nations, a gathering of peoples from all parts of the world that America is unique, entrancing, ever-progressive, lovable. It is because of the traits and personal characteristics of the nation from which they or their forebears hailed that the people of this continent have welded together that inspirational, driving, dynamic idealistic force which we call the American spirit. May those native and inherited personal characteristics never be lost to the United States.

Who would want, on the basis of assimilation or standardization, to wipe out the provincial color of the various parts of this land? How could we get along without the attractive Southern leisureness of speech, the New England incisive intonation, Virginia ham, Pennsylvania pancakes, Georgia peaches, California grapes, Maine lobster, Maryland shad roe, Idaho potatoes, Milwaukee beer? Who would want to scratch off the American menus Mulligan stew, sauerkraut, kolbassi, bagels, gefilte fish, chop suey, borscht, shish kebab, and crepes suzettes? Who would want to travel through a country as if on a treadmill of sameness and monotony? Why, therefore, find fault with Italian mandolins and guitars, pizza, vino, tarantella and celebrations of saintly *feste?*

Some of the anti-immigrationists argued that the Italian could never assimilate because he did not speak English when he arrived. Neither did Lafayette, when he presented himself to the Continental Congress in Philadelphia, speak any more English than a few words he was able to learn on the voyage across the ocean. Felix Frankfurter did not speak English when he arrived in America and he rose to become a Justice of the Supreme Court of the United States, nor did John Peter Altgeld who became Governor of Illinois, nor did Walter Damrosch who became one of America's most popular orchestra conductors. Nor did Igor Sikorsky, the inventor of the helicopter and developer of America's multi-engine airplanes.

The Italian may not have known any more English than did Lafayette when he arrived here, but no one could question the eloquence of his muscles, the fluency of his brawn, the speech of his industriousness, the articulateness of his loyalty to his work and his adopted country. The Italians learned English as quickly as they could and some became extremely proficient in its use, as we have seen with Pascal D'Angelo, immigrant "pick and shovel man."

There were those who complained because the Italian immigrant read Italian newspapers, but this in no way impeded him in his assimilation program. On the contrary, it speeded him in achieving necessary knowledge to obtain his naturalization papers and then to keep pace with the rapid tempo of America.

In spite of the constant disparaging of the southern European by the anti-immigrationists, no scientific revelations worthy of the name were ever presented in Congress during the immigration debates to support the theory that America could better absorb the Nordic newcomer than the Mediterranean arrival. The Nordic has not held up any better in the American mills, factories, mines, laboratories, on the railroads and farms and in the forests, than has the southern immigrant.

Those who have defended the southern immigrants against the onslaughts of the Nordic champions have pointed out that, regardless of background and antecedents, a willing, conscientious, eager person can adapt himself to environment easily, so that the processes of Americanization present no problem whatsoever. To this the Nordic protagonist has replied that heredity has a far greater influence on personality and character than environment. If that be true, how then can it possibly be argued that the Nordic has a supremely superior advantage in this respect? The historical facts are directly to the contrary. When Italy and Greece had attained a standard of civilization, which even today in many respects still inspires cultural simulation, the northerners were wearing the skins of wild beasts and living in caves. In his book *The Italian in America* Eliot Lord expressed it picturesquely:

> The far-reaching ancestry of the natives of South and Central Italy runs back to the dawn of the earliest Greek civilization in the peninsula and to the Etruscan, driving bronze chariots and glittering in artful gold when the Anglo-Saxons and Jutes, and all the wild men

of Northern Europe, were muffling their nakedness in the skins of wild beasts, and making their lair in rock caverns or the crudest of huts.

Nor is there any merit to the contention of the restrictive immigrationist that the heavy immigration into America of the late nineteenth and early twentieth centuries depressed the American standard of living. On the contrary, it played an important part in elevating it. When the immigrant workers reached the stage of maximum application to American industry, their numbers strengthened the argument presented by labor unions for improved working conditions, fair and decent wages, reasonable vacations, and increased safety. The difference between what the working man received in return for his labor prior to 1880 and what he gets now is almost the difference between economic serfdom and freedom.

Nothing can be so disconcerting as dishonest propaganda. Even those who can see with their own eyes that certain representations are false will yet go on believing what has been dinned into their ears. Despite what their minds clearly tell them, and what observation and experience have proved to them, they still go on believing and acting on what has been imparted to them through their innate prejudices and antipathies.

In 1926 I launched my first candidacy for public office, the Pennsylvania State Legislature, from the Twelfth Legislative District, made up of two Pittsburgh city wards and about forty-five boroughs and townships, including Mt. Lebanon Township, in which, in all likelihood, no "foreigners" resided. One day a friend of mine brought me a leaflet which he had picked up in Mt. Lebanon, where he lived. It called on the voters of the Twelfth Legislative District to defeat Musmanno because he was not an American. "Who is this person with the foreign-sounding name," the leaflet inquired, "who wants to represent Americans of this district in our State Legislature?"

If this anonymous interrogator had examined the official records of the United States Army he would have discovered many "foreign-sounding" names as recipients of the highest military honors that America can offer. On September 14, 1918, Company D of the 107th Infantry was pinned down by German machine guns which were taking a deadly toll of American troops and holding up the advance which was to crack the Hindenburg Line. Private Michael Valente, later joined by Joe Mastine, another Italian, stole out of his trench and, with bullets splashing about him, destroyed three German machine guns, killed ten of the foe, and rounded up some forty prisoners, all in strategic positions. Company D moved forward, and the Hindenburg Line was on the way to collapse.

If this questioner had dipped further into the war records, he would have learned also that the first American seaman to make the supreme sacrifice in World War I was a young man bearing the "foreign-sounding" name of John Isidore Eopolucci.

The American army citation next in importance to the Congressional Medal of Honor is the Distinguished Service Cross. Eighty-three of these awe-inspiring medals were awarded to American soldiers who were born in Italy. A score more went to American soldiers of Italian lineage. It has been estimated that about 400,000 American soldiers with Italian names served under the Stars and Stripes in World War I. It is to be noted in this connection that Italy itself had entered the war two years before the United States and that some 90,000 Italians in America returned to Italy in 1915 to join the Italian colors. Had they been here in 1917 it can be assumed that most of them would have served under the American flag.

That the American soldiers of Italian descent shed blood in equal if not greater share than other nationalities on our side would seem obvious from the statement made by George Creel, who headed the Public Relations section of the Department of War:

"The Italians in the United States are about four percent of the whole population but the list of casualties shows a full ten percent of Italian names."

I went to Mt. Lebanon, where a custom obtained in every political campaign to open the high school auditorium one night to all candidates. I knew no one in Mt. Lebanon and I doubt that anybody there knew me. Since the program had not yet begun, I walked up to the meeting chairman and informed him I wished to speak in behalf of a candidate. He asked me my name and I said: "Don't introduce me by name but just say, when my turn comes: "'Here's the next speaker.'" He indifferently handed me a slip of paper which listed me as No. 9 of the speakers of the evening.

When the eighth speaker had concluded his remarks the chairman said: "And here's the next speaker." I advanced to the platform and spoke:

"Ladies and gentlemen, I come to speak to you in behalf of a legislative candidate I know well. He was born in Stowe Township on the banks of the Ohio River: he attended and graduated from our local public schools and then attended and graduated from the Georgetown, George Washington, National and American Universities, all in Washington, the capital of our nation. He served in the United States Army. The candidate for whom I speak is a lawyer and articles by him have appeared in the *American Bar Association Journal*, the *American Law Review*, and the New York *Times*. He is a candidate for the Pennsylvania legislature."

"What's his name?" someone called out.

"Michael Angelo Musmanno," I replied.

A gasp of silence followed. I could feel in the air a sense of general incredulity that a person with such a name could be an American. Then an elderly gentleman sitting in the third or fourth row rose and asked: "Why doesn't this Michael Angelo fellow speak for himself?"

"He is here," I replied.

"Where?"

"I am he."

Another gasp of silence followed this, a more startled one than its predecessor, and then most of the audience applauded. I wouldn't say the applause was vociferous. Certainly it didn't endanger the roof, but it was encouraging.

Several days later the people of Mt. Lebanon, together with the voters in the rest of the Twelfth Legislative District, went to the polls and buried me under their adverse ballots. Of course, only a few of those who voted had seen me at the "open night" meeting, but it is a question whether those who applauded on that evening opened their minds enough to let out the prejudice which prevailed in that area against so-called foreigners. I might add that in the next campaign I carried Mt. Lebanon by a very narrow margin and was elected throughout the District. In my third campaign I carried Mt. Lebanon by a large majority.

13 PREJUDICE AND GENIUS

Nothing is so impervious as prejudice. A cannon projectile can penetrate a wall of steel sixteen inches thick, but it would bounce like a rubber ball off a wall of prejudice. An earthquake can shake a city and topple every building in it, but it cannot bend one weed of bigotry growing in the soil of hate. This is not the place to talk at length about the case of Nicola Sacco and Bartolomeo Vanzetti, but it must remain as a mark of everlasting shame in the history of law and in the temple of justice that Harry H. Ripley, the foreman of the jury which passed upon the fate of those two Italians, always referred to Italians as dagoes. He also made the remark, which was never refuted, that "if he had the power" he would "keep them out of the country." Before hearing a word of testimony in the case he said to a friend: "Damn them [Sacco and Vanzetti]; they ought to hang anyway!"

Prejudice is by no means an encrustation which attaches only to the uneducated mind. The most well-trained brain, if dipped in the acid of bias, can no more reason justly than a bent auger can bore a straight hole. When, following their conviction, Sacco and Vanzetti appealed to Alvan T. Fuller, the Governor of Massachusetts, for a pardon, the Governor appointed a commission of three distinguished citizens to review the case: A. Lawrence Lowell, President of Harvard University; Samuel W. Stratton, President of Massachusetts Institute of Technology; and former Probate Judge Robert Grant. The statement of Ripley's prejudice was presented to the commission in behalf of the condemned men. Lowell, the chairman of the commission, brushed it aside with the preposterous observation that "it is extremely improbable that Ripley was so different from other men that he desired the disagreeable task of serving on this jury, and he had only to reveal what he had said to be excused." The simple truth, of course, is that Ripley had no desire *not* to serve on the jury which was trying the "dagoes" he disliked. In fact, he relished the opportunity to sit in judgment on two "wops" he would have kept out of the country.

The second member of the commission, Judge Grant, had already manifested his prejudice against the Italians and had once referred to them as a "race of pickpockets." In addition, he had already stated, before starting to review the case, that he believed the defendants guilty. What chance did Sacco and Vanzetti have before a three-man reviewing body, two of whom walked into the reviewing chamber with ropes of prejudice in their pockets?

The district attorney, who prosecuted Sacco and Vanzetti, was not lacking in similar intolerance. At the Plymouth trial where Vanzetti had stood trial on a charge of attempted robbery in Bridgewater, sixteen Italian witnesses testified to having seen Vanzetti on the day of the crime some twenty miles away from the scene of the holdup. In his final speech to the jury District Attorney Frederick Katzmann ridiculed Vanzetti's alibi because his witnesses were Italians (one of the jurors had been overheard to refer to the witnesses as dagoes), and charged that as Italians they "stood together." Governor Fuller, in his review of the case, "dismissed the Italian witnesses in scathing terms as unworthy of belief because they were Italians."*

The judge who presided at the trial, Webster Thayer, had a special prejudice of his own against the defendants. Off the bench he referred to them as "anarchistic bastards" and said he "would get them good and proper."

When Judge Thayer finally sentenced Sacco and Vanzetti to death by electrocution, who can believe that Vanzetti was not justified in saying, in his eloquent courtroom address:

* Judiciary Committee hearing, Massachusetts Legislature, April 2, 1959.

"I am suffering because I am a radical and indeed I am a radical; I have suffered because *I was an Italian, and indeed I am an Italian.*"

In the latter phases of that tragic case I participated in it as one of defense counsel. When the Supreme Court of Massachusetts rejected our final appeal in the State Courts, I hurried to Washington to file a petition for a writ of certiorari in the Supreme Court of the United States. By this time the affair of Sacco-Vanzetti had fired the whole world of public opinion. Emotions and passions had reached almost explosive peaks. Humanity protested, paraded, and demonstrated in every part of the globe in behalf of the condemned men. The feeling was universal that Sacco and Vanzetti would never have been convicted, or at least would have been granted a new trial after conviction, were it not for the fact that they entertained unpopular views on government and were Italian workers, both of whom had been "pick and shovel men," and, just prior to their arrest, had been working at their humble callings of shoemaking and fish peddling, respectively.

The district attorney, Frederick Katzmann, had described the defendants as dangerous bandits, although prior to their arrest for robbery-murder they had never once been convicted of any crime. In order to portray Sacco and Vanzetti as menacing desperadoes, the district attorney and county sheriff filled the courtroom with armed guards and circled the courthouse with mounted constabulary. Policemen, bristling with firearms, marched the defendants, manacled to one another, into and out of the courtroom. All this was done with the connivance of the judge, although there had never been any incident to justify this daily parading of armed might.

The propaganda emanating from the office of the district attorney, aided and abetted by Judge Webster Thayer, and further swelled to fantastic proportions by Governor Alvan T. Fuller, made of Sacco and Vanzetti, in the public mind, such images of ferocious outlawry, that when I arrived in Washington to proceed to the Supreme Court, the newspaper reporters missed me at the railroad station because they thought that any attorney for Sacco and Vanzetti had to be decidedly "foreign looking," and probably quite ferocious in appearance also.

As I got off the train I saw a score of newspapermen and photographers at the station platform (they had learned that the Sacco-

Vanzetti lawyer was on that train). Since I had no idea they were looking for me, I walked straight through them, no one questioning me. However, ten or fifteen minutes after I had arrived at my hotel, a dozen reporters with notebooks and pencils burst into my room expressing considerable astonishment.

"No wonder we missed you at the station," they exclaimed, in varying phraseology. "We expected a man with a beard and certainly someone much older." The reporter of the Washington *Times* wrote in the afternoon edition of his newspaper: "Musmanno, despite his Italian name, speaks without the trace of a foreign accent." I could not help but recall in that instant my experience in Mt. Lebanon where the political audience also expected that with a name like mine I should talk like one just off the boat. In his surprise at not finding me "bearded like the pard," the writer went on to say that I was "smooth-shaven with skin inclined toward fairness." And then as if to startle the reader all the more in the revelation that I was truly American, even though defending Sacco and Vanzetti, the observant journalist added: "He wears the bronze emblem of the United States Army in his coat lapel."

Continuing his description he wrote: "He is not tall but is exceedingly brisk in all his movements." I was indeed brisk that morning —confidence and assurance kindled in my heart. I thought that now at last my two Italian clients would be accorded the justice which had been denied them for seven cruel years, but Katzmann, Thayer, and Fuller had set their trap too cleverly. In consequence, the shoemaker and the fish peddler, who never received the fair trial guaranteed by the Constitution of the United States, and, to save and protect which, countless Americans of Italian lineage had given of their brawn, talents, blood, and their lives, walked into it and never emerged alive.

While Henry Cabot Lodge and H. H. Boyensen were proclaiming their prejudices against the Mediterranean immigrants, while Madison Grant and Kenneth Roberts were propagating their animosities against Italy and countries of the south, while Edgerton was expressing his intolerance of the Latin peoples, while Alvan T. Fuller was making millions of dollars and developing the acumen which would enable him to weigh his chances for the Presidency of the United States against the lives of two Italians who could have been innocent, while Lawrence Lowell was building up that arrogance which would not permit him to believe that two Italians could be other than criminals, while Judge Grant was feeding that meanness of spirit which permitted him to libel a nation of Italians because he had been piqued by the assumed fault of one, while Webster Thayer was fueling his fires of bias with the fagots of ignorance, ineptitude, and vulgar vanity, while Harry Ripley was fattening his hatred against Italians which was eventually to send two guiltless ones to the electric chair, the greatest scientific achievement of all times was being accomplished and demonstrated by an Italian.

Ever since man learned to voyage into waters of such expanse that he could see neither shore, he sailed at the mercy of the destructive storm, the perils of the deep, and the infirmities of the craft beneath his feet. Once the unbidden waters stole into his ship, once the vessel began to lose level, once the bow dipped deeply into the trough of the sea, the captain could appeal to no one for assistance, guidance, or comfort.

Nautical history abounded with melancholy pages which told of ships that sailed for distant ports and were never heard from again, while relatives of the crews and passengers lived out their grieving lives in ever-continuing agony and torturing doubt as to what had been the fate of their vanished loved ones. Nor could man through the centuries ever even hope to dream that a way could be found for the master of an imperiled vessel to appeal for help to other vessels beyond his vision. Without bridges, wires, or cables, how could any message be transmitted across the wastes of water and through the empty air?

Guglielmo Marconi, an Italian, found the way. His brain saw substance more durable than bridges, more imperishable than wires, more communicative than any other medium that had previously informed, enlightened, ensaddened or engladdened the world.

On April 10, 1912, the S.S. *Titanic*, queen of the seas and empress of comfort and luxury, sailed on her maiden voyage from Southampton carrying over two thousand persons and crew. To the accompaniment of music and a singing crew, she cut through the waters with the grace and speed of a racing yacht on her way to winning the coveted blue ribbon for the most rapid transatlantic crossing. Then, with most of the journey behind her and only two days out of her destined port of New York, she crashed into an iceberg. The icy monster slashed along three hundred feet of the hull like a can opener into a can of sardines. Heralded as unsinkable, the *Titanic* quivered like a whale that had been harpooned. Passengers ran to the rail to see what had happened. A great white shadow loomed in the darkness, but there seemed no cause for alarm. Soon, however, the deck beneath their feet began to slant and they heard a cascading sound within the vessel. Torrents of the sea, unstoppable and undikable, were pouring into her longitudinal wound.

The captain dashed to a little cabin on the top deck and ordered the young man at a table with a telegraph key before him to "Send the call for assistance!"

The telegrapher's fingers swiftly tapped the instrument key, and from the wires swung between the masts, fiery sparks cut grooves into the air and, through the microscopic tunnels, electric energy sped with a velocity that outdistanced lightning.

Sixty miles away another luxury liner, the S.S. *Carpathia*, speeding in the opposite direction, suddenly turned in her course, churning a gigantic white horseshoe in the black sea. The telegraph operator on this ship had heard, instantaneously with the *Titanic* operator's tapping it out, the message:

C.Q.D. (Come Quick Disaster) We've struck a berg. Sinking fast. Come to our assistance. Position, Latitude 41.46 North, Longitude 50.14 West. S.O.S. Titanic.

No bridge spanned the expanse between the *Titanic* and the *Carpathia*. No wire or cable joined the vessels. Sixty miles of empty air yawned between them. But it was really not empty. Some 250,000 volts of high tension energy, like irresistible horsemen, rode that air, charioting the awesome dispatch: "S.O.S.! S.O.S.!" Other sounds were in the air. The ship's band of the *Titanic* had assembled on deck and the director was leading the sorrowing musicians in "Nearer My God to Thee" as the palatial liner headed for its unannounced final port. Sixteen lifeboats creaked down into the sea. There were not enough boats for all those aboard, so that those who were left behind, sang. Throats that were soon to taste the gushing salt waters, sang with the salt of tears in their voices.

The *Carpathia's* wireless receiving apparatus listened again to what the *Titanic* was saying: "Come quick, our engine room is flooded to the boilers." Every wheel, piston, and belt of the *Carpathia's* strained to its utmost as the liner was driven forward, her prow knifing fiercely through the ocean and night's darkness.

At last she arrived at the *Titanic's* position, but the *Titanic* was no more. Sixteen lifeboats, however, were bobbing on the debris-strewn, ice-clogged waters. In them were 717 living men, women, and children.

Guglielmo Marconi, the Italian, although a thousand miles away, had thrown a life bridge across the intervening watery distance. Ten years before, in February 1902, while crossing the Atlantic on the S.S. *Philadelphia*, he had completed his wonder-struck experimentations in the circumambient air and had electrified the world with the revelation that he had transmitted and received wireless messages over a distance of 1551 miles. This Guglielmo Marconi, who had his origin in the "inferior races" in the Mediterranean, had discovered a new world in space, as Christopher Columbus, who also was of the maligned Mediterranean, had discovered a new world on land.

As the *Carpathia* steamed into New York Bay, Marconi paced the dock waiting to welcome the people his genius had rescued from the voracious sea. When they saw him they cried out: "Ti dobbiamo la vita!" (We owe you our lives!) Later, at a thanksgiving ceremony, they conferred on their rescuer a golden plaque depicting Marconi as Apollo releasing from his fingertips sparks to the winds.

On October 10, 1913, the S.S. *Volturno* caught fire in mid-Atlantic. Nothing can be more terrifying to an ocean voyager than to see his ship yellow with flames eating away her life to the water's edge. Voyagers aboard the *Volturno* turned their eyes prayerfully to the wireless mast as it clicked out its summoning "S.O.S.! S.O.S.! Come quick, ship afire." "S.O.S.! S.O.S.!" The fire alarm of the sea. Ten ships equipped with Marconi's lifesaving wireless caught the cry of mortal distress and swiftly turned their prows in the direction of the nautical torch to which clung 667 human beings. The S.S. *Carmania* arrived, then the *Grosser Kurfuerst*. One by one—each with its Marconigram on the chart—the ships heaved into view amid splash and foam. Ten ships from six different nations formed a circle about the flaming *Volturno*, but then a monstrous storm came up, transforming the ocean into heaving mountains and sinking valleys. No small boat could possibly survive.

"Call for an oil tanker!" the captain of the *Carmania* ordered his wireless operator. In an instant the searching arm of the wireless was combing the sea. It located an oil tanker, the S.S. *Narragansett*, whose captain translated the dots and dashes flashing to him through the tempest: "Come quick. Need oil to calm stormy waters to take off passengers from *Volturno* on fire and sinking." The *Narragansett* skipper tapped out a jocular but comforting reply: "Arriving at dawn with necessary milk." At 5 A.M. the *Narragansett* was spreading mollifying oil over the troubled waves, and the small boats of the other vessels took off 521 men, women, and children from the burning *Volturno*. The others, in hysteria and panic, had leaped into the sea.

On October 15, 1913, the London *Daily Telegraph* spoke editorially:

> But for the invention of Marconi, we should be mourning today a holocaust of the seas of unparalleled horror, the overwhelming by fire in mid-Atlantic of six or seven hundred men, women, and children. There is nothing, perhaps, less noble in the record of our times than the indifference with which the patient research in the service of humanity is rewarded. The practical scientist who bridged the oceans and contracted continents within the span of electric impulse, never received from any state a fitting recognition of his triumph.

Marconi did later receive "fitting recognition of his triumph," but no honors conferred upon him, including the coveted Nobel Prize in physics, could equal the gratification that must have been his to know of the ships and lives his invention delivered from watery entombment. Up to 1927 it was estimated that more than three thousand ships on the verge of shipwreck achieved survival because of their wireless and that thirty to forty thousand persons who might have vanished in the mystery of the sea were saved simply because Guglielmo Marconi "was able to endow the ether with the power of speech." Since 1927 there is no counting the thousands of vessels and perhaps millions of lives, considering the fearful havoc at sea of World War II, that were liberated from certain disaster because Marconi had turned "the abyss of the air into the mouthpiece of man."

Today the wireless is as commonplace as putting on one's shoes, and how many moons would a parent have to promise his child in exchange if he took away his television? Yet, it is within the span of our own lifetime that this miracle achieved reality. In 1930 I followed on the radio Marconi's projection of electrical energy halfway around the world. Marconi was off Genoa in his yacht *Elletra*. He was sepa-

rated from the other end of his experiment by four seas, ten countries, vast deserts, mountains, every variety of weather, vegetation,
and climate, from icebergs to palm trees. No wire, no cable connected the two termini. Marconi picked up the telephone instrument
and called: "Hello, Australia."

Australia replied: "Hello, Genoa."

Marconi had hurled his voice to the other side of the spinning
earth as if it were an astral baseball.

"Are you ready for the experiment?"

The Australian replied: "Yes."

The Australian was the president of the Radio Electric Exposition
at Sidney, about to inaugurate its season. The exposition was in
darkness. Thousands of people had gathered to witness with incredulous eyes the magic of Marconi, 11,000 miles away.

"Ready?"

"Ready!"

The words went hurtling over the earth, the Mediterranean, the
Red Sea, the Arabian Sea, the Indian Ocean.

Marconi turned to his switchboard—glittering knobs, scintillating
bulbs, sparkling tubes. One could almost visualize the mythical god
Thor on the mountaintop preparing to hurl thunderbolts into the
world beneath.

The wireless wizard threw a switch, he pressed a button. The Exposition resounded to the shouts of the multitude. Three thousand
lights had been illuminated by Marconi in his yacht off Genoa. With
the accuracy of a sunbeam Marconi had hurled energy around the
globe.

On February 12, 1931, Marconi stood in the presence of Pope Pius
XI at the radio station of Vatican City. It was noontime in Pitts-
burgh, late afternoon in Rome. Sitting by my radio I heard the great
Marconi:

> "For nearly twenty centuries the Roman Pontiffs have given their
> inspired messages to all people, but this is the first time in history
> that the living voice of the Pope will have been heard simultane-
> ously in all parts of the globe."

> "With the help of Almighty God, Who places such mysterious forces
> of nature at mankind's disposal, I have been able to prepare this
> instrument that will give to the faithful throughout the world the
> consolation of hearing the voice of the Holy Father."

Then, addressing the Pope:

"Holy Father, I have today the happiness of consigning to your Holiness the work entrusted to me. Its completion is now consecrated by your august presence. Be pleased, I pray you, to let your voice be heard all over the world."

And in the twinkling of an eye the voice of the Pope was heard throughout the six continents! Not long after this, the Pope's photograph was sent through the air. And now it is routine, through the magic of wireless, to see in our newspapers pictures of events which occurred only two or three hours before, at the other end of the world. In addition, it is standard procedure, no less exciting, for that reason, to see and hear on our television sets in our living room, through the intercession of the Telstar, news events in Rome, Paris, or London, simultaneously with their happening. Still lounging in our easy chair, while munching a piece of chocolate cake and sipping coffee, we turn a knob and a symphony orchestra performs for us, another turn and we are transported to orchestra seats to the best of dramatic plays, another turn and we are attending interviews with famous people. Without stepping out into the rain or the snow, we cheer our sports heroes at baseball and football games, we take lessons in every field of knowledge. Our home has become a university, a theater, a political auditorium, an athletic field, an opera house, and it all began with Guglielmo Marconi.

While Marconi was bridging the seas with controlled electrical energy, another Italian was experimenting on bridging the ocean with man-made birds. The Wright brothers had achieved their spectacular victory over the air by actually propelling man-carrying vehicles through it. Giuseppe Bellanca in Italy was aiming at long-distance flights, and, within five years after the Wright successes, had perfected a plane of such durability that it could be depended on for sustained atmospheric buoyance and mobility. He came to America and established a laboratory for special aviation research. In 1922 he designed and built a five-seater cabin monoplane, winning first prize in thirteen events. He designed and built the monoplane *Columbia* which made two successful transatlantic flights.

In 1933 General Italo Balbo headed the first mass long-distance flight in history, piloting twenty-four huge eleven-ton seaplanes from

Orbetto, Italy, to Chicago, alighting, after five stops en route, in the waters of Lake Michigan to participate in Chicago's Century of Progress Exposition. In the speeches of the day the flight was described as the most memorable event in the annals of navigation since 1492.

14 THE PORTALS OF HISTORY

In the summer of 1924 the S.S. *Graf Waldersee*, after a stormy crossing of the Atlantic, glided serenely into the Bay of Naples, an unparalleled expanse of Mediterranean loveliness. One enters into that bay, which is some twenty miles wide at the mouth and ten miles deep, as one might pass through the portals of history. At the right terminus of the semicircular panorama, but separated from it by a narrow strait, stands the sentinel of the Isle of Capri, a pile of picturesque white limestone rising to a sheer height of two thousand feet. To the left, one sees the island of Ischia, a pastoral heaven of green.

As the ship steams into the azure waters, their gentle undulations suggesting the story of the thousands of fleets that have passed over their surface, one gets his first view of legendary and chronicled Italy. One almost expects to hear the enchanting hillsides burst into music. The towns lining the coast seem, with their vibrant names, to be characters in an opera: Sorrento, Vico Equense, Castellammare, Torre Annunziata, Torre del Greco, Portici, San Giovanni a Teduccio, Posilipo, Baia, Pozzuoli. As we move by these operatic figures wearing their rosy capes of soft morning light, embroidered with flowers, vineyards, and orchards of orange and lemon, we see off to the right, like the enormous backdrop of a titanic stage, a gigantic, cone-shaped, purple-clad mass rising from a vast plain and ascending to a dominating apex with an open crater a half mile in diameter. This is the world-famous Vesuvius, which has threatened, rumbled, and grumbled down through the centuries and at times has rained destruction on the surrounding regions, on one occasion covering with petrifying lava the ancient cities of Herculaneum, Pompeii, and Stabiae. But now it is as peaceful as a farmhouse chimney, white clouds rising from its crest and hovering above it in opalescent majesty, as if proclaiming its concord with the world. The pearly mists float over the little harbor of Pozzuoli, which in Roman days was Italy's greatest port. It was here on a spring day in A.D. 63 that a vigorous personality descended the gangplank of a ship which hailed from Alexandria. The voyager was demanding his rights as a Roman citizen to appeal to the Emperor. The voyager was St. Paul, the Emperor, Nero.

As our ship cleaves a lacy spray through the mirroring bay I begin to sense the full impact of what is happening. Naples lies straight ahead in all its dramatic and spectacular beauty. The curving harbor berths vessels of many colors flying flags of every hue from the most distant corners of the world. The waters lap at the walls of Castel dell'Ovo. The Castel Nuovo on the beach bespeaks its turreted and battlemented welcome. The sun has reached meridian, pouring dyes of every tint over the sea, which in its genial agitation now resembles a vast oriental carpet with the richest of colors and fabric.

Behind the harbor, white stone and marble buildings climb the hillside in amphitheatrical symmetry to the summit, where they join the snowy expanse of Castel Sant'Elmo. Wide avenues and spacious boulevards gird the city like satin sashes; parks and groves of trees ornament it like emerald brooches; flowers of every species become the reddest of roses in the sunlight, which veils the whole world in a golden mist, transforming it into a felicitous fantasy of living. I stand on the deck of the *Graf Waldersee* and weep. For centuries poets have been singing, "Vedere Napoli e poi morire" (See Naples and die). They believe that, once one has witnessed and lived the magic and entrancement of this view of Naples from the sea, he has seen and felt everything.

How can I absorb, how can I visually encompass, how can I spiritually embrace such overwhelming harmony in color, form, shape, and atmosphere? Here is poetry, romance, and symphonic music, and then, I am young. Young with all the enthusiasm and health of irrepressible youth to enjoy *la bella Italia,* the mecca for millennia of poets, troubadors, romanticists, dreamers—and doers.

Much of the emotion that overwhelmed me on that summer day in 1924 was undoubtedly due to kinship asserting itself. My blood recognized that here was the land whence came my forefathers. And my eyes beheld the land that from childhood had held me in a spell —the land of the Caesars, Columbus, Dante, Michelangelo, and the others of the immortals whose bright shadows dwelt in Arcadia on the other side of the distant, towering Apennines.

I must also admit that no small part of my joy was due to the fact that I had at last arrived where I could obtain some edible food. I had crossed the ocean in steerage and, after the first day out at sea, it was impossible for me even to look at the amorphous conglomeration of supposed edibles, which was thrown into our tin plates as we lined up in the dark and dreary hold of the ship, three times a day. As I was wearing clothes which one does not normally associate with steerage passengers and as I was obviously American-born, the query was constantly being put to me as to why I was not traveling cabin class. I explained that my parents had made the crossing in steerage and I wanted to see what it was like. This was true, but there was even a more cogent reason—I didn't have the funds with which to travel first or second class.

In the crossing I lost eight pounds, and my mouth watered for that first sumptuous meal to which I intended to treat myself. When I sat down to the repast in a restaurant overlooking fabled Santa Lucia, the rich marinara sauce piled over the spaghetti was diluted by the happy tears of the half-starved pilgrim as he contemplated not only the savory feast before him, but also the soulful feast which was to be his to enjoy at all the fabulous places of the fabulous itinerary forming in his mind.

Italy! I had to keep pinching myself to believe I was truly here. And as this country's romantic, momentous history raced through my mind I wondered how so much could have happened in so small a territory. It extends 700 miles, from the snow-crowned Alps into the sparkling Mediterranean, but its overall size is smaller than our own state of Montana. In 1924 its population was 40,000,000, now it is over 50,000,000. It is divided into 19 regions, which are subdivided into 92 provinces and 8007 communes. Although Italy is a peninsula, it could almost be considered an island because the Alps shut it off from continental Europe as effectively as the surrounding water sets it apart in the Mediterranean, Adriatic, and Tyrrhenian Seas. Giovanni Mariotti describes it poetically in his book *Here's Italy:*

> Running out into the middle of the Mediterranean, like a flower-bedecked bridge between the Alps and Africa, this land has all the charms that may be found in a country. . . . Her superb crown of snowy peaks and glaciers, which cut her off sharply from the northern world; the fruitful valley of the Po, studded with towns, villages, and factories; the long spine of the Apennines from which the most charming hills branch out; the terraces hanging high over the valleys; her long beaches bathed in sunshine; the islands, great and small, like gems in the azure sea. . . .

And now I am here and, of all exciting places, at Santa Lucia, known throughout the world because of the melodic song which has made it immortal and whose nostalgic strains I had heard even in my cradle. I am here to see and enjoy—not through books, maps, or songs, but with my own eyes which, in my desire to behold everything simultaneously, seem now to me to be as large as the oranges smiling at me from the trees whose branches sag at the windows. And my heart is thumping like the white-crested waves breaking on the Santa Lucia beach, which greets me through the open door.

I pay for my lunch (about fifteen cents in American money) and hurry out of the restaurant so as not to lose time in beginning my odyssey. The first place I hasten to, because it happens to be close by, is the Borgo Marinaro. It was here that the gallant Lord Nelson, forgetting for a moment Napoleon and the French fleet, launched his infatuation for the beauteous Lady Hamilton. Then in Posilipo I pay my respects at the tomb of the great Latin poet Vergil. And now I climb to the top of Mt. Vesuvius by funicolare (whence comes the rollicking *Funicoli! Funicola!*). And here I am standing on top of the world. I shiver with ecstasy at the incredible universe below. The ocean seems an amethyst lake, the castles look like toys for children to play with, the streets and boulevards are silver threads. Close by is old gruff Vesuvius himself, smoking his pipe with no hint that he might, as he has done in the past, empty the ashes from the pipe onto that fairyland below.

Back to sea level again, I clamber aboard the bus which takes us out to, and bowls along, the Amalfi Drive, the most startling roadway in the world, having been chopped out of tall cliffs hugging the churning sea. For thirty miles it winds in and out of mountainous formations which seem to be rococo clouds in a thunderous sky, petrified into deathless stone. Suddenly one cliff ends and does not appear again for a fifth of a mile. In the meanwhile our bus is sailing through the air with the rocky coast and tiny fishermen's villages five hundred feet below. I breathe again when the airy viaduct, which is not visible from the auto's portholes, has shot us safely to the shelf of the next cliff.

From time to time we stop, and this enables me to get my heart back into its proper cavity. But what stops they are! Here is the storied Amalfi with its fragrant citrus groves and magnificent cathedral of Lombard-Norman architecture, here is romantic Ravello, lovely beyond compare, the inspiration of composers and authors. Here is Positano, which cannot be real but only a souvenir picture card momentarily transfigured into breathing life. You linger to drink *un caffè espresso* on the beach while listening to mandolins and guitars, and sirens who apparently come in close enough to the shore to join in the serenade.

And now I am back in Naples, the most kaleidoscopically animated city in the world. Here commotion is king and tumult is queen. The streets could not be more actively in motion if they were carousels. People, horses, wagons, carriages, bicycles, donkeys, autos, wagons, hearses, wheelbarrows, flower carts, fruit carts, vegetable carts pass as if on a revolving stage. Everybody is talking, gesticulating, singing, laughing, as though there was just so much action to be gotten out of life, and this was the last day. It is all contagious, electrifying, and I find myself trying out my Italian on merchants, waiters, passersby, asking a million questions and getting two million replies. Everyone is willing to help. If I ask someone for directions, he drops everything to guide or even accompany me to my destination.

Despite the seeming chaos, however, of Neapolitan life, there is a pattern and system to it. It is not organized confusion but melodic enthusiasm. It is like the furious sawing of the violins, the crashing of cymbals, the flashing of the trombones from which emerges the great symphony. Naples is a tonal symphony of life, love, laughter, work, and achievement. It is wonderful.

The next day is not so uproariously alive. I visit Pompeii. Anyone who immerses himself in an era of long ago instinctively wishes, as he reads, that the printed pages might portray three-dimensionally the life, locale, dramatis personae, and the *modus vivendi* of the period which is the object of his concentrated absorption. This wish can be realized in Pompeii. The disaster that overtook it in A.D. 79, when an eruption of Vesuvius buried it under thick layers of ashes and lava fragments, preserved this Roman colony so that today we can walk through the streets and enter the buildings of this ancient city just as the Pompeians did nineteen centuries ago. When we reflect that in A.D. 79 there were people living who had seen Christ in Palestine we can realize the depth of the sensations which must grip one as he passes over the threshold from the nineteenth to the first century.

The bodies of some of these people have been preserved in stone as they were on that fatal day—only forty-six years after the Crucifixion. I visited a bakery and saw the loaves of bread which had also turned to stone. I stepped into a wine shop where a circular splotch with reddish radiations on the mosaic floor told the probable story of a customer from whose hands an amphora slipped and crashed as he dashed out into the hurricane of death.

Pompeii was an enlightened city. With running water, steam heat, public schools, public baths and parks, the citizens proudly displayed their names outside their comfortable homes. Large bulletin boards announced news in the manner of modern newspaper dispatches. The street intersections were equipped with a convenient feature which could well be used today. High stepping stones crossed the thoroughfares so that pedestrians in inclement weather could pass over dryshod.

In their petrified form I saw people who had traversed those streets eighteen hundred years ago. I beheld beautiful women, I looked into the faces of the sweetest children. I entered the kitchens in which the women cooked; I lingered in the yards in which the children played; I observed the recreation centers, the work tables at which craftsmen produced all the beautiful and useful things which adorned and distinguished this highly enlightened society. I felt myself back in A.D. 79. The sensational was real, tangible, palpable, but something was lacking. I heard no sound. Not a shout penetrated the stillness, not a conversation buzzed in the tranquil air, not a merchant praised his wares, not a chariot wheel turned, not a voice lifted high in song. And yet I heard whispers. They were whispers coming down through the centuries, replying to those who said that the inhabitants of southern Europe were of an inferior race.

From A.D. 79 I pursued my pilgrimage through the chasms and valleys of time back to 753 B.C., the founding of Rome. Here, mythology supplied the fleece; and then legend, on the loom of romance, wove the fetching story of Rhea Silvia, a Vestal, who was loved of Mars and bore twins, Romulus and Remus, whom Amulius, the King of Latium ordered thrown into the Tiber. Somehow they survived this plunge and were befriended and mothered by a she-wolf. Sufficiently grown, they took their poetic revenge on Amulius and threw him into the Tiber, placed a suddenly-produced grandfather Numitor on the Latium throne, and departed to erect for themselves a new city on one of the seven hills sleeping by the tawny Tiber.

Although in every souvenir shop in Rome one sees statuettes of Romulus and Remus being suckled by the she-wolf, and indeed they have become the traditional symbol of ancient Rome, it is enough to accept in the symbolism the Palatine Hill where the Eternal City was truly born. From the Palatine Hill, Rome extended to six other hills: Aventine, Capitoline, Quirinal, Viminal, Esquiline, and Caelian, later spreading to two more hills, the Pincian and the Janiculum. Rome traditionally, however, has always remained the City of the Seven Hills.

North of the Tiber lived the Sabines, a brave, stern, and religious race with women reputed to be beautiful and alluring. Rome in its early days had a preponderence of males. The bachelors, it is said, looked longingly toward the north and the Roman king approved of their thoughts. Population was needed, so he sent his most handsome warriors across the Tiber to court the Sabine ladies and invite them to Rome. The warriors went and did not return, as Romans never returned, empty-handed. This episode has been termed *The Rape of the Sabines.* The noun is not to be taken too seriously. Canvases have been painted of the husky Romans seizing the virgins, throwing them into chariots and making off to the seven hills. It cannot be doubted that an occasional centurion or legionnaire, in an excess of spirit, traveled beyond the call of duty in winning for himself a wife. But, on the other hand, it has also been reported that many of the Sabine women, when they learned of the intended Roman raid, kept impatiently asking when the "abduction" was to begin.

Certain it is that the Romans generated a hearty race. In many ways it was an amalgam of many peoples. America was not the first continent to stir the melting pot. Latins, Etruscans, Sabines, Ligurians, Villanovans, and others furnished the fibers that entwined into the sinews of the race that was to rule the world.

The early Romans quickly developed a genius for government. They knew that an increasing population without sociological restraint would make them weak, not strong. The people should have the right to speak, to assert their prerogatives, but they had also to accept duties and responsibilities. They chose a senate, the word deriving from the Latin *senex* (meaning men of years), which would legislate for the people, laying down rules and standards of conduct, providing for the common defense, establishing courts and law enforcers. Some limitations were also placed on the privileges of the king. While the people wanted him to be a virile, aggressive ruler, they desired also that there should be a check on his actions so that impetuosity might not lead to harm, and energy might not degenerate into disorder. Thus, the senate resolved itself into a keeper of the king's conscience, with authority to advise and consent with him.

However, even the wisdom of the senate failed to keep King Tarquinius within bounds. His son Sexton performed a deed of dreadful note. He broke one night into the chambers of Lucrezia, matron of distinguished virtue, and threatened to kill her unless she yielded to his demands. If she spurned him, he told her, he would kill also a slave and then publicly state he had slain both because of their adulterous conduct. Lucrezia was able to elude him, but the shock of her humiliation was such that, after relating to her husband what had happened, she stabbed herself to death. The scandal struck Rome like an earthquake and the populace demanded that Sexton be punished. The king refused to allow the law to take his son, and the indignant citizens rebelled, driving Tarquinius from his throne and banishing him for all time. The people went further. They abolished kingly rule entirely. They had had enough of kings.

They formed a republic with two chief executives known as consuls with one-year terms. They provided also for the choosing of a dictator in the event of a national emergency, the dictatorship, however, not to exceed a period of six months.

Their first full-fledged dictator was Julius Caesar, who has supplied history, poetry, and romance with more copy than any other ruler in ancient or modern times. In 49 B.C. he contested the ruling authority which gave him his power. While he was conquering the Gauls, winning over vast territories for Rome, Pompey, his former son-in-law, prevailed upon the senate to make himself—a member of the ruling triumvirate—sole consul. The senate commanded Caesar either to resign his military command or to suffer exile. It was at this juncture that Caesar added a cubit to his stature and, at the same time, added a colorful phrase to our language. He had to decide between political extinction and defiance of the majesty of Rome.

Bivouacked on the northern bank of the Rubicon River, he asked himself whether he should remain there or cross the Rubicon, precipitating civil war. Robert E. Lee was to debate the same question for himself two thousand years later.

Night had fallen and Caesar had retired to his tent. As he lay on his cot, the Rubicon kept flowing through his mind. As the reddening dawn heralded a new day, he leaped to his feet, summoned his staff, and in a voice which cut through the frosty air like a sword, he shouted: "We will cross the Rubicon!" From then on, crossing the Rubicon has meant decisive action.

Tents fell, barges headed into the current, horses and men found fording passages, and the army moved to the southern side of the stream like a determined rain. With flags flying, Caesar marched on his recalcitrant kinsman. Pompey promptly decided to cross his own Rubicon, which was the Adriatic Sea, hoping that this barrier would stay the advance of his irate ex-father-in-law. But Caesar would not be stayed and the armies clashed on the plains of Pharsalus. Pompey crossed the Mediterranean to Egypt and Caesar pursued, but before they could meet again, Pompey had crossed the Rubicon of death and disturbed Caesar no more.

Flush with his multiple victories Caesar decided to rest for a few days in the shade of the Pyramids. Here he was to meet with an extraordinary defeat which no one, including his astonished self, could ever have anticipated.

While happily engaged one day in literary creation, adding a few more chapters to his *Commentaries*, which were later to harass so many high school students, he was informed that the Queen of Egypt had sent him a present, a large rug. A couple of servants carried the gift into his chambers and deposited it, rolled up in cylindrical form, on the floor and departed. As Caesar continued with his memoirs, he glanced over to the rolled-up rug and saw it undulate as no rug had ever undulated before. In a moment the cylinder opened, and there emerged Cleopatra, the sorceress of the Nile.

She glided forth and, with exceeding grace and royal aplomb, curt- sied before the great general, who, with an amused smile, put down his pen. One would think he always received his visitors in this fashion. In due time he returned to his *Commentaries* but, in the meanwhile, the young agile Egyptian queen had sent a message to her ladies-in- waiting. It was short but told all: "*Veni, vidi, vici.*"

After a dalliance which one does not usually associate with so serious-minded a man as Caesar, the world leader shook Cleopatra's perfumed fingers out of his laurel-leafed hair, buckled on his armor, climbed into his chariot behind his plunging, plumed steeds and rolled away in a cloud of dust to conquests untouched by female guile. In Syria he fell pell-mell on the Pharnacesan army, which had hurriedly drawn up to oppose him, and crushed it with such ease and celerity that in reporting to the senate the nature of the en- gagement, he said simply: "*Veni, vidi, vici.*"

The senate, beside itself with pride and joy over the exploits of Rome's favorite son, unanimously and enthusiastically acclaimed him dictator and *praefectus morum* for life. As eager for administrative glory as for military exaltation, Caesar returned to Rome and em- barked at once on his new stewardship. He announced an ambitious program for public works, he would drain the Pontine marshes, cut a canal through the Isthmus of Corinth, codify the laws, build public libraries, and take a general census.

He arose early one morning to deliver in the senate an address which he was confident would initiate one of the most ambitious legislative programs in Roman history. His wife Calpurnia was silent and even moody at their early breakfast. When he asked why, she replied that she wished so much he would not go out that day because she had dreamed he would be killed. He took her by the hand and smiled. "What? Caesar afraid of dreams?" Danger simply did not dare confront him:

> "Danger knows full well
> That Caesar is more dangerous than he.
> We were two lions littered in one day,
> And I the elder and more terrible.
> And Caesar shall go forth."

And so he went forth. A soothsayer on the street pushed his way through the throngs that had gathered to cheer the dictator and called out: "Beware of the Ides of March," that is the fifteenth day of March, which day it was. Caesar asked that he be brought before him so that he might look at him. This was done and Caesar remarked: "He is a dreamer." Probably like Calpurnia, he thought. He gathered up his magnificent robe and strode on, the crowds renewing their cheers.

As he swept into the ornately decorated, marble senate chamber with its magnificent porphyry columns, the entire membership stood in homage. A senator by the name of Brutus, swathed in his white toga, hastened forward to greet him. Caesar was very fond of Brutus and had even pardoned him after Brutus had sided with Pompey against Caesar. In addition, Caesar had appointed him governor of Cisalpine Gaul. Further he had proclaimed him a praetor of Rome. Brutus made a great show of gratitude, taking Caesar's hand warmly. Caesar smiled in acknowledging Brutus' display of friendship, and, while addressing some words of affection to him, Brutus whipped a dagger from the folds of his toga and plunged it into Caesar's breast. Caesar's knees buckled and tears coursed down his cheeks as he cried: "*Et tu, Brute.*" A dozen other senators now fell on Caesar and sank their daggers into vital parts of his body, but the blows were all superfluous, for Brutus' blade of ingratitude had been quite enough.

Several hours later Marc Antony stood over the hacked and mutilated body of his chief and sadly mused:

> "Thou art the ruins of the noblest man
> That ever lived in the tide of times."

Caesar in his will had named his grandnephew Octavius his heir and successor. Octavius, who was only nineteen years old at the time of his granduncle's death, turned for comfort and advice to Marc Antony who was demanding revenge against Caesar's murderers. Brutus and Cassius, of the lean and hungry look, who had been the principal instigators of Caesar's assassination, mobilized an army to oppose Octavius and Marc Antony, who were now joined by General Lepidus. These latter three, who called themselves the second triumvirate, met the Brutus-Cassius challenge and defeated the conspirators at the Battle of Philippi.

This having been accomplished, the triumvirate sat down to survey the situation. In perhaps the most gigantic demonstration of modesty on record, the three warriors decided to divide the world among themselves. Octavius took Italy, Spain, Gaul, and all the West; Marc Antony was satisfied to have Greece, Syria, Asia Minor, and all the East; Lepidus said he would be content with Africa.

Ever faithful to the memory of his beloved Caesar, Marc Antony fretted over reports that Cleopatra had given military and monetary aid to the Brutus-Cassius forces. He proceeded to Tarsus* in the southern part of what is now Turkey and from that vantage point sent a dispatch to the Queen of Egypt demanding that she come to him to make an accounting of what she had done. Antony might better have remained at home.

Cleopatra did not complain when she received the summons. She welcomed it. She ordered that her largest ship (some historians call it a barge) be remodeled for the voyage. The ablest craftsmen and artists at once set about decorating it. They hoisted purple sails, installed silver oars, and built a golden quarter-deck. They loaded the vessel with musicians, beautiful girls, and barrels of perfume, which was ingeniously sprayed on the sails, making the air heavy with languor and innate rejoicing.

Cleopatra outdid the shipmakers. With a portrait of Aphrodite to give her guidance, she arrayed herself in multicolored finery as soft, delicate, and clinging as the gentle breezes of Tarsus into whose harbor her ship, at the end of the voyage, glided like a swan over a lake of lilies and roses. The population of Tarsus rushed to the shore to stare at the fairy queen and her fairy ship. Although Marc Antony had intended to order Cleopatra ashore and administer to her some rough military justice, tempered of course with mercy, he found himself instinctively following the crowds. When he reached the dock to which the ship had now been warped, a couple of Egyptian generals in resplendent uniforms met him, saluted obsequiously, and said: "Your Liege, Unparalleled Great Marc Antony, Her Majesty the Queen awaits you."

For three days there was the sound of revelry aboard the queen's ship. Laughter, voices raised in song, music, and dancing enlivened the harbor and the country around. At night the decks sparkled with

* The birthplace of St. Paul.

thousands of incense candles, their illumination and fragrance turning the world into a garden of paradise.

Finally came the day of departure. With lutes, harps, and flutes producing music that made of the universe a melody of peace, harmony, and love, the ship headed out into the turquoise Mediterranean. On the golden quarter-deck there was to be seen half reclining on a gorgeously-draped divan an apparition of beauty, her eyes filled with stars, her hands languidly waving a fan. At her feet lay the unparalleled Marc Antony, conqueror of the world, but not of Marc Antony.

For fourteen years the Roman chieftain remained in Egypt. From time to time he made short hurried trips back to Rome, but his heart always remained in the queen's palace on the Nile. Eventually Octavius, who had taken over from Lepidus even his part of the world and now reigned alone, sent word to Antony that if he did not return to Rome and to his wife, who, incidentally happened to be Octavius' sister, he ran the risk of expatriation.

And still Antony dreamed away his life in faraway Egypt, somehow believing that he was burning incense at the shrine of Julius Caesar by enjoying the companionship of the woman the great Caesar had loved and who had borne him a child. When Antony continued to ignore Octavius' demands, Octavius sailed for Alexandria with a battle fleet. Off the coast of Epirus, Antony warned Octavius to sail no farther. It was a brave challenge, but the Egyptian fleet which he now commanded, refused to fight. With the exception of the ship Antony personally commanded, not one of them fired a single catapult or shot a quart of burning oil at the Roman vessels. As if the Egyptians were bent on pleasure they hailed the Roman sailors and soldiers with shouts of welcome, joined their ships to those of Octavius, and sailed away with them.

Antony's world had crashed and he returned to Alexandria, ready to cross his own Rubicon. Schooled in all the traditions of Roman courage and honor, he ran on his sword, and with his last breath, gasped: "Hail, Caesar!"

Cleopatra, schooled in all the indulgences of an absolute monarch, tried out a half dozen poisons on her slaves to determine which one might kill without inflicting pain. One by one, the slaves fell before her, writhing in agony. And so she turned to the basket of fig leaves, in which lurked the deadly asp.

15 THE ROMAN EMPERORS

Although Octavius had battled Antony, his personal affection for him had never ceased and he grieved over his passing. He also dropped a flower of sorrow on the coffin of Cleopatra. She had been loved by both Caesar and Antony, the persons closest to him in the vast-ranged empire of Rome. He ordered an imposing double funeral and after the last strain of elegiac music had died away in the Egyptian air, and the last centurion had dipped Rome's banners before the remains of the star-crossed lovers, he returned to Rome where the senate conferred upon him the Latin title Augustus (majestic) and declared him Imperator. The Roman Republic had ended. Emperor Augustus reigned from 27 B.C. to A.D. 14.

It was during his reign that there came into the world at Bethlehem an Infant, Whose empire was to extend far beyond any that Augustus might have envisioned.

It was said of Augustus that he found Rome brick and left it marble. This is not entirely accurate because one can see even today in the Roman Forum marble architecture which antedates Augustus. Even so, Augustus proved a great builder. He erected not only wholesome and artistic edifices, monuments, and buildings, but also an organized society of responsibility, with the Law supreme. Displaying considerable engineering talent he ordered the construction of canals, roads, aqueducts, and bridges throughout the realm. He also encouraged literature. The greatest poets of ancient Rome— Vergil, Horace, and Ovid—sang their verses during the Augustan Age. Livy, the classic historian, often visited Augustus.

The Roman senate, fully acknowledging his genius and goodness, immortalized him by naming the eighth month of the year August, as a previous appreciative senate had dedicated the seventh month, July, to his granduncle, Julius.

At the age of seventy-nine Augustus, realizing that his final days were upon him, called for a mirror, and, studying his reflection, asked of those about him: "Have I played my part well?" When they answered in the affirmative he said, using the language of actors: "*Valente et plaudite*" (Farewell and applaud). Thus passed the first Roman Emperor. The Romans would never look upon his like again.

Augustus was succeeded by Tiberius. It was during his reign that Christ walked the earth in distant Galilee. Tiberius' head was stamped on all Roman coins and it was one of those coins the Pharisees showed to Jesus, thinking to trick him into treasonable utterance by asking Him: "Is it lawful to give tribute unto Caesar, or not?" Christ asked them to name the person whose image appeared on the coin and when they replied, "Caesar," He said to them: "Render, therefore unto Caesar the things that are Caesar's; and unto God the things that are God's." And Saint Matthew observed, after relating the episode, that the Pharisees "marveled and left Him, and went their way."

Tiberius may be rated as a fairly good emperor. He maintained peace in the Roman Empire and accomplished some worthy domestic reforms. He spent most of the latter years of his life on the mountainous Isle of Capri, where one can still see remnants of his imperial villas. He died in A.D. 37 and was succeeded by Caligula, whose name has become a synonym for despotism, profligacy, and cruelty in office. He once wrathfully declared that the whole Roman population should have but one head so that he could decapitate the people with one blow. He ordered the senate to make his horse a consul of Rome, he declared himself a god, had temples erected in his name, and ordered sacrifices in his honor. Four years of him was more than enough for even his own imperial bodyguard who one morning buried their swords in his imperial body. He was twenty-nine at the time.

Caligula was followed by Tiberius' nephew Claudius who constructed the famous aqueducts Aqua Claudia and Anvio Novus, remains of which, the former especially, decorate to the present day the Roman landscape and offer silent testimony to the engineering genius of ancient Rome. In A.D. 43 Claudius led an expedition into Britain and made the southern part of it a Roman colony.

Claudius governed well, but he had a failing not restricted to emperors: he liked women. He married four times. His fourth marriage was a disaster. He had a niece called Agrippina, sister to his predecessor Caligula. She was now a young widow, beautiful and talented with a young son who had displayed musical proclivities. He particularly enjoyed performing on the instrument which was the precursor of the violin. His name was Nero.

When Claudius' third wife died under mysterious circumstances, Agrippina had a heart-to-heart talk with her uncle Claudius and pointed out to him that it would be a desirable thing to keep the emperorship in the family. She proposed matrimony and they married.

Agrippina thus became empress. She had been sister to one emperor; she was now the wife of another. Her cup was full, but it wasn't slopping over into the vast saucer of her boundless ambitions. She wished to be mother to a third emperor. This could not happen, of course, while Claudius was living and reigning. She persuaded him to give the imperial cooks a short vacation and, for her liege, she said she would prepare dishes of which he had never dreamed. Her viands, dressings, sauces were indeed out of this Roman world. One day she served a particularly savory roast pheasant with delicious stuffing. Claudius heartily enjoyed several portions, each one of which contained enough subtle poison to kill off the entire Praetorian Guard.

Nero was fifteen—and emperor. Under the tutelage of the great philosopher Seneca, he ruled well for five years. The people prospered and rejoiced. Nero enjoyed himself too. He danced, wrote poetry, composed songs, and twanged a lyre. Then he began to resent Agrippina who, mother-jealous, objected to his marrying Poppaea, the superlative beauty of Rome. Nero persuaded his mother to take a long sea voyage. It would give her, he said, the rest and relaxation she needed and restore to her fading cheeks the color which had once thrilled all imperial suitors. Nero instructed his architects to build a special ship, one that, by the withdrawal of a few strategic bolts, would collapse and sink in minutes. He selected a conspiratorial crew, and Agrippina sailed.

When the vessel reached a point beyond sight of land the crucial bolts were withdrawn and the ship fell apart. It was night and Agrippina's lady-in-waiting, Aceronia, finding herself sinking, cried out: "I am Agrippina!" assuming that this was the surest way to be rescued. She erred slightly. The sailors broke their oars over her head, and Aceronia plummeted to the bottom of the sea. Agrippina herself, who was a better swimmer than her son gave her credit for, saw in the glinting moonlight what had happened and quickly deduced the situation. She dived beneath the wreckage and came up on the other side, and then made for shore with a speed not ordinarily associated with empresses.

The citizens at whose door she knocked recognized the regal comportment of their unannounced guest, even though somewhat disheveled and in disarray, and treated her with all the honors due a female monarch. She could not restrain her exaltation in having worsted her son's scheming, knowing that as she was somewhat of a schemer herself, she had triumphed in a contest of champions. With a fine show of irony, she sent off a courier to Nero with the message: "You should hire better ship architects." Her elation was short. She had revealed her whereabouts and four centurions accompanied the courier on his return. One of them confronted her with upraised sword, and she exclaimed: "Strike deep, but you cannot take away my glory of having made three Emperors of Rome!"

Nero went into public mourning, praising in a public speech the virtues of his mother, and ordered the execution of the centurion who had "misunderstood" orders.

The people guessed at the truth but said nothing. They publicly sympathized with the bereaved emperor and turned out in multitudes to do him honor wherever he appeared. Nothing could please Nero more. He thirsted for applause as a camel craves rain. He appeared in theaters to recite poetry he had composed, accompanying himself on a lute. He organized claques who were trained in the gradations of applauding. The mildest applause was produced by bringing the hands together in cup fashion; this was called *imbrix*; then came the *testa*, when the hands smashed together like bricks; then there was the *bombus*, which sounded like bulls bellowing in a tunnel; and, finally, came the *tempestas cum tonitribus*, the unabated storm which shakes the rafters and imperils the foundations of the theater.

From excessive vanity Nero degenerated into excessive cruelty. Disturbed by an insurrection which broke out in his colony in Britain, and criticized for the failure of his armies in Armenia, he lashed out at the Christians who had now come to the surface from the catacombs where they had originally been worshiping. In A.D. 64 a small fire, which could not be controlled, spread into a vast conflagration. Nero enjoyed the spectacle, comparing it to the burning of Troy. He stood on the balcony of his palace, gargling his verses, while wildly strumming his lyre. His conspicuous enjoyment of the flames, which crackled and ravaged for a week, reducing three-fourths of Rome to cinders, produced not unnaturally the accusation that he had been the incendiary. He retaliated by blaming the fire on the Christians, rounded them up en masse and marched them into the arena while beasts from Africa roared their hungry welcome.

Without necessarily expressing any sympathy for the martyred Christians, the Roman senate began to tire of Nero's homicidal buffoonery and gently hinted that he should behave in a manner befitting the Roman purple. Nero's reply was to castigate the senate. The senate filed a refutation, condemning him as Public Enemy No. 1. Nero fled and the Praetorian Guard pursued. As the guard surrounded the building in which he was at last cornered, he ordered one of his lieutenants to stab him. Before the sword was drawn, however, he prepared the scene. He arrayed himself in his purplest robes and made a speech: "Rome loses in me not only a great emperor but a great poet, a great musician, and a great actor." He closed his books, which belied all these accomplishments, at thirty-two.

With the death of Nero, the bloodstream of Caesar dried up. No succeeding emperor could claim kinship with the mighty Julius. Most of the Roman emperors who followed measured up to the regal concept of character, outstanding courage, and great ability associated with Roman authority. A few were profligates, unworthy of the imperial purple. However, whether wisdom or folly wielded the scepter of authority, the majesty of Rome never faltered. Government functioned with competence, and commerce marched with the solidity of the military phalanxes which penetrated into every section of the known world. The continent rang with the shovels, hammers, and chisels of the road builders constructing the famous Roman highways, many of which even today are serviceable. Stone and marble monuments, temples, colosseums, and theaters rose in all parts of the empire, sturdy bridges spanned brawling streams. Art and literature rolled forward in the golden chariots of Latin culture. The era of the Roman Empire until the barbarian invasions is still the era which launched the civilization we enjoy today.

Constantine, who became the first Christian emperor, set up in A.D. 330 an additional capital in Constantinople, which was known for a period as Nova Roma (new Rome). The vast Roman world was now divided into the Western Empire and the Eastern Empire.

In 452 Attila, the Hun, with a half million savage warriors at his back, tore through Gaul and Italy pillaging, burning, destroying as no combined tempest, earthquake, and conflagration had ever destroyed before. It was Attila's proud boast that "the grass never grows where my horse has placed his hoof."

He stopped before Rome, where it is said Pope Leo I subdued him by the majesty of his presence. The next year, however, he renounced his promise not to invade Rome and mounted his grass-destroying charger, shouting defiance and destruction to all civilization. Perhaps his own blood rebelled against his fiery denunciation and one day he collapsed on the ground, expiring from hemorrhage.

Other so-called barbarian rulers followed. In 568 the German Lombards swept down and occupied northern Italy. Their king, Alboin, established Pavia as the capital of his realm and he contested the Byzantine power, which derived its vitality from Constantinople. He destroyed the power of the East over Italy and then went the way of all flesh.

The Lombards, strangely enough, could not find a king to rule them and they divided their realm into regions, each headed by a leader called Duce.* Finally the Lombards did get a king, Agiluf, who made the mistake of encroaching upon papal territory, menacing Rome itself. The Pope, Stephen II, called upon the Franks who had acknowledged the spiritual authority of the Church to aid him, and they sent their leader, Pepin the Short, who made brief work of the Lombards, deposing the last Lombard king in 774. Pepin the Short had a tall son called Charlemagne, who had been his father's right arm in defeating the Lombards. On Christmas Day, Pope Leo III crowned Charlemagne Emperor of the Holy Roman Empire.

* This was the title taken by Mussolini.

Charlemagne ruled for forty years and when he hung up his sword in Valhalla he was succeeded by his son, who in turn was succeeded by *his* son. The Charlemagnes produced eight kings, the last one bearing the unglorious title of Charles the Fat. He spent more time at the table than in the field, and when the people finally tore away from him his knives and dishes, he languished and passed away.

For several centuries Italy was the arena for civil wars and foreign invasion. Troops in lustrous armor, horses prancing under steel flanks and flying plumes, warriors flashing bright swords and gleaming shields, charged into battle against other warriors similarly glittering in the sun. They jousted, lunged, and stabbed at one another, the air thick with arrows, stones, lances, and pikes. The skies resounded with war whoops, shouts, and the moans of men being quartered and left dying on the field. The next morning a king, prince, or general cantered onto the battlefield, with silken banners fluttering from staffs held by aides, and pronounced a victory which, in a day, week, or year became a defeat, and another king, prince, or general gloried in the burst of triumphant music.

During all this time the civilian population lived a terrorized existence, toiling amid war's devastation and being bled white because of sons forced into battle and by confiscatory taxes which reduced them to serfdom.

In 1122 Pope Calixtus II and the Holy Roman Emperor Henry V signed the agreement called the Concordat of Worms which guaranteed to the cardinals of the Roman Catholic Church authority to elect the Pope, who would thus rule independently of the will of the emperor. With the papacy, in this way, acquiring a sovereignty of its own, the city-states of Italy took heart and courage and began to manifest their own independence.

In time, France, Spain, and Austria came to look upon Italy as their legitimate prey and warred on one another for the unhappy land, periodically agreeing to armistices and promising to withdraw and then, disregarding all treaties and pacts, invading again. The Bourbon family, with monarchs in both France and Spain, put their Charles IV on the throne of the Two Sicilies in 1734. He was succeeded by Ferdinand IV. Then in 1796 the young French military genius, Napoleon Bonaparte, with Italian blood in his veins, returned to the land of his forefathers and spectacularly chased the Austrians out of northern Italy. As soon, however, as he departed from Italy,

Austria plotted with Great Britain, Russia, and Turkey to seize his Italian conquests.

Learning of these developments while in faraway Egypt, whither he had gone to destroy Great Britain's colonial empire, Napoleon hurried back to France, made himself first consul, and then swung down into Italy, defeating the Austrians at Marengo and annexing Piedmont, Parma, and Piacenza to France. He now sped back to Paris to attend to a detail in his career, that of making himself emperor. Literally he did just that. As Pope Pius VII was about to lift the crown to the conquering Corsican's head, the latter pulled it out of the pontiff's hand and crowned himself.

In 1805 he crossed the Alps with his wife Josephine and, in Milan, adorned his brow with the iron crown of Charlemagne, proclaiming himself King of Italy. Later Waterloo exploded like a bomb under his feet and he landed in St. Helena. All the petty princes who had tyrannized over Italy and who had gone into hiding during the Corsican's reign, now fled back to their former despotic haunts like crows winging to a newly-discovered cornfield.

The Congress of Vienna approved of the chains newly riveted on the Italian people. The returning despots prohibited freedom of speech, and even of thought, and decreed confiscations and torture for those who dared to speak of liberty.

In spite of their chains, the Italian people rebelled against serfdom. It was at this juncture that the Carbonari societies, already described, sprang into being. For fifty-five years the Italians, through secret organizations and conspiracies, insurrections and revolutions, strove mightily for the inherent right to govern themselves. Their oppressors strove just as mightily to hold the chains in place. Thus, the peninsula of Italy, projecting into the sea, like the bridge of a ship plowing through a storm, trembled in the hurricane and typhoon of war. Cannon belched their clouds of inferno, muskets propelled their streams of lead, bayonets pierced living flesh, sabers slashed at arteries, and the blood cascaded. In 1821 the people of Naples rose in rebellion and demanded a constitution. The people of Piedmont followed suit. Ferdinand of Naples, fearing for his life, yielded the constitution. The King of Piedmont vacillated, abdicated, and transferred his crown to his brother Felix, placing the regency in Charles Albert, who offered a semblance of representative government to his subjects.

This yielding to the people enraged Austria, Russia, and Prussia whose monarchs feared their own crowns might slip from their heads if the people were allowed encouragement in self-government.

These three nations sent hundreds of thousands of bayonets into Italy to suppress popular rule. The leaders of the various rebellions were seized and hanged, armies of occupation were forced on the people at their expense, taxes became all-destructive, and the Italian people were pinned beneath the steel-nailed boots of the foreign tyrants.

16 ITALY ACHIEVES INDEPENDENCE

In 1830, encouraged by the revolution in France which had dethroned the Bourbon king, the people of the Lombardo-Venetian kingdom rose en masse, even the women joining their husbands as they furiously attacked the Austrian army of occupation which numbered 80,000. Before so resolute an onslaught the Austrians fled and the Italians took heart again. Charles Albert, now King of Piedmont, conferred a free constitution on his people and drew his sword against Austria.

The Neapolitans once more raised the standard of revolt. So did the Romans. The grand duchy of Tuscany joined in the insurrectionary movement. The Austrians, however, 130,000 strong, re-invaded Venetian Lombardy and swept the Italian army, made up mostly of raw volunteers, before them. Charles Albert abdicated in favor of his son, Victor Emmanuel II.

Garibaldi fought valiantly to hold Rome, which had declared itself a republic, but he, as already recounted, being over-whelmingly outnumbered, had to withdraw. The forces of independence had been smashed, but the spirit of freedom still breathed amid the wreckage and ruin. From the shrine of liberty in America, Garibaldi sailed for his homeland, and from Genoa he sailed to take up the battle in Sicily. Count Camillo Benso di Cavour, prime minister to King Emmanuel II, dispatched an army to join the liberating forces in southern Italy, and then, through astute diplomatic moves, he brought about a referendum at which the Kingdom of the Two Sicilies voted for union with the Sardinian Kingdom. On March 17, 1861, at Turin, Cavour proclaimed Victor Emmanuel II the King of Italy.

In 1866 Italy redeemed Venice by allying herself with Prussia in her war against Austria. In 1870, when Prussia attacked France, necessitating the latter's withdrawal of her troops from Rome, General Raffaele Cadorna breached the walls at Porta Pia and the Italian *bersaglieri* marched to Campidoglio. Rome was now the capital of Italy.

Even so, two of Italy's children were still denied a place at the family hearth. Trente and Trieste, Italian cities on this side of the Alps, Italy's natural northern boundary, were held captive by Austria and became known as the Italia Irredenta (unredeemed Italy). In World War I, Italy allied herself with England and France and fought with tenacious valor in the Alps against Austria, her legendary foe. In October 1918 General Armando Diaz launched one of the mightiest offensives in military history. Advancing on a fifty-mile front, the Italians doggedly drove ahead, inflicting on the foe a stupendous defeat. At Vittorio Veneto the whole Austrian defense collapsed and Austria was knocked out of the war. Germany, now losing support on her eastern flank, had to throw reserves into the breach, thus weakening herself on the western front. On November 11, 1918, she sued for peace.

Italia Irredenta was at last redeemed and the whole Italian family could warm itself at the common hearth, but the reunited family did not rejoice long. The Bolshevists in Russia had forcibly taken control of government and now rolled out their world-bolshevizing blueprints. Revolutionary cadres poured into Finland, Hungary, Poland, Germany, and Italy, recruiting heavily from the ranks of the discontented and the after-war unemployed. In Italy they seized factories and drove farmers from their lands. In two thousand towns they raised the red flag of Communism over municipal buildings.

It was at this juncture in the drama of Italian history that Benito Mussolini, the blacksmith's son and ex-socialist, strode to the center of the national stage in a black shirt and took up the battle with the Communists. He organized the *Fasci di Combattimento* (combat groups), which drove the Communists from the public buildings and the mills they had occupied.

With these combat groups ready to do his bidding, he decided on a revolution of his own. With jutting jaw and fiery speeches he declaimed against the status quo. In 1922 his four principal lieutenants, Balbo, Bianchi, De Bono, and De Vecchi, organized what was called "The March on Rome." One hundred thousand men, from the large cities of Italy, most of them war veterans, clad in their military uniforms but wearing the inevitable black shirt, headed for Italy's capital. Mussolini, with reflective circumspection, remained in Milan. Facta, the prime minister, resigned and the King asked Mussolini to form a cabinet. Mussolini boarded a night sleeper, arriving in Rome the next morning to take his place at the head of the column of men who had already completed the march.

He formed a cabinet, modestly taking for himself the three most vital posts: the premiership, ministry of foreign affairs, and ministry of internal affairs. Later he was to hold seven ministry posts.

A skilled propagandist, Mussolini set out to make himself a popular idol. He paraded, postured, and performed. He strutted before clicking cameras, mounted a horse, strode into the cage of a toothless lion at the zoo and fondled a kittenish cub, while motion pictures ground out film. Visiting dignitaries from abroad asked to be photographed with him. The press, foreign and domestic, besieged him.

The story of this swaggering egomaniac is so recent and has been told so often, not only in contemporary periodicals, but also in books, that no point would be served in relating it here at length. He abolished representative government, reduced the Chamber of Deputies to a rubber stamp and made the Fascist Party supreme. Hand in hand with this usurpation of powers never embraced in the concept of the Italian prime ministry he proclaimed a military belligerency entirely out of harmony with the spirit of the Italian people. In a mad flight of moral irresponsibility he declared that war was desirable for war's sake. And yet, in an event or two, he demonstrated firm statesmanship. When Hitler threatened a German-Austrian union, England and France protested but Mussolini blocked Hitler by entering into a commercial treaty with Austria. When Hitler spoke of annexing Austria forcibly, Mussolini ordered 75,000 troops to the frontier and Hitler dismissed the project. Events proved later, however, that the dismissal was only temporary.

But in all this show of protecting the rights of national sovereignties, the blacksmith's son was not motivated by principle. He was hammering away on the anvil of his own vainglorious ambitions. In 1935–36 he struck with the sledge of military might and annexed Ethiopia. Later, with Hitler, he sent troops to support the dictator Franco in Spain.

In September 1937 Hitler received Mussolini in Berlin with pomp and ceremony. Several months later Mussolini received Hitler in Rome with pomp and ceremony. With each succeeding ceremonious encounter, however, Mussolini lost more and more of his stiff-necked, metallic self-sufficiency. By March 1938 the blacksmith's son was no longer the hammer or the anvil, but wallpaper paste, being molded into whatever shape the paperhanger of Munich desired.

Even so, when the Nazis invaded Poland, precipitating war with France and England, the black shirt swelled with some of its former independence of spirit, and the wearer refused to join in Hitler's barbarous aggression. Had he persisted, there would still have been time for him to break away from his partnership with doom and damnation. But in June 1940 his pathological vanity, added to his belief that Hitler was invincible, induced him to declare war against France and England.

In August 1940 he attacked the British in Africa and in the following month he invaded Greece. He was ignominiously routed on both fronts and in May 1941 he had to give back Ethiopia. When Japan treacherously attacked the United States at Pearl Harbor, Mussolini, by this time apparently wholly mad, declared war on the United States.

In 1942 he began to reap the whirlwind he had sown. Tragically, however, it was the people of Italy, rather than he, who felt the tornado of war's destructiveness. Allied planes rained ruin and disaster on the entire peninsula while Mussolini, with the reasoning of a Pulcinella, assumed he could avert the inevitable by dismissing his cabinet and taking over complete political and military control of the nation. Like an infant playing at soldiers, he piped orders for movements of troops which did not exist and commanded the building of defenses for which there were no materials.

In July 1943 Patton's Seventh Army landed in Sicily, and Mussolini, even in Rome, felt the hot blast of retribution on its way. He cried to Hitler, who flew down from his own troubles on the Western front, and the unholy pair met in Verona. Mussolini tried to tell his partner that Italy had to conclude a separate peace, because further resistance was hopeless. However, he could not get in a word as the voluble Fuehrer shouted and screamed at him for two hours, ordering him to drive the Allies into the sea, but not telling him how.

Mussolini hurried back to Rome to his Fascist Grand Council and discovered what he thought could never happen. The Council demanded he resign the premiership. The King ordered his arrest. The balcony dictator began to drip sawdust. He was confined to a hotel on a mountaintop at Gran Sasso, where German paratroopers rescued him and flew him to Germany. Hitler treated him as a poor, despised relative. He set up for the sagging Black Shirt, a papier-mâché Fascist republic, north of the Allied lines in Italy, and here, continuing to pour sawdust at every turn, Mussolini lived out the rest of his wretched days. On April 26, 1945, he was captured by Communists, who, without any trial or formal legal procedure, murdered him in cold blood. On April 30, 1945, Hitler, anticipating a similar or even more humiliating end, took poison and shot himself in the mouth, simultaneously.

In 1925, while a student at the University of Rome, I interviewed Mussolini one day, as he sat astride his horse on the banks of the Tiber. I asked him what he thought of Hitler, who had raised the dust of revolt and menace in Germany. Mussolini laughed at my query and said: "Hitler is a joke."

"But he has declared a great admiration for you," I went on, "and seems to want to imitate you."

"I doubt he ever could. Furthermore, Fascism is not an article for exportation."

But Hitler did imitate Mussolini by adopting the Fascist salute, dissolving Parliament, and glorifying war for war's sake. The impersonation went so far that, twenty years later, they were both heading straight for the cliff of irremediable disaster.

On May 9, 1946, King Victor Emmanuel III abdicated the throne, being succeeded by his son, Umberto II. On June 10, 1946, as the result of a popular referendum, Italy became a republic, with Enrico de Nicola as its first president. Alcide de Gasperi, one of the ablest Italian statesmen since Cavour and Crispi, retained the premiership, which had been conferred on him in December 1945. Italy made tremendous strides during his administration, which lasted eight years, in regaining economic, political, cultural, and diplomatic stability.

17 ITALIAN ODYSSEY

On the banks of the Tiber River, hard by the ancient Castel Sant'-Angelo, and close to the Basilica of St. Peter's, there rises in solemn majesty the Roman Palace of Justice. The massive proportions of this travertine, crenelated structure in its classic and historic setting take away one's breath. On either side of the pillared entrance there stand, as if to guard for all eternity the sacred principles of justice they crystallized into law, the figures of Caius, Cicero, Papinianus, Paulus, Hortensius, and others of the formidable Roman juriconsults who had kindled, two thousand years ago, the torch by whose light I studied, at the University of Rome, the living, vital rudiments of justice. What is Justice? It could not be better defined than it is at the very beginning of Justinian's Institutes: "The constant and perpetual desire to render to every one his due."

The achievements of ancient Rome resulted more from its promulgation of law than from its conquest by arms. Giovanni Marioti well stated:

> If the power of Rome had lain only in its arms the downfall of the empire would have coincided with the downfall of an entire civilization. But, as is well known, this was not the case.

Herbert Bittner and Ernest Nash in their book on Rome, put it this way:

Rome and law are synonymous, and one always suggests the other. . . . The Romans were . . . the first and greatest creators of conceptions framing social life, such as the study of the just and legitimate, right and wrong, family relations, property, inheritance, crime and so on through the whole economy of human experience. This intellectual monument raised by the Romans has remained because they worked according to rules of reason, with a clear and direct mind, and with the uncanny genius for precise definition.*

These three titanic structures, St. Peter's, Castel Sant'Angelo, and the Roman Palace of Justice, form perhaps the greatest and most imposing group of monuments anywhere dedicated to the spirit and the progress of man. As already stated, the Castel Sant'Angelo was constructed to be the tomb of Hadrian. It was during his reign that Roman civilization marched with the soldiers, colonists, artists, and artisans to England and all of continental Europe, including the far reaches of the Mid-East. And it was over the excellent roads built by the Romans that Christianity, symbolized by St. Peter's, "spread the wealth of its spiritual value all over the world."

Through these indomitable forces Rome became a world capital and so it spiritually remains. One senses it in the vibrant atmosphere, the overwhelming monuments, the classic panorama, the gigantic statuary, the splashing fountains, the wide boulevards, the globe-encircling diplomatic corps. Rome is the only national capital that hosts two sets of ambassadors from nearly every country: those accredited to the Republic of Italy and those accredited to the Vatican.

One can read in the venerable ruins of ancient Rome its impassioned dedication to physical and mental health, by the abundance of its public baths, gymnasia, aqueducts, stadia for sports, parks and gardens. One can see the glowing devotion of the Romans to education in their debating forums, theaters, lecture halls, libraries. One can almost feel the community spirit which brought the citizens running to celebrate together events which had thrilled them with pride. Apathy, listlessness, and *laissez faire* were unknown in ancient Rome. The development and progress of man was a science, an art, and an achievement that Rome lived for, excited over, fought for, and, if need be, died for, with a deep sense of nobility, honor, and glory.

Henry James felt that electrifying spirit as soon as his feet touched

* Bittner and Nash, *Rome*, Henry Regnery Co., Chicago, 1950, p. 58.

the storied pavements. "At last—for the first time—I live!" he exclaimed, describing his sensations. "I went reeling and moaning through the streets in a fever of enjoyment. . . . The effect is something indescribable."

He not only regarded himself a Roman citizen, but also felt himself living with the Romans of old.* By simulating mental or even physical participation in any event of the past one becomes a contemporary of the era recalled. I felt myself living in 508 B.C. when one memorable day in the summer of 1924 I stripped to the waist and dived into the Tiber near Ponte Palatino where Horatius had dived. Heavy armor did not weigh me down as it had Horatius, nor were Etruscan soldiers throwing big ugly spears at me, but I did have to keep an eye on the *carabiniere* guard on the bridge.

As I cut through the water with a vigorous overhead stroke, I imagined I could hear the roar of thousands of Romans awaiting me. No one actually greeted me as I climbed to the empty shore, but I felt a fever of exhilaration over that historical plunge, and rejoiced to see that the *carabiniere* walked away uninterested, even though he was shrugging his shoulders as if to say: "You can't tell what these Americans will do."

Nothing would satisfy me now unless and until I could also make a speech in the Roman Forum. I found the Orator's Platform from which Marc Antony declaimed and I there announced to the few tourists who had gathered at that point that I had "come to bury Caesar, not to praise him."

Thoroughly enjoying this fancied reincarnation I visited what was left of the Roman senate and denounced Catiline as Cicero had done, only much more briefly. I walked over the renowned Appian Way and genuflected where Saint Peter beheld the Vision asking him not to forsake Rome. In a building across from the Basilica of St. John Lateran I ascended on my knees the *Scala Santa*. I prayed in the catacombs where early Christians lived, died, and were buried; I slept one night in the Colosseum in an attempt to experience the feeling of one who is to be eaten by lions the next day. With a Roman signorina on my arm, I strolled through the gardens which had known

* When Longfellow beheld the Colosseum for the first time he exclaimed: "The arbitrary distinctions of time, years, ages, centuries were annihilated! I was a citizen of Rome! Mighty is the spirit of the past, amid the ruins of the Eternal City!"

Michelangelo and Vittoria Colonna; I stood where Garibaldi had directed the defense of Rome.

But Rome is not merely a classical temple of echoing memories. It is the pulsating heart of the Roman Catholic Church with its 558,-000,000 members. And, like every one of the faithful, I desired to see the Pope and be blessed by him. I attended one of the audiences in the Throne Room of the Vatican and Pope Pius XI blessed for me a statuette of St. Anthony which I had taken along and later brought back to America for my father. That statuette remained in my father's room until he passed away at the age of eighty-three, serenely content as he said: "I have lived an interesting life, and I now go happily into the New Adventure with St. Anthony."

My sojourn in Rome included the Holy Year of 1925 when the Holy Door at St. Peter's, which had been sealed for a quarter of a century, was opened at the Pope's command. Silver trumpets saluted the holy event and a five-hundred-voice choir sang, while half a million pilgrims in the Piazza applauded and cheered. The church itself accommodated eighty thousand.

Unparalleled in size and artistry as is St. Peter's Basilica, it is only one of more than four hundred churches in Rome. And when, on a holy day, the bell-ringers of all these churches take a high hold on their ropes, and ride with them to the floor, the belfries vibrate and tremble as the bells boom in their cradles, rolling and turning. The serene azure skies become a vast resounding vault of deep-throated melody, resounding chimes, resonant roaring, tuneful reverberations, and soft treble chiming, and one's own heart responds. In those moments one does not think or reflect, one is carried along on an ocean of sensation that knows no shores of mood, sorrow or care. God bless the bells of Rome.

Rome exalts you also with its hundreds of fountains, more than any other city in the world. All of them are artistically unique and mesmerizing. No matter where your feet take you as you bask in the glory that was and is Rome, you will surely receive a cheerful and refreshing welcome from the fountains. You will be greeted by little birds, their beaks playfully squirting water; you will be saluted by gruff lions, their jaws roaring water; you will be hailed by turtles playfully dashing water at you; you will be honored by every type of medieval and mythical figure geysering water into the air; you will be spoken to by maidens of the seas, inviting you to join with them in the glistening, exhilarating cascades.

In St. Peter's Square, two towering, double-tiered fountains, discharging rivers of water, seem to speak of the greatness and the grandness of the human soul, typified by the Basilica itself. Nor will one ever forget the Fontana di Trevi which sweeps across the width of a palazzo. A huge Neptune presides at the center of the aqueous stage, standing triumphantly in a winged chariot, driving before him seagods and galloping horses. The water pours, gushes, roars and thunders at you in rivers, cascades, and niagaras. It is no wonder that many a lover of Rome tosses a coin into the bubbling waters before he leaves, the tradition being that this act will ensure his returning to the Eternal City. It is said that ancient Rome, with its fountains, public baths, and domestic uses, consumed 340,000,000 gallons of water a day. No one can doubt it.

If Italy had only the city of Rome to attract religious pilgrims, artists, authors, scientists, archaeologists, and tourists, it would still rate among the No. 1 tourist countries. But Rome, stupendous as it is, the center of Christendom as it is, unequaled in history and art, does not stand alone in this peninsula of wonders. Cities like Florence, Venice, Genoa, Milan, Naples, and Palermo also conjure up visions of historical sublimity, panoramic delights, intellectual and spiritual feasts. There is no nation where cities differ so much in appearance and in their own distinctive personalities as do the cities of Italy.

Florence, known as the City of Flowers, appeals at once to the world of the spirit and the mind. Florence sounded the reveille of the Renaissance. It was Florence which stirred man out of his medieval torpor and led him to the mountain heights of awareness of what could be in store for him if he would only use the gifts God has conferred on him.

The guidebooks rapturously describe the museums and art galleries of Florence, and with reason, but Florence itself is an open air museum and depositary of art. Particularly enchanting is the Piazza Signoria, a vast open square, ornamented with the Fountain of Neptune and dominated by the Palazzo della Signoria, whose graceful crenelated tower rises three hundred and eight feet into the cloudless skies.

Architecturally and artistically captivating as is the Piazza Signoria, it marks a very sad and tragic episode in the city's history, for it was here that the dread sentence pronounced by the Council of Eight against Girolamo Savonarola was executed. A brass disk in the pavement marks the spot where the fagots were piled, and, as I stood there, I felt myself with aching heart looking upon that fearful scene of 1498. I see the raised platform where the brave Dominican friar, having been hanged, is now being burned. The flames shoot higher. The body of Savonarola is now no longer visible. It is enveloped in smoke.

Venice is the next logical city to visit after Florence. A traveler in Italy should never go to Venice first because he runs the risk, after looking upon that incredible marvel, of refusing to believe anything else he sees in Italy. Venice is the ultimate paradox, the final perplexity, the impenetrable mystery of man-made wonders. One who reads or hears of Venice can only refuse to accept as fact what is told him. So he decides to go to see Venice to believe it, and it is precisely when he sees it that he cannot believe it all. The palazzi, churches, and public buildings are constructed of stone and marble but they appear as light as fragile china. The multiple-domed Basilica of Saint Mark, the breath-taking façade of the Doge's Palace, the richly ornamented Church of Santa Maria della Salute, the Ca d'oro, the Logetta, and palazzi too numerous to mention and too beautiful to describe, all seem to be delicately assembled from the finest laces, all finely turned as jewel boxes, and yet they are constructed of unbreakable marble of a hundred hues.

But this is only a whisper of the visual symphony which is Venice. Every one of these sublimely beautiful structures in their myriads of colors rests on the gentlest of lapping waters which reflect in their ripples this city of dreams, fantasies, wonders, and a thousand prodigies. The streets, avenues, and boulevards are shapely canals over which gondolas glide like swans in the daytime and, with their bobbing lanterns, like fireflies at night. If one prefers not to exert himself in visiting the sights of Venice, he can recline comfortably in his gondola and Venice will come to him. As the gondolier in his immaculate, freshly starched shirt, garlanded by a satin sash, gracefully propels his craft, the languorous tourist need merely look into the mirroring surface of the magic waters on either side and he will be enchanted by the lacy palazzi, the shimmering cupolas, the tessellated towers, the wedding-cake exteriors of public buildings and private homes in this heavenly, incomparably gorgeous Venice.

If all the most talented artists, architects, and engineers of today were assigned a section of the Adriatic Sea and commissioned to build a Venice, unconcerned about cost, I do not believe they could do it. And yet, a thousand years ago, with none of the construction equipment of today, the Venetians began the building of this legendary metropolis which has well been termed the Queen City of the Adriatic.

Four hundred bridges span the watercourses, most of them architectural gems, not the least of which is the renowned Rialto where some of Shakespeare's characters gathered to get the news of the world. Another attention-fixing bridge is the Bridge of Sighs, over which persons convicted of crime passed from the Ducal Palace into the prison.

As already recalled, the Neapolitans say: "See Naples and die." Robert Browning literally saw Venice and died. It was here on December 12, 1889, that his spirit rose above the lagoons he loved, soaring into the Alpine winds refreshing his revered Italy. Above the door of the palace where he spent his last hours there appears a bronze tablet with the moving inscription: "Open my heart and you will see graved upon it—Italy."

Lord Byron, the votary of incandescent beauty, burnt much of the candle of his impetuous youth in Venice, but its flame lighted up the pages on which he produced some of his most romantic and ever-enduring poetry. Richard Wagner completed the second act of his opera *Tristan und Isolde* in Venice.

Shakespeare pitched his poetic-dramatic tents also in Verona where he created the valiantly loving Juliet. In that city I stood on the Via Capello and looked up at the balcony of the Capulet palazzo where the star-crossed Juliet sighed farewell to her star-crossed Romeo in the garden below:

> "Good night, good night! parting is such sweet sorrow
> That I shall say good night till it be morrow."

Among the regrets that one can work up into a full-blown infelicity is the fact that Shakespeare never wrote a play about Christopher Columbus, for here indeed was an epic story of the highest dramatic tension, heart-rending frustration, continental conflict, romantic love, supreme triumph, and then tragic ingratitude, a play which would have majestically ranked with his *King Lear* and *Coriolanus*.

The first place I sought out in Genoa, naturally, was the birthplace of the discoverer of America. It is modest, small, and with no architectural elegance, as one would expect it to be, his father having been a woolcomber and, therefore, not one habituated to a palazzo. Genoa is proud of her illustrious son and has immortalized him in statuary in various parts of the city, as Columbus has perpetrated Genoa in the heart of all mankind for having given birth to the greatest, most daring, most knowledgeable, and most competent navigator of all time. His noble character was strengthened and fortified by four devotions, symbolized in marble figures surrounding the gigantic statue of the great sailor in the harbor: Religion, Wisdom, Fortitude, and Geography.

We see some of the New World in Italy. Milan and Turin particularly could, in some aspects, be taken for American cities. Their tall buildings, large factories, thoroughfares teeming with automobiles, the wearing apparel of the people on the streets, all give these metropolises a modern appearance. However, no twentieth-century patina can hide the architectural and artistic riches which still make and hold these cities in the mold of true Italian tradition of dedication to religion and beauty.

The translator who transformed the softly-spoken musical name of Livorno into the guttural, awkward Leghorn, should be required, for punishment, to feed and water at least a thousand Leghorn hens for a week and weave underwater a thousand Leghorn hats. Throughout the day that I spent in Livorno I failed to see one white hen and I saw only three of the straw hats inexplicably called Leghorns.

From Livorno I traveled by automobile to Pisa, my eyes eagerly awaiting the first view of the world's architectural phenomenon and this city's trademark. The children sing:

"Evviva la torre di Pisa
Che pende, pende
Ma non mai vien giù."

"Three cheers for the Tower of Pisa, which leans and leans, but never falls down." I thought, however, that that sooner-or-later-to-happen day had arrived when I climbed the tower with its 293 steps. When I reached the top level I was instructed by the guide to lie flat on my stomach and look down from the lowering side. The effect is staggering. One gets the feeling that the tower is falling and you are hurtling down to the earth, together with the masses of white marble columns which will complete the destruction of what will be left of you after the fall of 179 feet. However, after a few moments, one realizes he is still stationary and manages to get his heart, which is in his throat, back to its place in the chest, and his stomach, which is in his chest, back to its normal depository. He smiles wanly and starts down the spiral stairway, seeking to lean heavily on the upper side.

I shall not refer to all the cities and places my feet, as if winged, took me in that enchanting odyssey of 1924–25 because this is not a book of my journeyings, but I must mention my visit to Padua to worship in the Basilica of Sant'Antonio where Saint Anthony, the patron saint of my father, is sepulchered. This church is one of the most unique and spectacular in Italy. Its seven domes, numerous spires and minarets all blend together in a grand harmony of soul-inspiring intensity.

Nor could one in Padua, or anywhere near it, fail to enter the venerable University where the great Galileo Galilei lectured for eighteen years, having among his students princes, scientists, and savants from all of Europe. Awesomely I touched the podium which had felt the vibrations of his voice and I could easily understand why it became necessary to enlarge the hall to accommodate the thousands who came to drink in the wisdom he imparted.

Bologna is known as La Città Dotta, the City of the Wise. Its university, one of the oldest in Europe, counted among its distinguished lecturers Copernicus, Dante, Galvani, Marconi, Carducci. The city itself is a vast arcade of charm. By constructing the second stories of their buildings above the sidewalks, the Bolognese have developed a style of promenade which is enchanting as well as extremely practical. No one needs to worry, in a sudden downpour, that he will be drenched. Umbrellas are practically unknown here, because gracefully-arched and colonnaded roofs protect the pedestrian no matter where he visits.

Bologna rejoices in its culinary fame, for the Bolognese regard their city as the epicurean capital of Italy. I indeed found the fare there supreme, but it has been my experience that there is no restaurant, hotel or home in Italy from Bolzano to Ragusa where the food and wines do not titillate the palate, excite the salivary glands, and often make you wish you had eaten less, such is the strain on the will power to refuse dishes which captivate, entrance, enrapture, and enlarge the diner.

It can be believed that the checkered tablecloth in Italy's restaurants, inevitably ornamented with its carafe of sparkling red wine, golden bread sticks and menus large enough for a painting, attracts tourists as much as her dramatic mountains, entrancing lakes, and historic ruins. Italian cooking has become a universal favorite. Dishes which at one time were regarded frugal and suitable only for the *contadini*, are today eagerly sought as gourmet items in hostelries throughout continental Europe and America.

Many of the dishes trace their origin to those of the ancient Romans, enriched by the Renaissance. Much of what is considered *haute cuisine* of France derives in reality from delicacies introduced to the court by Catherine de' Medici, who left Florence with her Florentine chefs when she departed to become the bride of the Duke of Orleans, and a future queen of France.

Because of its independently evolving city-states, Italy seems outwardly more like a collection of nations than a homogeneous country, and in no way is this more evident than in the cuisines of the various regions. Thus, what one eats in Milan, for instance, might seem wholly exotic in Palermo, and vice versa. Every province, every city, nearly every village claims a specialty, the flavors of each reflecting fine nuances of Italian temperament as well as the foods available in each region.

Ossobuco (veal knuckle in gravy), *risi e bisi* (Venetian rice and peas), *taglierini in brodo con fegatino di polla* (pasta in broth with chicken livers), *lasagne al pesto* (sauce of basil, olive oil and goat cheese) are favorites in northern cities. In Florence and Pisa one enjoys *minestrone, arrosto misto* (mixed grill: chicken, pigeon and veal), *porchetto* (roast suckling pig), *zucchini con funghi e peperoni* (green squash with mushrooms and peppers), *carni alla spiedo* (meat on a skewer), *pomidori ripieni al forno* (pasta-stuffed baked tomatoes). Bologna has a style distinctly and famously its own, and it is enough to add "*alla Bolognese*" to know that no matter what the dish, one leaves the table with regret, knowing that capacity can never reach satiety.

Rome commands the appetite as her history commands the intellect, and they go together in this most majestically enchanting of cities. There is scarcely a restaurant that does not have a window or a vista overlooking some ancient ruin, a splashing fountain, or renowned site. Dante supped here, Garibaldi drew his sword there. Caesar passed at this point, on that spot Augustus proclaimed his imperial edicts, and as one enjoys this instantaneous journey into the adventure and romance of the ages, one relishes his *saltimbocca* (literally "jump into the mouth," veal with *prosciutto*), *fettuccine*, *gnocchi*, *trippa alla romana*, *manzo con vino* (top-sirloin roast with wine), *anitra con lasagne* (duck with *lasagne*), accompanied by the famed Frascati and Grottaferrata wines.

In Naples one takes in the enchanting view of its matchless, turquoise bay while dining on *veal piccata* (sauced in tomatoes, garlic and oregano), *pizza* in luscious reds rivaling the most magnificent sunsets, *bracioula di vitello alla napolitana* (roulatine of veal Neapolitan), *pollo alla cacciatora* (chicken cacciatora), *sfogliatine di crema* (leaf mounds with cream). Sicily has so many specialties that the island is a smörgåsbord of gastronomical delights, among them *caponatina* (eggplant appetizer), *prosciutto* with figs, seafood of every description with *salse rosse*, *carciofi sotto olio ed aceto* (pickled artichokes), and *zabaglione* (hot, foamy egg dessert with a fortified wine). There is no place in Italy which serves more delicious and a greater variety of sweets and desserts than Palermo.

Pasta (any kind of alimentary dough) of course, is the undisputed monarch of the Italian table. Those not too familiar with Italian phraseology list every type of *pasta* under spaghetti or macaroni, but *pasta* can have and does have hundreds of forms and tastes, among them the most well-known being *spaghetti, ravioli, cannelloni, bucatini, fettuccine, gnocchi, zitoni, linguine, perciatelli, fidelini, lasagne, manicotti, spaghettini, rigatoni, cappelli, cappelletti, maccheroni, conchiglie, stelline, fusilli*, all manifestations of the imagination of the Italian menu and a measurement of its exciting variety. In the north and central regions, rice and corn are staples of diet and *risottos* and *polenta* dishes prevail, adding further diversity to the Italian table.

My favorite dish is *melanzana alla parmigiana*: eggplant cut into slices, dredged with bread crumbs, rolled in well-beaten eggs, dipped in boiling olive oil until brown and then baked in layers with *moz-*

zarella and tomato sauce, all sprinkled over with anticipatory delight, masticatory enjoyment, and postprandial sweet contentment.

A friend of mine, knowing I was writing this book, sent along the following newspaper item:

> Thomas Jefferson is credited with introducing spaghetti to this country. He served it at a formal dinner when he was Secretary of State under President George Washington, according to researchers.
>
> Food historians tell us that Jefferson sent his aide, William Short, on a special mission to Naples to find out how the Neapolitans prepared the famed Italian specialty.

The city of Siena—with its battlemented massive stone structures, its narrow, winding streets, and its main square called the Piazza di Campo—is a city lifted bodily out of the Middle Ages. Its municipal building, called the Palazzo Pubblico, was built in 1297–1310. A geometrically perfect, dignified, chaste tower with a crenelated belfry rises sheer from the Palazzo to the height of 334 feet. It is called "the noblest tower in Italy." The Piazza di Campo, with its bewitching levels, seems always to be marching with banners flying.

One goes to Assisi as one calls on a close relative. He knows that while there, he will be the companion of one of the kindliest men who ever trod the earth. No one wants to be isolated from humanity. Perhaps even the person of outward coldness and austerity would like at heart to be regarded with respect and affection. Let such a person go to Assisi and he will not come away lonely or feeling sorry for himself. The geniality of St. Francis greets every visitor like the dawn spangling the nocturnal hills. The Convent and the Basilica of San Francesco surmount the hills of Monte Subasio. The Basilica is built over the tomb of St. Francis. One says "tomb" because one sees the vault in which his body rests, but he really is not dead. I felt St. Francis at my side, guiding me through the town, pointing out the monuments of Roman temples, medieval castles, and modern landmarks, and conversing about the Order of Franciscans, which he founded.

I cannot linger too long on the odyssey of my youth when I savored the wonders and the beauty of Italy in boundless ecstasy: the snowy Alps which form a crown to this majestic land; its lyrical lakes which are gems in a matchless panorama; the stately Apennines which are the backbone of the peninsula; its vine-covered hills and smiling orchards; its rivers large and small, ribbons of commerce and silken sashes of scenic delight; its long enchanting shoreline courted by azure seas; the Dolomites, mountains of dramatic grandeur, all under clear Mediterranean skies.

I crossed the Straits of Messina into Sicily, an island of superlative natural beauty which has been further enhanced by the engineering skills and the artistic talents of its wonderful people. Sicily has produced some of Italy's greatest statesmen and many of her children in America have attained eminence in nearly every field of endeavor.

I crossed the Tyrrhenian Sea over to Sardinia, where the kind and gentle folk unobtrusively produce the farm and dairy products that are shipped to the mainland. I saw all of Italy's magnificent seaports from which are shipped the fruits of her orchards, the golden streams of her olive oil, and the sunset-tinted wine of her vineyards. I visited countless little towns and talked with the people, a hard-working, God-fearing people, who know how to smile in the face of every adversity and who have an unconquerable optimism that all will come out right in the end. I visited its bathing beaches and spas, entered into its concert halls and listened to the divine music of Italian masters. Italy is a land of creativity, of workers and worshipers, and its people were deserving of a kindlier fortune than the one they faced through centuries of subjugation, invasion, and exploitation.

18 THE MAFIA

For centuries Sicily had been the prey of invaders. First the Greeks landed, then came the Romans, the Greeks left but returned, the Romans left but returned, then the Saracens stormed ashore, the Arabs, also the French, the Spanish. The island seethed with foreign occupation and the population had no native representatives or officials to turn to for assistance, protection, or comfort. Government became but another word for oppression, crushing taxation, and tyranny. The viceroys and all those serving the occupying governments looked upon Sicily as a land where they could revel in a luxurious, licentious, and riotous existence. The progress recorded during this despotic era in trade, commerce, arts, agriculture, and artisanry was permitted only because it meant for the rulers a more opulent living.

By the beginning of the sixteenth century, law in Sicily had become a mockery of Justice. Those who committed crimes were taken into custody, but once in jail the accused criminal found that money was a key which could unlock any prison door. It was also a broom which could wipe away incriminating evidence. Thus bribery became part of government because the sums levied against the criminals did not go to the police alone. Prosecuting officials and those in the higher strata of administration harkened also to the jingle of the corrupting gold.

In time the criminals—thieves, burglars, bandits—began to regard themselves as part of the government. Invisible, to be sure, but still an integral part of the "law and order" of the land. The police themselves often extorted in their own right.

Many of the usurpers, after seizing large estates and enormous properties, returned to their original home countries, leaving agents to superintend and supervise, and to collect rents and royalties. When tenants failed to meet the landlord's demands the agents often hired thugs to warn the tenants that if they did not pay up, broken bones could follow. At first, anonymous threats were disregarded, but when tenants fell under nocturnal cudgels and their livestock was driven away, others who received similar threats responded with more alacrity than they might have, to notices from the sheriff.

All Sicilian governments recruited their armies through military conscription. People of means never served because they could purchase exemptions. Thus the poor people were the ones who had to fight the wars of their despotic rulers. Once conscripted, ten years could pass before the conscript was released. Consequently, many draftees took to the mountains where eventually they joined up with malefactors who lived on violence and extortion.

Since the judiciary was appointive, the judge who attempted to hew to the line of the law, imposing suitable punishment where justified, could be transferred to a distant jurisdiction known for its lack of body comforts and conveniences. All this favored the chronic violators of the law who began to acquire a certain standing of their own. Corrupt government, venal absenteeism, and poverty combined, consciously and unconsciously, to create an invisible but very tangible part of the society of the land which in time became known as the Mafia. The origin of the word is shrouded in mystery but one explanation is that a well-known gang of criminals which lived in the stone quarries of Mafie was called the Mafie gang. When other criminal bands were identified they were also called Mafie, and in time the whole concept of criminality operating through terrorism and extortion acquired the distinctive name of Mafia. It was not long until romanticists began to weave fanciful tales around the Mafia and, in a land where illiteracy was common, superstition rife, and means of communication primitive, the Mafia soon was wearing a legendary cloak such as that which enveloped the Molly Maguires of Ireland and the Robin Hood bands of England.

The Mafia was a thoroughly disreputable, criminal operation which, in the accomplishment of its nefarious objectives, practiced kidnaping, extortion, burglary, and even murder, but it is seriously to be doubted that it was a closely-knit, highly disciplined, island-wide organization with a supreme chief, deputy chiefs, and regional chiefs. Its activities were local and provincial. It is possible and even probable that the individual bands in their own territories worked out arrangements with bands in other territories as a matter of mutual convenience in the perpetration of their respective criminal deeds, but it was never established that there was a centralized headquarters with a high mogul who could issue edicts and commands to district leaders and gangs throughout all Sicily. Nevertheless, by 1840 the Mafia was a hideous reality in that unhappy island, and it gained additionally monstrous power through the advancing years.

When Mafia adherents were charged with crime, they enjoyed immunities in the ensuing trials which could not have been theirs except through the connivance of a substantial segment of officialdom. Even when murders occurred in open daylight with people unavoidably looking on, it was impossible to get the witnesses to testify because of their fear of Mafia reprisals. At the same time, persons could be found living in towns far away who would testify to alibis for the defendants.

The Mafia terrorized the farmers, fishermen, shopkeepers, craftsmen into paying tribute. Otherwise cattle would disappear, crops would be destroyed, tools would be ruined, fishing nets would be torn apart. If, after sustaining this property damage, the victims still refused to pay over money for "protection," personal violence could be forthcoming.

Even after Italy achieved independence and unification, little, if anything, was done effectively to strike down this terrible evil. An Italian member of Parliament, Leopoldo Franchetti of Florence, after conducting a survey of economic conditions in Sicily, wrote in 1876:

> The Mafia is a union of persons of every class, of every profession, who, without any apparent continuous and regular ties, are always found together in order to promote their own mutual interests, without any consideration for the law, for justice, for public order; it is the medieval sentiment of those who believe that they can take care of their own safety and interests through their own personal ability and influence, independently of the legal authorities. In a few words,

the Mafia is the tendency to substitute individual violence for law and order.

Sicilian parliament members were aware of the Mafia cancer festering in their homeland, but they were loath to take action because, individually, they felt incapable of successfully fighting it, and, collectively, they had not reached that state of cohesion which would guarantee success to an anti-Mafia campaign.

Mussolini's sins were many, and most of them unforgivable, but it is to his credit that he dared to declare war on the odious Mafia when the conventional politicians looked away. It is said that Mussolini's anti-Mafiaism followed a personal affront. It was reported that while traveling in Sicily, a Mafia leader told him that he should fear no physical harm because the Mafia would protect him. The black-shirted chief of state raged that anyone should dare to regard himself more powerful than Mussolini, and he at once resolved to demonstrate to the *mafioso* how inconsequential he could be, compared to the Duce.

Whether this story has factual basis or not, Mussolini instituted vigorous action. He invested Prefect Cesare Mori of Lombardy with full powers to prosecute. This dedicated official, who had spent a lifetime in police work, lost no time, spared no efforts, and withheld no weapon in the mighty offensive which he at once launched against the Mafia outlaws. He assembled a small army of police agents who scoured the island obtaining evidence on all Mafia depredations. Then, in an island-wide raid, he rounded up the reputed bandit leaders and clapped them into jail. He assigned police to protect the prosecution witnesses.

At the ensuing trials, the defendants were confounded and consternated to see that witnesses boldly testified to their criminal deeds. Three hundred were convicted and sent to prison to serve out sentences totaling two thousand years. The Mafia was smashed.

Currently there have been stories of its revival in Sicily and it cannot be doubted that crime stalks the streets of Palermo and other large cities in Sicily. Whether this spells out a new Mafia, or represents modern gangsterism* which is preying on the public in large

* Robert Neville, writing in the New York *Times Magazine*, January 12, 1964, says: "The new Mafia is pure gangsterism. Its operators are sleek, well-dressed young men who drive high-powered cars, live in lavish modern apartments, are seen

cities throughout the world, is not definitely established. Smugglers, extortionists, dope peddlers are plying their vicious rackets, but the government is fighting them with all the modern weapons of crime detection, fast pursuit cars, radio communication, plus detective infiltration into the ranks of the criminals themselves.

With the interment of the Mafia during Mussolini's regime, there were those who said that its ghost crossed the ocean to extort and terrorize in America. This story still persists. Italians have committed crimes in America, just as persons from other nations have committed crimes. Italian names appear in lists of racketeers, gangsters, and various types of misdemeanants and felons. They are a disgrace to the names they bear and no law-abiding Italian seeks in any way to defend them and their crimes against society. But this is far from saying that there exists in the United States a national syndicate of crime operated exclusively by Italians.

It is interesting to note in this connection that one of the most renowned heroes in American police history was Giuseppe Petrosino who brought many an Italian criminal to justice. In pursuing some of them back to Italy he was shot and killed on the streets of Palermo.

On May 26, 1959, the New York *Herald Tribune*, speaking of another Italian police officer, said:

> Police heroism is a commonplace around our town . . . but we can recall nothing that for sheer courage matches the performance of Detective Lieutenant Mario Biaggi, who, with a gun pointed at his head, chose to shoot it out with a thug, and emerged triumphant.

In twenty-one years of police service, Biaggi received twenty-seven commendations for bravery, was wounded eight times in line of duty, and has been elected to the National Police Hall of Fame.

It may be in order to interpolate here, also, that Charles J. Bonaparte, who, in 1908, founded the Federal Bureau of Investigation, was of Italian lineage.

In October 1963 newspaper readers, radio listeners, and television viewers obtained a great deal of interesting information on gangsterism by the testimony of one Joseph Valachi who was serving a life

---

in expensive hotels and bars and in general throw their newly-found money around very carelessly. The police estimate that there are now in Palermo around 1800 Mafia *nouveaux riches*, the majority of whom until a few years ago were boys on farms."

sentence for murder. He testified before the Rackets Committee of
the Senate Governmental Operations Committee on the criminal
ramifications and activities of an organization which he called Cosa
Nostra (our thing). Valachi's testimony did not reveal him to be a
person of a very high order of intelligence. When Senator Carl T.
Curtis of Nebraska asked him: "Do you know of any Cosa Nostra
groups in Omaha?" Valachi replied: "I never heard of Omaha."

Murray Kempton, writing in *The New Republic*, October 12, 1963,
said:

> Never before Joseph Valachi has a witness given such broad circu-
> lation to the myth of the American Mafia and never before him has
> a witness left that myth with less illusion of substance.

One year after Valachi's testimony, Jack Vandenberg of the
United Press International (October 31, 1964) wrote:

> His guttural, semi-literal ramblings have given little evidence they
> could use in court though many cases have been developed as an in-
> direct result of his stories. Those who had hoped for quick conviction
> of the top leaders of organized crime became thoroughly disillusioned
> by what at first had been hailed as a big breakthrough.

Several Italian societies and fraternal organizations resented the
Valachi hearings, protesting that Italians throughout the country
were being held up to humiliation. John N. LaCorte, director of the
Italian Historical Society in America, complained that the hearings
embarrassed "21,000,000 Americans of Italian descent who have
shown their loyalty to America in peace and war." These groups and
the individuals who spoke for them were, of course, motivated by the
best intentions, but they undoubtedly exaggerated in their minds the
effect of Valachi's testimony. Nothing was said at the hearings which
would suggest, rationally, that, because of the bad Italian characters
put on display, all Italians were suspect. Police Commissioner of New
York, Michael J. Murphy, stated it well at the hearings: "Crimes are
committed by individuals, not by racial groups. Italians have no monopoly on crimes in our city."*

Italian organizations and individuals as well, however, properly re-

* Albert Q. Maisel in his book *They All Chose America* said: "The idea that
Italians—or other immigrants, for that matter—are especially given to lawbreaking
is a myth, refuted by every serious study of the records. . . . The FBI's lists of
most-wanted criminals contain no dominating proportion of Italian names."

sented radio and television shows which constantly assigned Italian names to criminal types. The unceasing, repetitive portrayal of Italians as men engaged in defying the law could not help but create in the public mind an image which was entirely untrue. Harry Golden in his best seller *Only in America* said:

> In crime books and in radio and TV dramas the Italian has become almost a stereotype for the gangster and the mobster. This, of course, is not only unfair, but untrue.

A fictional character incessantly exposed to the millions who watch television can become more of a reality to them than a historical one. Who can doubt that the Lone Ranger is more real to millions of the younger generation than Henry Clay or Daniel Webster? It is to be said to the credit of the sponsors and owners of such offending television shows that their formats have been revised to exclude the gratuitous slandering of the Italian name.

There are, of course, Italian gangsters who are not fictional. The New York *Times* on February 14, 1965, carried an article on a survey of crime in which were listed over thirty Italian names connected with illegal enterprises of various descriptions, some operating behind seemingly legitimate façades. All Americans, whether of Italian origin or not, applaud the vigorous efforts being made by prosecuting and police authorities to apprehend, convict, and punish criminals, regardless of nationality, race, or creed. In New York, Alfred J. Scotti, Chief Assistant of the Rackets Bureau, is assigned to investigating criminal activities where it appears that Italians may be involved. In Brooklyn, Assistant District Attorney Albert V. DeMeo has a special squad of eight detectives committed to the same kind of work.

Detective Sergeant Ralph Salerno in the New York Police Department said:

> "Call it Mafia, Cosa Nostra or what you will, but organized crime has become one of the big test businesses in the United States and is trying to act like big business. 'Hoods' like Dutch Schultz never went without two bodyguards. Today's bosses of organized crime have a lawyer and accountant instead."

Charles Grutzner, author of the *Times* article, said that "the strength of the Mafia does not mean that Italians have a monopoly on organized crime."

William G. Hundley, chief of the Organized Crime and Racketeering section of the United States Department of Justice said: "The organization has a working relationship with other criminal organizations made up of people of varying ethnic and religious backgrounds."

All this would indicate that there does not exist in America any kind of monopolistic network of Italian malefactors.* In 1957 a group of some sixty Italians, practically all of whom had at some time run afoul of the law, met in the village of Apalachin, New York, for an unannounced and never publicly explained reason. A book published in 1959† referred to the Apalachin gathering as a meeting of the "Grand Council of the Mafia." The author said:

> In the history of crime the Mafia is unique. There have been many secret societies devoted to evil-doing, but nothing like the strange combine of Sicilian families which forms this company of born lawbreakers, and which has produced such men as Lucky Luciano, Albert Anastasia, Frank Costello, and Joe Adonis, to name only a few.

But, after definitely projecting the concept of the Mafia as an organization, the author explained:

> To understand the Mafia, one must realize that this unique society of lawbreakers is not a rigid, monolithic organization, as most powerful secret societies of the past have been. There is no president, no formal roster; there is no initiation or oath.

If it is not an organization, the "Mafia" which the author has in mind is made up of law violators who have here and there banded together into individual gangs, of which there have been many in American criminal history, such as the Jesse James gang, the Dillinger gang, the Baby Face Nelson gang, the Al Capone gang, the Anastasia gang, Murder, Inc., and others.

The author said that the Apalachin affair was a meeting of the "Grand Council" of the American Mafia "in formal session," but how can there be a Grand Council of an organization which he says does

* A survey made by the U. S. Bureau of Prisons, Department of Justice, indicates that the Federal prison population with Italian names is less than three percent (*Il Progresso*, March 26, 1961). Letter from Chief Research and Statistics Branch of Federal Bureau of Prisons to Congressman Alfred E. Santangelo.

† *Brotherhood of Evil: the Mafia*, by Frederic Sondern, Jr., New York, Farrar, Straus & Cudahy, 1959.

not exist? The New York State Police, the Federal Bureau of Investigation, and a Federal grand jury probed all phases and background involved in the Apalachin meeting, but at no time unearthed evidence which even remotely suggested the existence of an America-wide Mafia.

The National Broadcasting Company, after an investigation of its own, said through Frank McGee, on August 29, 1958:

> "And we have come to the conclusion that the Mafia in this country is a foolish and distracting myth. . . . We arrived at this conclusion long before being petitioned by organized groups of Americans of Italian descent. We sympathized then and now with their resentment at being stigmatized with the label, Mafia, but their complaints—made before knowing what we were going to say—have not changed one word of the report."

Virgil Peterson, a former FBI agent and Chairman of the Chicago Crime Commission, said on the same NBC program:

> "I have never seen any convincing evidence of the Mafia as an organization which governs organized crime today."

William J. Keating, former Assistant Attorney General, and Counsel for the New York Crime Commission, said:

> "There isn't any one organization involved in crime, on such a widespread basis as the Mafia is supposed to exist, that could last two weeks against our law enforcement."

On July 1, 1959, United States Senator Kenneth B. Keating, of New York, wrote to United States Attorney General William P. Rogers, inquiring as to whether there existed "a nationwide organization of criminals . . . of any national origin." The Attorney General replied: "To my knowledge there is no nationwide ring consisting solely of criminals of any particular national origin."

Twenty of the sixty men who had attended the Apalachin meeting were indicted and convicted of conspiring to obstruct justice and commit perjury and drew substantial prison terms. The sentenced defendants appealed to the United States Court of Appeals, Second Circuit, which reversed the convictions.* The opinion in the case

* U. S. v. Bufalino, et al., 285 F. 2d 408.

was written by Chief Judge Lumbard. In a concurring opinion, Judge Clark said:

> Perhaps the most curious feature of this strange case is the fact that after all these years there is not a shred of legal evidence that the Apalachin gathering was illegal or even improper in either purpose or fact.

He said further that

> the government has never taken the position that the defendants were guilty of wrongdoing by merely failing to reveal what occurred at the Apalachin meeting.

To the extent that the word Mafia is used as a synonym for criminal, the word has validity because there can be no doubt that those Italians who participate in crimes of violence, where collective action is required, may be called *mafiosi*. Thus the Mafia exists, as organized crime exists, but no authoritative evidence has yet been forthcoming which establishes a Mafia as a monopolistic nationwide syndicate with branches in the various parts of the nation. Take, for example, an article that appeared in the *Saturday Evening Post*, October 31, 1964. It is entitled "How Mafia Killers Got Their Man." The man in question was James V. Delmont, whose body was found in a field near Ontario, California. The California police identified him as a "small-time hoodlum closely associated with the Mafia element in Buffalo." If one substitutes the word "criminal" for "Mafia" here, the description is undoubtedly correct, but when the article goes on to say that the dead man was a "soldier" or "button man," "the lowest rank in the Mafia hierarchy," it simply is using vivid but unprecise language.

The author states that Delmont got in bad with the Buffalo Mafia and fled to Miami, that he told several people later that he went to the FBI in Miami and offered to divulge secrets of the Mafia in exchange for information about the members of the Buffalo Mafia who might be looking for him. But the author admits that the FBI has no record of any visit made by Delmont to its Miami offices. Later, Delmont said that "the Mafia is stronger than the FBI."

On May 25, 1960, he walked into the offices of the FBI in Los Angeles and said he wanted to know who was in Southern California from the Buffalo Mafia, in exchange for which he would reveal secrets of the Mafia generally. The author of the article then says:

> Delmont told a garbled story of his predicament, filled with lies and half-truths, and the clerk who interviewed him dismissed him as a nut.

In spite of this, the author ends his article with the statement:

> Thus, an insignificant soldier in crime's shadow army died. The Mafia had scored another humiliating victory over law enforcement.

The non sequitur is glaring. Delmont had been in trouble with the law from the time he was fifteen years of age. For twenty-nine years he lived in crimeland. The fact that he was murdered in California, and the history of his numerous crimes, plus numerous jail sentences, probations, and flight, hardly offer substantive evidence of the existence of a Mafia in the United States in the sense intended by the author. Certainly something more convincing is required than the word of a felon who says that the Mafia is stronger than the FBI, recognized globally as the most efficient and powerful police organization in the world. Certainly there can be but little evidentiary value in the word of a man who, after being interviewed by an FBI agent, is appraised as a "nut."

The whole theme of the Mafia, as it existed in Sicily, was that its members were so powerful, its ramifications so widespread, and its control over the police and the judiciary so complete, that no matter what crime the *mafiosi* committed, they could never be punished because the victims of their depredations and the witnesses to their crimes were so terrorized, the police so linked up with the criminals by bribery and graft, and the judges so beholden to the criminal element for their continuing incumbency that no prosecution could be initiated, much less carried to a convicting conclusion. To suggest that there could be any such demoralization of law and order on a national scale in America is so preposterous as to be unworthy of serious discussion. The fact remains that Al Capone, Lucky Luciano, Joseph Valachi, Vito Genoveso, and scores of so-called *mafiosi* have been sent to prison.

United States Marine Band, about 1896. Leader Francisco Fanciulli.
COURTESY, UNITED STATES MARINE CORPS.

Amadeo P. Giannini, founder of Bank of Italy in California, which evolved into Bank of America, largest banking institution in the world. UNITED PRESS INTERNATIONAL PHOTO.

Giuseppe Verdi, famous composer of *Rigoletto*, *Il Trovatore*, *Otello*, *Aida*, and other immortal operatic works.

Arturo Toscanini, most famous symphony conductor of the twentieth century, here directing the National Broadcasting Company Orchestra. COURTESY, NBC.

Enrico Fermi. He "unlocked the door to the Atomic Age." Nobel Prize Winner in Physics, recipient of Congressional Medal of Merit.
COURTESY, UNIVERSITY OF CHICAGO.

Sergeant John Basilone, described by General Douglas MacArthur as a "one-man army." His Congressional Medal of Honor citation states Basilone contributed "in a large measure to the virtual annihilation of a Japanese regiment." COURTESY, UNITED STATES MARINE CORPS.

Fiorello LaGuardia, United States Congressman and Mayor of New York. He is shown here at the throttle of a subway train when the BMT was taken over by the City, June 2, 1940. UNITED PRESS INTERNATIONAL PHOTO.

Benedetto Croce, Italian philosopher, referred to by the Manchester *Guardian* during World War II as the "greatest living Italian." Here he is at his villa in Sorrento conversing with the author.

19 WORLD WAR II

During World War II, from September 1943 to May 1945, much of Italy suffered mutilation from both friend and foe. The German artillery and air bombs bombarded terrain held by the Allies. The Allies blasted away at positions possessed by the Germans. Since all this happened in Italy, the Italians suffered no matter who was attacking and who was defending.

The most melancholy toll was that taken of the children. In the late summer of 1944, after the American Fifth Army, to which I was attached, had liberated Rome, Prince Humbert invited me to the Royal Palace. As I passed through the royal gardens I was struck by the peculiar walk of some thirty boys and girls of seven to twelve years playing on the great lawns. They all moved as if they were catching themselves just before an anticipated fall. Although engaged in games, they did not laugh and shout.

I heard from them no joyous cries as only children make. As I got closer to them I gasped. Many of these tots were missing an arm or leg. Practically all of them were disfigured by the telltale marks of shrapnel and bomb fragments. These hapless victims of the inexorable god of war had been gathered by Prince Humbert from the sections of Italy liberated by our troops and he had made them his special wards.

He took me to them and said: "Fanciulli, vi presento il Comandante Musmanno, un'Americano ed un grand'amico dell'Italia."
("Children, I want you to meet Commander Musmanno, an American and a great friend of Italy.") I knelt, held out my arms and, with
my voice almost breaking, I said: "Ragazzi, venite da me, vorrei ab-
braciarvi." ("Children, please come to me, I would like to embrace
you.")

With their little pathetic voices, they cried out: "Grazie, Comandante, Grazie!" And with hands extended before them they advanced
with that peculiar walk of theirs. From that moment I could see nothing. A mist clouded my eyes. I could feel the babbling children tumbling over me, pulling at my jacket, kissing at my hands, my neck,
my face.

Every one of those God's children was blind. Blind from the bombs
which fell from the war engines which flew through the blue skies of
Italy, blue skies never again to be seen by those tumbling, searching,
affection-seeking lambs. The war left in Italy fifteen thousand mutilated children—blind, armless, crippled, paralyzed, or burned.

The Italians made an enormous contribution to winning World
War II. It is perhaps impossible to know precisely how many Americans of Italian lineage, wearing the American uniform, advanced
under shell fire, kept vigil in muddy and freezing foxholes, patrolled
the seas on battleships, cruisers, and destroyers, and sailed the under-
seas in submarines, but there can be little doubt that the number
considerably surpassed a million.* They fought on every battlefield
and many covered themselves with glory, while adding, with their
blood, a deeper red of loyalty to the Stars and Stripes.

There was Lieutenant Willibald C. Bianchi, who charged an enemy
machine-gun nest on the Bataan peninsula. Hit by a grenade, he kept
running forward to silence a Japanese pillbox. Climbing to the top
of a tank he manned an antiaircraft gun, mowing down the enemy
until he was hit by a rifle bullet. He continued at the trigger until
the splinter of an artillery shell struck him and disabled him completely. A grateful nation conferred on him the Congressional Medal

* Governor Nelson Rockefeller, in a speech delivered August 25, 1961, before
Italian-American War Veterans of the United States, said: "Throughout America,
the services mustered over one million five hundred thousand of Italian descent—
over ten percent of the might of America."

of Honor. There was Salvatore Battaglia, recipient of the Distinguished Service Cross for the gallant part he played in a torpedo attack on enemy ships in the battle of Midway. There was Sergeant George Braga, who made a dash across no-man's-land on Bataan, running a gauntlet of machine-gun fire to carry vital information to Americans holding another position.

And then there was Sergeant John Basilone, whom General Douglas MacArthur called a "one-man army." Born of Italian immigrant parents he joined the Marines and soon after Pearl Harbor sailed with his outfit to Guadalcanal where he held up a whole Japanese regiment for three days and nights with his machine gun, which he had maneuvered into a strategic position. In his ceaseless vigil and action, he could not stop for food, sleep, or rest. Over and over again the enemy stormed his position, until at last Basilone had to move because the Japanese he had killed piled to a height above which his machine gun could not fire.

The citation for the Congressional Medal of Honor described what followed:

In a fierce frontal attack with the Japanese blasting his guns with grenades and mortar fire, one of Sergeant Basilone's sections, with its gun crews, was put out of action, leaving only two men able to carry on. Moving an extra gun into position, Sergeant Basilone placed it in action. Then under continual fire, repaired another and personally manned it, gallantly holding his line until replacements arrived. A little later, with ammunition critically low and the supply lines cut off, Sergeant Basilone, at great risk of his life and in the face of continued enemy attack, battled his way through hostile lines with urgently needed shells for his gunners, thereby contributing in a large measure to the virtual annihilation of a Japanese regiment.

After this exploit and the awarding of the Medal of Honor, Basilone was returned to his hometown of Raritan, New Jersey, where he was welcomed with speeches, flowers, and bands as befitted a great war hero. The Secretary of the Navy now assigned Basilone to inland duty, as instructor at Marine camps. Here he was safe from artillery shells, grenades and machine guns, but he kept thinking of his Marine comrades fighting and dying in the Pacific. He wanted to help them end the war so peace could smile again all over the world. He requested assignment to active war duty and sailed once again for the battlefront. He was killed in action in the landing at Iwo Jima. The

208 THE STORY OF THE ITALIANS IN AMERICA

Navy Cross was bestowed on Basilone posthumously and a Navy destroyer was named in his honor. Corporal Anthony Peter Damato of Shenandoah, Pennsylvania, was another Marine to be similarly honored. Others awarded the Congressional Medal of Honor were Ralph Cheli and Gino J. Merli of Pennsylvania, Arthur De Franzo of Massachusetts, Peter Dalessandro of New York, Michael Colalillo of Minnesota, Vito Bertoldi of Decatur, Illinois, Robert Vial of California, Joseph Cicchetti of Ohio. Ten more Italians won the Navy Cross.

Captain Don Salvatore Gentile of Ohio, one of the leading American aces of the war, shot down thirty Nazi planes. Major A. Martini of San Francisco, in a cat-and-dog fight with the Nazis over Paris, downed twenty-two of them in a fifteen-minute battle.

In February 1945 Lieutenant Colonel Henry A. Mucci, commanding the 6th Ranger Battalion, blasted ashore on Dinagat Island in the Gulf of Leyte to liberate starving American and other Allied prisoners held in a Japanese stockade twenty-five miles from the nearest American line. The Rangers liberated 513 men, killing 532 of the enemy in the process. Associated Press correspondent Fred Hampson enthusiastically radioed from Luzon:

> Put Lieutenant Colonel Henry Mucci's 6th Rangers with Rogers' Rangers. Put 'em with Allen's Green Mountain Boys. After what happened last night that is where they belong.

Four Americans of Italian lineage achieved the rank of brigadier general in World War II: Daniel Noce of Denver, Robert V. Ignico of Boston, Ralph Palladino of Winchester, Massachusetts, Joseph T. Michela of Duluth, Minnesota. Several Americans of Italian lineage also achieved Navy flag rank.

One of the great heroes of the war, although he did not march in military ranks, was Enrico Fermi, who has been appropriately called the architect of the Atomic Age. It is not too much to say that had it not been for this Italian's genius, World War II might well not have ended on August 14, 1945. It could have raged for another year or more with its incalculably further devastation, misery, and death. Indeed, as early as 1938, two German scientists, while working at the Kaiser Wilhelm Institute in Berlin, had split uranium atoms, establishing the dire potentialities of atomic fission. With Hitler bent on world domination, he ordered his scientists to man the laboratories to perfect an atom bomb. Had they achieved this objective before July 16, 1945, when we exploded our bomb at Los Alamos, New Mexico, the war might have taken a very tragic turn for America.

Not only Germany was prying into the vast mysteries of atomic fission. England and Russia were overworking their scientific laboratories in the same frantic search. In Japan the military overlords had ordered their scientists to develop a bomb with an explosive power of at least 10,000 tons of TNT. It was to be the fate of Japan that a bomb twice the size of the one she had visualized would be dropped on Hiroshima, bringing the Nipponese kingdom to her knees, begging for the mercy conspicuously absent at Pearl Harbor.

Throughout the war Hitler kept screaming at his Uran Verein (Uranium Society) to invent the weapon with which he could annihilate his enemies in a matter of days, perhaps hours. Up to those last groveling final moments in the Berlin underground bunker he was sure his scientists would hand to him the magic torch with which he could incinerate every country and person opposed to him.

Meanwhile, Enrico Fermi, born in Rome and educated at the University of Pisa, was delving into the intricacies, complexities, and mysteries of the atom. His mental endowments and dedication to science made him a worthy historical associate of the immortal Galileo Galilei, the site of whose experiments in Pisa, where Fermi was studying, were a constant inspiration to him. Mathematics came to Fermi as simply as boiling an egg and he picked up languages like suitcases. At seventeen years of age while reading a book on mathematical physics which he found highly exciting, he exclaimed to his sister Maria: "It's wonderful! I am learning the propagation of all sorts of waves! It explains the motion of the planets!" When he got to the end of the book, he said to his sister: "Do you know it is written in Latin? I hadn't noticed."

As a child he built electric motors and drew plans for airplanes. At college his teacher asked Fermi to instruct him on Einstein's theory of relativity, which Fermi was pleased to do. In 1922 he received his degree of Doctor in Physics, *magna cum laude*. Two years later he was teaching at the University of Rome. I was a student at the University at the same time but little could I realize that a member of the faculty of that same university would one day receive the highest civilian decoration of my country, the Congressional Medal for Merit, proclaiming him "the first man in all the world to achieve nuclear chain reaction" in "the development of the greatest military weapon of all time, the atomic bomb."

At twenty-four years of age Fermi published a work entitled *On the Quantization of a Perfect Monatomic Gas,* and at the early age of twenty-seven he was named to the Royal Academy of Italy, an honor that usually falls to men twenty to forty years older. A predecessor in greatness in the portentous world of science, Sir Isaac Newton, had achieved a similar honor at the age of twenty-seven when he was elected the Lucasian Professor of Mathematics at Trinity. Never before had so young a man held this formidable chair.

In 1930 Fermi was invited to lecture at the University of Michigan on "The Quantum Theory of Radiation." He lectured also in Argentina and Brazil. In 1936 the scientific world learned that Enrico Fermi had been awarded the internationally famous Nobel Prize in Physics, the citation reading:

> To Professor Enrico Fermi of Rome for his identification of new radioactive elements produced by neutron bombardment and his discovery, made in connection with his work, of nuclear reactions effected by slow neutrons.

In 1939 he was appointed Professor of Physics at Columbia University in New York. His remarkable experiments in the laboratories of that famous institution inspired the head of the Department of Physics to urge the military authorities in Washington to listen to what this Italian scientist had to say about atomic energy, declaring that "there is no man more competent in this field of nuclear physics than Professor Fermi."

By this time Fermi's name had come to the admiring attention of perhaps the most illustrious name of the day in the scientific world, Albert Einstein, who, on August 2, 1939, wrote to President Roosevelt an urgent letter in which he said:

> Some recent work by E. Fermi and L. Szilard . . . leads me to expect that the element of uranium may be turned into a new and important source of energy in the immediate future . . . it may become possible to set up a nuclear chain reaction in a large mass of uranium, by which vast amounts of power and large quantities of new radium-like elements would be generated. . . . This new phenome-

non would also lead to construction of bombs, and it is conceivable
—though much less certain—that extremely powerful bombs of a new
type may thus be constructed.

On the twenty-fifth anniversary of the writing of this momentous
communication, the New York *Times* referred to it as a letter "that
changed the course of history." Upon its receipt President Roosevelt at once set up a Special Uranium Committee which immediately
made available to Professor Fermi four tons of graphite and fifty tons
of uranium for his experimentations. Uranium, as it occurs in nature,
consists of a mixture of two kinds of uranium isotopes—one called
U-235, the other U-238. The U-235 isotope is fissionable with relative ease, that is, its atoms can be split for the release of nuclear energy. In contrast, U-238 is fissionable only under special circumstance.

Fermi knew that when neutrons were emitted in the process of
fission, it was done with such rapidity that they could not be utilized
to produce fission in uranium, which was the one ideal medium for
producing a super-explosive bomb. He saw that the problem he faced,
therefore, was how to reduce the speed of neutrons and accordingly
prevent their neutralization in air before he could employ them as
splitters of uranium. It would not be enough to capture only a few of
the neutrons because a small number would not be enough to set off
chain reaction.

He had found that neutrons could be decelerated by having them
pass through paraffin and water, so he directed his efforts toward ascertaining the effect of fission of uranium in water, which acted as a
moderator. But it developed that water or any medium containing
hydrogen absorbed too much of the neutrons to make a chain reaction feasible. With his fellow scientist, Leo Szilard, Fermi now concluded that the neutrons could be slowed down and made effective
by producing them in uranium scattered between layers of graphite.
This arrangement was to be called a "pile" or "reactor."

In the latter part of 1941 the Uranium Project ordered by President Roosevelt was moved to the University of Chicago and placed
under the direction of Professor Arthur H. Compton. A narration of
the further experimentations, the extensive research, the days and
nights of toil and study needed to bring about the final testing of
Fermi's theory on chain reaction would be too long and embody too
much technical language to form part of this story. It is enough to

say that in order to achieve success, Fermi had to bring about a chain reaction whereby in a sequence of fissions in uranium or plutonium, neutrons would be released in one generation of fissions so as to cause splitting of a sufficient number of other atoms to propagate a chain of nuclear reactions. "In an atomic bomb the chain reaction *may race through eighty generations in less than one millionth of a second.*"* Fermi described the process in the following way:

> The fundamental point in fabricating a chain-reacting machine is of course to see to it that each fission produces a certain number of neutrons and some of these neutrons will again produce fission. If an original fission causes more than one subsequent fission then of course the reaction goes. If an original fission causes less than one subsequent fission then the reaction does not go.

From now on Fermi lived for but one purpose and that was to force his way through the whole universal planetary system of chemistry, physics, natural and physical science to get to the precise combinations, time coordination, mixtures, contacts, and fusions which would provoke the chain reaction, from which could be built the instrument that would bring to an end the war that was killing tens of thousands of people every day and inflicting torture on innocent millions. Pursuing this critical search he was in the laboratory at an early hour every day, and, with but brief intermissions for food would continue until late evening.

At last, on December 2, 1942, came the final testing which would determine if all the agonizing work had been fruitless or fruitful. The climacteric event was to unfold in the squash court of the University of Chicago under the West Stands of the Stagg Field Stadium where Fermi and his collaborators had assembled a graphite-uranium pile. Herbert Anderson described what happened:

> "When, on December 2, 1942, Enrico Fermi stood before that silent monster he was its acknowledged master. Whatever he commanded it obeyed. When he called for it to come alive and pour forth its neutrons, it responded with remarkable alacrity; and when at his command it quieted down again, it had become clear to all who watched that Fermi had indeed unlocked the door to the Atomic Age."†

* *Atoms and People*, by Ralph E. Lapp, Harper & Brothers, New York, 1956.
† Ibid.

Arthur Compton, the project leader, leaped to the telephone to call Dr. James Conant of the Office of Scientific Research and Development at Harvard, and exclaimed, employing guarded language which did not minimize the expression of his elation: "The Italian navigator has landed in the New World!"

No less enthusiastic at his end, Conant asked: "How were the natives?"

"Very friendly," Compton replied, all smiles.

What the Italian navigator Columbus had accomplished in the terrestrial world, what the Italian navigator Marconi had attained in the atmospheric world, the Italian navigator Fermi had now achieved in the nuclear world.

The atomic bomb was at last assured! Tremendous work—physical, scientific, experimental—still remained, but Fermi had opened the heavily locked door to the Atomic Age. The monumental project with the strange name of "Manhattan" now rose in the deserts of New Mexico and there Fermi, and an army of scientists, laboratory technicians, chemists, engineers, and mechanics, toiled continuously for the great triumph. Those who had unleashed the treacherous attack on Pearl Harbor and those who would enslave humanity would now face a force which all their evil and all their crafty machinations could not possibly overcome.

On July 16, 1945, the first incredibly devastating agency known as the atomic bomb rent the heavens with such a series of earthquake shocks as to provoke realistically the fear that the world was in the last throes of extinction:

> The whole country was lighted by a searching light with the intensity many times that of the midday sun. It was golden, purple, violet, gray, and blue. It lighted every peak, crevasse, and ridge of the nearby mountain range with a clarity and beauty that cannot be described. . . . Thirty seconds after the explosion came first the air blast, pressing hard against the people and things; to be followed almost immediately by the strong, sustained, awesome roar which warned of doomsday. (General Farrell's Report to War Department. *Atoms in the Family*, p. 23a).

It warned of doomsday, yes, but in its golden light shone also the promise of peace.

The bomb over Hiroshima fell on August 6, 1945, the bomb over

Nagasaki fell on August 9. On August 10 the Japanese announced they were ready to surrender. On August 14 they surrendered. And the bloodiest, cruelest war of all time ended.

General Douglas MacArthur and Admiral Chester Nimitz had planned an attack on the Japanese mainland for the fall of 1945, the second phase of the mammoth operation to be carried out in the early spring of 1946, with numerous armies engaged. The Japanese, in preparation for the attack, had massed two million troops and had honeycombed the country with pillboxes and land mines. It was the opinion of Secretary of War Henry L. Stimson that, had it not been for the intervention of the atom bomb, the planned operations could be expected "to cost over a million casualties to American forces alone."

Countless homes in America which would have worn wreaths of bereavement now rang with shouts of joy at the return of these soldiers who had escaped mangling, crippling, possible death, and all the horrors of jungle conflict with the intransigent Japanese soldiers. The atomic bomb not only saved America a million casualties but also held back the Communist hordes.

After the war Fermi continued with his experimentations, addressing himself to the adaptation of nuclear power to the ways of peace. Physically he was not strong, his frame was small. His body was not built to withstand the demands of sleepless and unceasing toil which he made on it. On November 28, 1954, when he was only fifty-three, the candle burned out, but the flame of his genius still burns in the watchtowers of America where the weapons of his forging now hold at bay all enemies of the peace he loved, and for which he offered his life in the laboratories of devotion and exhaustion.

20 "TAKE ME OUT TO THE BALL GAME!"

At the termination of World War II, General Mark W. Clark, who then became American High Commissioner in Austria, assigned me to the presidency in that country of a commission known as the United States Forcible Board of Repatriation. The work of this commission has nothing to do with the subject of this book so I will not dwell on it except to say that, with the authority vested in me by General Clark, I was enabled to save thousands of Russian refugees (who had sought asylum under the American flag) from forcible repatriation to Russia where they could have faced firing squads or Siberian exile. In the latter part of 1946 President Harry Truman appointed me to the International War Crimes Tribunal in Nuremberg where I presided over the Einsatzgruppen Trial, described by the Associated Press as "the biggest murder trial in history."

Returning to America in the summer of 1948 I had ample reason to be happy about the status of Italians, both in their home country and in the United States. The maniacal efforts of Mussolini to lead the Italian people against America had ended in a miserable fiasco. Moreover, once the Italians had rid themselves of his odious dictatorship, they fought side by side with the Allies in the liberation of their native land. The American soldiers of Italian descent had, as I have already shown, covered themselves with glory and were now once again fully enmeshed in the American way of life, bringing credit to themselves, to their heritage, and to the land whose flag they had defended on every sea and in every continent.

It was one of the happiest days of my life when I disembarked in New York from the ship that brought me back to America after five years overseas in the Navy and at Nuremberg. Several nephews and a brother jubilantly welcomed me and marched me off to one of the fine Italian restaurants in Manhattan where we celebrated. For dessert we motored out to the Yankee Stadium to watch the mighty Yanks perform. Here my yearning to see Americans of Italian lineage recognized for demonstrated merit obtained thrilling realization. Four of the redoubtable Bronx Bombers were full-blooded sons of parents hailing from the Italian peninsula: Joe DiMaggio, center fielder; Phil Rizzuto, shortstop; Yogi Berra, catcher; and Vic Raschi, pitcher.

No phase of life in America is more thoroughly and completely American than baseball. There is scarcely a man in our whole country who has not at some time desperately clutched a baseball bat or furiously fielded a baseball in some fiercely contested game of his youth. Whether it was on the green grass at the school picnic in the country, on a sandlot in the suburban areas, in the backwash streets of a big city, or on an improvised high school diamond, every American boy has felt the electric thrill of that hickory club smashing against the horsehide sphere and has sensed the exultation in his soul as he plunged toward first, second, or third base or even home plate, his very life depending on getting there before the ball banged into the glove of the enemy sentinel guarding the sack. As he grew up, the sandlot and the grassy field faded away before the onrush of the responsibilities of adult life, but the excitement of baseball always remained with the grown-up boy. Every one of the lads of yesteryear lives again the romance of the game through his championing of the home team in the professional pennant race.

Baseball is as American as the Plymouth Rock, the Rocky Mountains, and the cheeseburger. The President of the United States throws out the first ball of the season at the Nation's capital, and then when the World Series turns the nation into two good-natured opposing armies of rooting fans, everyone feels the excitement engendered by the American and National Leagues battling for global supremacy on the diamond. The daily box scores ride banner headlines in the newspapers. Queues form before radio and TV to capture every one of the thrills that punctuate the games as hot pepper enlivens *polenta*.

And so, this day my heart beat a delightful tune as I sat in the mammoth Yankee Stadium eating a savory hot dog, downing a Coca-Cola, and following with keen eye every movement of perhaps the greatest ballplayer of all time, certainly the greatest of his day—the incomparable, graceful, personable Joe DiMaggio. The son of Sicilian immigrants living in San Francisco, young DiMaggio as a teenager had no money for bus fare, so that three or four times a week he jogged two miles to the baseball field where he trained for that mastery which was later to enthrall every sport lover from the Atlantic to the Pacific. Just a moment!

A batter of the visiting team has hit a fast pitch and the ball, like a meteor, is in the sky shooting toward the center field fence. Joe DiMaggio wheels about and in a flash is heading for that fence. How will he see the ball which is at his back? But he heard the sound and he knew the batter's hitting pattern. His instincts are guiding him beneath the coming trajectory of the soaring missile. A sepulchral hush envelops the grandstands. Hot dogs, cigarettes, cigars, peanut bags become immobilized in mid-air as 100,000 eyes rivet the back of the lightning-speeding Joe DiMaggio. He is looking ahead at the fence against which he must not crash; a few more feet remain. His head turns over his left shoulder, up goes his gloved hand. And now the stands roar with the explosion of a mighty cataract as the ball smashes into that lofty leather pocket.

But that isn't the end of it. A runner who was on first base took off at the crack of the bat, certain that a home run was in the making and he did not intend stopping until he circled the bases. But he did not figure on DiMaggio's miraculous fielding and his rifle arm which has now released the ball like a Winchester pushing a bullet. When the runner sees the catch and tries to scurry back to first base, it is too late. The first baseman is waiting for him like one waiting for a streetcar. That makes the third out and Joe comes trotting in with his typical lope, the fans on their feet cheering like a shipload of passengers who have just been saved from a catastrophe at sea. The center fielder modestly touches his cap in recognition and disappears into the dugout.

Joe DiMaggio could turn apparent defeat into victory as spectacularly at bat as in the field. I watch him as he approaches home plate.

It is the last half of the ninth and the Yankees are one run behind. DiMaggio is second up. His predecessor has connected with the first ball for a clean single. A double will put him on third, a triple will score him and tie the game, and a home run will win the game. That, of course, is too much for me to hope for. I will not allow myself any daydreaming. I must not be selfish and expect too much. Nevertheless, despite my modest philosophizing, I am hoping, hoping—as Joe stands at the plate in his super-wide, flatfooted stance, calm as a palm tree, cool as a tall drink.

He does not nervously brandish and wiggle his bat as many batters do; he does not pull and yank at his cap, he does not tap away the imagined dirt between the cleats of his shoes. Tall, sinuous, untensed, he looks toward the mound almost with an air of curiosity as to just what may be the pitcher's intentions. The ball has left the pitcher's hand and I follow its whiteness on its lightning trajectory toward the catcher. What will DiMaggio do? He does not even lift his bat from his shoulder. "Ball one!" the umpire intones. I knew it was a bad one, I say to myself, but I wish I could be as much at ease as DiMaggio, who still calmly waits as a confident matador awaits the charge of the bull. The catcher drops his hand beneath his glove and signals to the pitcher. The pitcher nods and goes into an elaborate windup. The whole world stands still as the sphere hurtles toward the catcher's glove with the speed of an uninhibited jet.

One sees the flash of a swinging club, followed by a crack like the snapping of a planet's axis and a white rocket streaks for the left field fence. The pitcher drops his arms helplessly, so do the fielders, the ball carries on as if bearing a message to Mars. The roar of the bandstands would make a battery of 16-inch guns seem like the smack of bubblegum in comparison. The game is over! The Yanks have won again! The Yankee Clipper is circling the bases, he is accepting the eager hands awaiting him at the home plate.

The father and mother of this Yankee, this American ballplayer, this idol of the American public, came from Italy. Joe DiMaggio is thus the product of that race which Henry Cabot Lodge, Madison Grant, and Senator Heflin called the "inferior race," and which they said would never assimilate in America. Nevertheless, the Baseball Writers Association of America three times awarded to this immigrants' son the most coveted award of America's favorite game, *The Most Valuable Player*. His uniform glows in the American Baseball

Hall of Fame. He achieved records that never have been surpassed. In 1941 he hit consecutively in 56 games, for a batting average of .408, crossing the plate 56 times and batting in 55 runs in addition, achieving 15 home runs, 4 triples, and 16 doubles during this single batting streak. In twelve active seasons with the Yankees, he participated in nine World Series.

Even before DiMaggio got to the major leagues he was a phenomenon. Playing in the Pacific Coast League when only eighteen years old, he batted safely in 61 consecutive games and in 1934 batted .398 for a total of 270 base hits, 34 of them home runs. In his first year with the Yankees he hit 29 home runs with a batting average of .323, and only four weeks after donning the Yankee uniform he had achieved such popularity that police had to escort him out of the stadium because of the crush of fans who fought to honor him.

Joe DiMaggio was not the first Italian to electrify Yankee fans. Anthony Michael Lazzeri was enlivening the bases ten years before Jolting Joe. His sensational accomplishments were many, but for the period May 21–24, 1936, he broke four major league records and one American League mark. He began this incredible performance on May 21 when he blasted a single homer. On the next playing day, which was May 23, he smashed three home runs in a doubleheader. Then, on the following day, May 24, he slammed out three more home runs, two of them coming with the bases full, plus a triple to drive in 11 runs in a single game. It eclipsed the previous mark of 9 set by Jimmy Foxx. And his triple just missed being a fourth home run by one foot as it hit the bastion on the lower left field stands. Altogether his field day produced these records: Most home runs in four consecutive games, 7; most home runs in three consecutive games, 6; most home runs in two consecutive games, 5; two home runs with the bases full in one game (this last record has since been tied); most runs batted in one game, 11.

Then there was Frank Crosetti, affectionately called "The Crow" by his teammates, who shone as shortstop on the Yankee team all through the late twenties and the entire thirties. When he retired in favor of Phil Rizzuto, he became a Yankee coach. He holds the distinction of having picked up more World Series checks, as player and coach, than any man in the history of baseball.

As far back as 1911 an Italian was wearing a baseball uniform, but no one knew he was an Italian. He had begun his major league career with the Chicago White Sox, but was informed by the management that he would have to change his name, so the handsome Francesco Pezzola became Ping Bodie, center fielder (Babe Ruth, right fielder) of the Yankees.

But there is no mistaking the lineage of Joe DiMaggio, Filippo Rizzuto, Vincenzo Raschi, and Lorenzo Berra, as I admiringly watch them in 1948 and in later years. Rizzuto is short and, because of his diminutive size, baseball scouts from the Boston Red Sox, St. Louis Cardinals, and New York Giants turned him down when, in his early days, he tried out for the big leagues. One of the coaches said: "Get away, kid. This is a man's game. Go home and get yourself a shoeshine box!" As a child when Rizzuto played with other children in the schoolyard they called him "Shrimp," "Midget," and "Little Dago."

This little fellow, who was born in Brooklyn of Rose Agnotti and Filippo Rizzuto, swallowed his humiliation and persevered as he pleaded with team after team, repeating: "Give me a chance. That's all I ask." Finally in 1941 the Yankees offered him a contract. Frank Crosetti was soon to retire and the Yankee scout, "on a hunch," thought it might be a good idea to replace an Italian with an Italian. The coach's hunch paid off. In his first season Rizzuto's superb talents won for him the title of "The Rookie of the Year." Each year he phenomenalized more and more as he turned infield play into spectacular fireworks. Fans got to calling him "The Scooter."

In 1947 Bucky Harris, manager of the Yanks, said of Rizzuto: "He pulls a miracle out there each day. I wouldn't trade him for any shortstop in baseball." Participating in 815 plays, he erred only 25 times. In 1950 he surpassed all shortstops in the game by fielding successfully 753 times out of 767 chances. In addition, he made 169 hits, scored 110 times, stole 18 bases, and slammed out 7 triples and 22 doubles. Tommy Henrich, one of the Yankee stars, said of Rizzuto:

"This ball club can get along without me or anyone else—except one. We just keep praying that nothing happens to that little scamp at shortstop. He's the one we have to have every day."

In 1949 he received the Most Valuable Player Award.

Every position on a baseball nine is indispensable, but who can doubt that the central figure is the pitcher? Before every big game, speculation is rife as to which pitchers will be called to the mound.

This was particularly true in the opening game of the 1950 World Series when Casey Stengel selected Vic Raschi to hurl for the Yankees as they lined up against the Phillies at Shibe Park. Raschi was big physically and stood high intellectually. Like so many Italian parents, his father and mother had determined that their boy should have the best in book learning and so they sent him to William and Mary College where he obtained a Bachelor of Science degree. But Casey Stengel did not book him to pitch the first game of a World Series because of his high I.Q. Stengel just had to win that first game. The psychological advantage of a first game winner in a short series is incalculable. The baseball scout who had watched young Raschi when he was pitching for the Springfield High School murmured to himself, as he saw the ball shoot from the mound into the catcher's mitt, with the batter swinging at the empty air, "Gee Whiz, that kid's a Springfield rifle." Raschi proved the aptness of the sobriquet in that 1950 World Series opener.

The first thirteen Phils to face him swung helplessly, muttering: "You can't hit 'em, if you can't see 'em." For the next two innings the Phils huffed and puffed and finally got a man on second base but no farther. Then the Springfield Rifle mowed down the last eleven to come before him, and Casey Stengel chalked up a resplendent opening victory. In that same year Raschi had treated American League batters to the same windstorm. He holds the record for having retired thirty-two consecutive batters, the last twenty Cleveland Indian batters in one game and the first twelve batters in the next game. In 1953 his pitching percentage in games won and lost surpassed that of any other pitcher in the American League. He wore the Yankee uniform in five straight World Championships.

In one of the crucial games of the 1947 World Series the Yankees desperately needed a hit. Bucky Harris looked along the bench and motioned to a short, squatty player who had not yet found a regular berth on the team. This player, who has been compared to a fire hydrant, an oak stump, and a hitching post, jumped up like a jack-in-the-box and moved with surprising agility to the plate. On the third pitch he knocked the ball into the bleacher seats, becoming the first pinch-hitter in World Series history to hit a home run. In the 1957 World Series, this "runt," as Yogi Berra has been called, hit a home run with three men on base, this being only the fifth "Grand Slam" in World Series history. The second one was scored by another Italian, Tony Lazzeri, who, as we have recorded, gleefully smacked seven home runs in a span of four consecutive games.

In 1951 the Baseball Writers Association of America voted Yogi Berra the Most Valuable Player. They repeated this honor in 1954 and 1955. And for a reason. He was rated the best catcher in the game. Besides being a perfect technician in throwing, catching, running, and batting, he knew the batting averages, strong and weak points of every player who came to bat in front of him, and he thus guided the pitcher, telling him what kind of ball to deliver. He was as fast as lightning in whipping off his mask and going after a foul ball or a bunt. With a slight threatening move of his throwing arm, he held runners hugging first, second, or third, because they knew that he had the accuracy and power of a .45 Navy Colt when it came to catching a man off base. This phenomenon, who in nine full seasons as a Yank played in seven World Series, and whose full name is Lawrence Peter Berra, was born of Italian parents in the Hill District (also known as Dago Hill) of St. Louis.

He holds the record for a catcher in home runs with 313, in consecutive chances without an error, 950; in consecutive games without an error, 148. His alertness was always evident. In a game with the Red Sox, the batter hit a bunt that took a short hop. Berra sprang to it like a cat and tagged out the batter. He then wheeled about and tagged out the runner dashing in from third, thus completing a double play unassisted. Arthur Daley of the New York *Times* said of Berra that he "has a wider knowledge of all baseball personnel than any other man in the sport."

This Italian baseball player, who had to leave school at the ninth grade to go to work as a coal-yard laborer in order to help his family, managed the Yankees to the 1963 American League championship.*

Berra is not the only Italian who reached managerial heights in the major leagues. Cookie Lavagetto managed the Senators and the Twins, Phil Cavarretta managed the Chicago Cubs, Sam Mele is manager of the Twins.

Cookie Lavagetto, as Brooklyn Dodgers third baseman, made history in the 1947 World Series. Up to October 3, 1947, no one had

* Berra is known for his wit, some intentional and some accidental. At bat one day he struck out, after reaching for three wide pitches in succession. On his way to the dugout, he muttered: "How does a pitcher like that stay in the league?"

ever pitched a no-hitter in a World Series, but Yankee pitcher Floyd (Bill) Bevens is now standing on the threshold of such immortality, being only one single out away from that phenomenal achievement. It is the last of the ninth, he has retired two Dodger hitters; runners are dancing off first and second. The Yankees lead 2–1 but the Dodgers had scored their run without benefit of a hit, so Bevens still has his no-hitter.

Pistol Pete Reiser comes to the plate. He is a power hitter and Bevens walks him intentionally to pitch to Eddie Stanky, a no power hitter. Dodger Manager Burt Shotton peers down the bench and points at Harold (Cookie) Lavagetto. Lavagetto moves contemplatively to the plate. Bevens rears back and fires. Strike one! Bevens throws again, and Lavagetto's bat explodes. The Yankee right fielder runs frantically in the direction of the wall and as the ball bangs against it, two runners cross the plate. Bevens stands on the mound, stunned. Lavagetto is being thumped by teammates, and hysterical fans pour onto the field. Bevens has lost his no-hitter, and Lavagetto has won the ball game.

To name all the great ballplayers of Italian lineage would make this chapter out of all proportion to the rest of the book, but it is something for Italians in America to be proud of, that in a span of seventeen years, the most capable judges of baseball talent selected ten Italians as the Most Valuable Player of the Year in either the American or National League.

Not only have Italians shone in many dramatic games and plays, but it has even happened that two famous Italian players have been pitted one against the other. In the sixth game of the same 1947 World Series, where Lavagetto starred, the Dodgers were leading the Yankees by three runs when Joe DiMaggio came to bat with two men on. The roar of his bat turned the grandstands into a paroxysm of delirium as the ball screamed on a line headed for the bullpen in left field, a sure home run. The Yankee fans are on their feet cheering their heads off, as the phrase goes, but hold! Another Italian is in the game. Al Gionfriddo, center fielder for the Dodgers, is racing like a madman for the fence, he is literally outrunning the ball. The two men ahead of DiMaggio are already about to cross the plate. The ball has started on its lowering parabola to clear the fence, when, without slackening speed, Gionfriddo leaps into the air and plucks the tiny white sphere out of the atmosphere just as it is falling into the bull pen. The catch saved the Dodgers, and they won the game 8–6.

Gionfriddo's catch has been recorded as one of the most phenomenal and unforgettable in all baseball history. DiMaggio brooded over what happened. After the game he got into his automobile and drove aimlessly for hours. He later said to a friend: "I couldn't get it out of my mind. That was the ball game, if he hadn't caught it."

The DiMaggio parents produced two other fine ballplayers, Dominic and Vince. Dominic, a consistent .300 hitter, was an outstanding center fielder for the Boston Red Sox. Toward the end of his career he was joined on the Red Sox by another Italian who became the league's perennial All-Star third baseman—Frank Malzone. Vince DiMaggio also performed brilliantly as a center fielder and, like Joe, could hit the long ball, although not so consistently.

The fame of Yogi Berra is such that he overshadows another fine Italian catcher, Ernie Lombardi, who played for Cincinnati during their championship years. Lombardi, who was frequently on the National League All-Star Squad, was a powerhouse at bat and an excellent handler of pitchers.

Italians have starred in so many ball clubs and in so many positions that an All-Star Italian team could easily be made up of Italian players alone: Yogi Berra, catcher; Vic Raschi, pitcher; Dolf Camilli, first baseman; Tony Lazzeri, second baseman; Phil Rizzuto, shortstop; "Cookie" Lavagetto, third baseman; Joe DiMaggio, center fielder; Dom DiMaggio, left fielder; Carl Furillo, right fielder; Crosetti, utility infielder; Frank Malzone, Ernie Lombardi, pinch-hitters. What a team! To that team may be added the phenomenal youngster first baseman, Joe Pepitone, in spite of that "white shirt error" in the 1963 World Series.

In the 1949 World Series Dolf Camilli performed so spectacularly that in the vociferous victory parade through Brooklyn which followed, banners proclaimed: "Camilli for President!" He never made it.

Italians have also scintillated in the popular companion sport, football. In 1931 Joe Savoldi, All-American fullback, terrorized his opponents in every game as he tore down the field sidestepping, zigzagging, leaping into the air to ensnare forward passes aimed at enemy players, to score touchdown after touchdown. On October 25 Notre Dame played the University of Pittsburgh which that year had such a team of indestructible defensive granite that not a single point had been scored against them all season. What happened in that first half completely shattered the dreams of glory which had been held by every Pittsburgh rooter.

Two young Italians in Knute Rockne's backfield caused the major portion of the destruction of Pittsburgh: Frank Carideo, the quarterback, and (Jumping) Joe Savoldi, the fullback. Five times in that riotous, demoralizing first half Carideo, with scarcely a temporary halt, drove his backfield down the field in marches that ended in touchdowns. It was indeed an exciting day as I watched in the crisp sunshine of a perfect fall afternoon these two magnificent ballplayers in their faultless performances. On the first play of the second quarter Carideo handed the ball to Savoldi who smashed over the center of the Pitt line for the third touchdown. Carideo then kicked his third successive point-after-touchdown and Notre Dame led 21–0.

Savoldi was only warming up. Pitt now received and, from deep within its own territory, tried its first forward pass of the game. It never reached its intended receiver. Savoldi speared the ball and raced unmolested across the goal line. Carideo then kicked his fourth straight point and the game was already a 28–0 rout. The merciful Rockne now pulled out his regulars and sent in a second team.

All the great Italian football players did not, of course, perform their feats for Notre Dame. During the Ivy League struggles of 1963 and 1964 hardly a Sunday went by without the sporting pages carrying headlines about a player whose name is as Italian as pizza and chianti. The large black letters proclaimed: IACAVAZZI BLASTS TRIUMPH FOR PRINCETON: IACAVAZZI NATION'S LEADING SCORER: COSMO IACAVAZZI SCORES THREE TOUCHDOWNS. And more, much more.* On November 20, 1964,

---

* Reporting the Princeton-Yale game of November 13, 1964, the New York *Times* used superlatives in describing Iacavazzi's playing: "Capt. Cosmo Iacavazzi put on a one-man stampede in the second half, shedding tacklers like a Samson on touchdown runs of 39 and 47 yards." "Iacavazzi wrecked a Yale team that had the crowd of 60,173 in the Bowl in an uproar as it went 85 yards for a touchdown." "Iacavazzi took charge in the manner of the fullback that his coach calls the greatest ever to wear the orange and black." "Within 2 minutes and 27 seconds the mighty Cosmo twice electrified the big gathering with his tremendous driving power as he bolted away for touchdowns." "In one swoop, Iacavazzi went the

the National Football Foundation and Hall of Fame named Iacavazzi a 1964 Scholar-Athlete At-Large. Majoring in aeronautical engineering, Iacavazzi maintained a B-plus average. Will someone please page John Cabot Lodge!

Nor will football fans ever forget Navy's phenomenal Joe Bellino and Colgate's All-American fullback of the early thirties, Len Macaluso. Another All-American, Charley Trippi, was almost a legend at the University of Georgia and went on to become a professional football star with the Chicago Cardinals.

All-Americans of Italian lineage number many more than these well-known super stars. There were Mike Getto and Jess Quatse at Pittsburgh; Leo Nomellini at Minnesota; Ralph Guglielmo at Notre Dame; and numerous others.

In the professional ranks, Andy Robustelli stood out as the No. 1 bulwark in the great defensive line of the New York Giants. Vince Lombardi, coach of the famous Packers, is one of the shining lights in sports coachdom. When asked what he impressed mostly on his players he replied: "Winning isn't everything. It's the *only* thing."

In 1954, for the first time in history, the New York Football Writers conferred a silver plaque on a coach—Lou Little, who is the son of an Italian-American contractor whose surname was "Piccolo," but when naturalized someone translated *Piccolo* to *Little*. And thus Luigi Piccolo became Lou Little. In accepting the Columbia coaching job, he made the memorable remark: "I did not come to Columbia to fail." At the ceremony attending the conferring of the Football Writers' plaque, Columbia's President Grayson Kirk said: "No coach is any finer than Lou. He is not only a great coach. He is a great man." Little was succeeded by another famous Italian coach, Aldo (Buff) Donelli.

Still another great football coach was Jordan Olivar (Giordano Olivieri) of Yale.

Not everyone likes boxing. I have an aversion to physical violence in any form and I should therefore regard prizefights with horror. Somehow, however, I enjoy the truly great fistic encounters. This is

---

distance, breaking off tackle and throwing off one blue-clad player after another in a demonstration of sheer strength that made the Elis (Yale) seem almost like lilliputians."

probably due to the fact that I am a good average American, and what excites the nation excites me. When newspapers carry first page headlines on battles like those of Dempsey versus Firpo, Dempsey versus Tunney, and Marciano versus Walcott, I cannot assume a superior attitude and say I'm not interested. I certainly was interested in the great sports event of September 23, 1952, which Pittsburgh's sportswriter, Harry Keck, described as "the famous Dempsey-Firpo fight of two rounds stretched out over 13 rounds."

It was one of those fine September evenings with the atmosphere as clear and mellow as wine, sparkling in a fine breeze. As we sat in comfortable chairs on the turf of the Philadelphia mammoth Municipal Stadium, there rose only twenty-five feet away a square platform bathed in silvery light, the surrounding ropes gleaming under the golden stars. We were to witness what had been advertised as the fight of the century. All prizefight promoters like to regard their productions as history-making. This one was to be actually that—in the pugilistic world. Rocky Marciano, who had not been defeated in forty-three bouts, was challenging world champion Jersey Joe Walcott, greatly admired for his pluck, skill, and endurance.

And now the young nimble Italian boy from Brockton, Massachusetts, who has earned the right to fight the champion by knocking out thirty-seven antagonists and has never been floored once, pluckily dances toward the champion. In several startling moments he learns this fight will be different. The venerable Walcott, who packs dynamite in his right fist, lunges, and the redoubtable Marciano finds himself, in the very first round, leveled out on the canvas. He allows himself several seconds to regain his breath and leaps to his feet only to find himself on the receiving end of continuing riveting hammer blows. Of course, he is not taking this punishment lying down or standing up. He fires back punch for punch, but even so, at the end of the twelfth round, all three ring officials are scoring Walcott ahead on number of rounds won.

But then that thirteenth—

Marciano advances to the center of the ring, his face bleeding from numerous cuts, the top of his head red from an accidental bumping of heads with his adversary in the sixth round. In the eleventh round he was badly hurt by a Walcott right under his heart, followed by volleys of furious lefts and rights to the head, face, and jaw. With my fellow 39,999 spectators I cannot believe that Marciano will win the championship this night.

Suddenly, with the spring of a jungle animal, Marciano rushes the champion. He connects with a wild left and a right that hurl Walcott against the ropes, which bounce him back into the ring. Walcott parries a left to his head and blocks a Marciano left to his body. Then for an instant he seems to sway slightly and his left arm and shoulder lower slightly. An exposed jaw gleams in the light of the stars. A right that does not seem to travel more than a foot shoots out like a hydraulic piston. Walcott sinks back against the ropes, then slides headfirst to the canvas. Rocky Marciano is the new heavyweight champion of the world.

He ranks along with the few great champions of modern times: Joe Louis, Jack Dempsey, Jess Willard, Jack Johnson. Since his departure from the scene the heavyweight championship has fallen into disrepute, but the memory of Rocky Marciano lingers on in the minds of the true boxing fans—he stood for something.

Another Italian heavyweight champion was Primo Carnera who battled the title away from Sharkey with a sixth-round knockout on June 29, 1933. The Italian, Tony Canzoneri, achieved the championship in three different divisions: featherweight, junior lightweight, and lightweight. Giuseppe Antonio Bernardinelli, known as Joey Maxim, also held the light-heavyweight championship. At various times the middleweight championship belt was worn by three different Italians: Jake La Motta, Johnny Wilson, and Rocco Barbella who fought under the popular name of Rocky Graziano.

The two brothers, Sam and Vince Lazzaro, fighting under the names of Joe and Vince Dundee, were respectively welterweight and middleweight champions. Peter Gulotto, fighting as Pete Herman, was twice the bantamweight champion. Melio Bettina and Willie Pastrano have been light-heavyweight champions. Carmen Basilio has been both welterweight and middleweight champion.

Other champions have been Battling Battalino, featherweight; Tony DeMarco and Young Corbett, welterweight; Willie Pep (Papaleo), featherweight; Frankie Genaro and Fidel La Barba, Olympic and world flyweight; Harry Jeffra, both bantamweight and featherweight titleholder; Bushy Graham and Petey Scalzo, featherweight.

The only prizefighter who ever knocked out Jack Dempsey was Andrea Chiariglione, although it is understandable why sportswriters preferred to refer to him simply as Jim Flynn.

I am not a golf player, but I respect and admire perfection in any wholesome endeavor. In 1936 I thrilled, with sports fans everywhere, to one of the greatest feats in golfing history. It happened at the famous Masters Tournament. Eugene Saraceni, whose professional name is Gene Sarazen, approached the par-5 fifteenth hole in the last round of the Masters, three strokes behind the leader, Craig Wood. His drive went off the tee, whistling 250 yards straight down the middle of the fairway. When he asked his caddie what score he'd have to finish with to beat Wood, the boy acted as if he had asked what Sarazen would have to do to get to the moon. "Why," he replied, "you'll have to shoot four birdies one right after the other." The great Walter Hagen, who was playing along with Sarazen, laughed.

The path that Sarazen's ball would have to follow toward the fifteenth green was guarded by a lake. His lie was not too clean in the tufted grass. Sarazen chewed grass as he pondered and then elected to play a No. 4 wood instead of the more conventional spoon. It was the wisest decision of his golfing life.

The shot that followed has been called the most dramatic single shot ever struck in a major tournament. As clubhead met ball, the ball screamed on a rising line toward the flagstick, then settled into a low trajectory no more than thirty feet in the air. It was dead on line with the pin. It took one big bounce as it hit the close-clipped grass blades of the green, then rolled straight into the cup for a double-eagle. Twenty years later golfers still talked about Sarazen's double-eagle shot in the '35 Masters.

In just one shot Sarazen had caught Wood. He parred his way into the clubhouse to discover he had finished in a dead heat for top money in the tournament. The next day, in a 36-hole play-off he trounced Wood to win the tournament, hands down.

This great golfer, who played a championship game for four decades, invented the modern sand iron, and in 1932, won the British Open, with considerable help from that device.

While Sarazen was by far the greatest of the Italian golf luminaries, there were others—Johnny Revolta, P.G.A. winner, Vic Ghezzi who triumphed in both P.G.A. and U. S. Amateur, and Tony Manero, winner of the U. S. Open. Golfdom also held in high esteem the seven Turnesa brothers. Of the seven, Willie Turnesa won the U. S. Amateur in 1938 and 1948 as well as the much coveted British Open. His brother Jim won the U. S. Amateur once as well as the P.G.A.

An interesting story is told about the golf-mad Turnesa brothers, who all learned the game at a country club where their father worked as a greenkeeper. In 1926, when it seemed that young Joe Turnesa might win the U. S. Open Championship, a member of the club, who had been listening to the game on the radio, rushed out excitedly to the elderly Mr. Turnesa, who was, at the moment, on his hands and knees on a green, picking crab grass with the concentration of a brain surgeon in the operating room.

"Mr. Turnesa!" the member shouted. "Joe's winning the National Open!"

Mr. Turnesa glanced curiously at him, turned back to the crab grass, and replied: "Why shouldn't he? He never did anything all his life but play golf."

Ken Venturi became the United States Open Golf Champion in June 1964. Commenting on his brilliant victory, Venturi, with characteristic Latin ebullience, said: "This may sound funny, and I hope it will be taken in the right way, but I've tasted the bitterness of defeat, now I'm going to enjoy success."

It is generally conceded by fans and sportswriters alike that until Angelo Enrico (Hank) Luisetti made his dazzling appearance upon the courts of America, basketball had been without a hero. Luisetti sensationalized basketball by making his baskets with one-handed shots. When he arrived at New York's Madison Square Garden in December 1936, with his Stanford team, Nat Holman, the famous coach of CCNY exclaimed: "Nobody can tell me shooting with one hand is sound basketball. They'll never get me to teach it to my boys."

That night Luisetti furiously passed and ran, shot baskets with both right hand and left, *though never the two together*. Stanford broke the LIU 43-game winning streak 45–31, Luisetti scoring one-third of Stanford's points. He was an All-American three times and was twice college-player-of-the-year.

Another great basketball player was Tony Lavelli of Yale.

The first two legendary immortals of automobile racing were Barney Oldfield and Ralph DePalma. During the period of 1900 to 1914 they both made the nation's headlines, driving the high, awkward wooden-wheeled cars of that dawning era in automotive speed history. In them the two men barnstormed the country, dazzling racetrack crowds everywhere. Of the two, the Italian Ralph DePalma was the only one to win America's most celebrated test of drivers' nerves: the annual 500-mile Memorial Day race at the colorful Indianapolis Motor Speedway. That was in 1915 when he averaged 89.84 mph for the 500-mile grind.

The influence of Ralph DePalma did not disappear from the Indianapolis scene along with his physical presence. In 1925 his nephew, Peter De Paolo, won the Indianapolis classic at an average speed of 101.13 mph for the 500 miles. Seven years passed before that record was surpassed.

Even people who do not follow the sport of horse racing and who have never so much as placed a two-dollar bet have heard the name of Eddie Arcaro, who reigned as king of the turf for so long that his name became a legend in his own time. By the end of 1958 Eddie Arcaro topped all jockeys in money-earning—his mounts had won a total of twenty-four million, eight hundred and ninety dollars. In the long history of American horse racing no one had ever won as much money with a single horse as he won with the great *Citation*— six hundred and forty-five thousand, one hundred and forty-five dollars. Arcaro, along with Earl Sande and George Woolf, was the first jockey elected to the newly-created Hall of Fame in 1955. His all-around success in the world of horse racing has never been equaled.

Perhaps it is because of the surface similarity of the popular Italian game called *bocci* to the American game of bowling that so many of the nation's best bowlers have been Italians. Andy Varipapa and Enrico (Hank) Marino and Frank Santore are probably the three enjoying the greatest national reputations, but there are others.

The biggest event of the year among topflight bowlers is the annual tournament of the American Bowling Congress. Past champions in the All-Events category of ABC tournaments include Barney Spinella in 1927, Frank Santore in 1953, and Al Faragalli in 1958. In

ABC singles competition, Santore won it all in that same year of 1953 and the following year the championship went to Tony Sparando.

I am not a bridge player as I am not a golfer, but here again I have a healthy admiration for those who excel in a contest of skill and wit. One of my best friends, General Alfred M. Gruenther, with whom I served in the Fifth Army, is recognized as one of the ablest strategists in bridge as he was equally rated among the best military strategists in World War II. The Italians seem to be particularly apt in bridge. Italy won the World Bridge Olympiad in May 1964, when it defeated the United States in a sixty-deal final match by a score of 158 to 112. The Olympiad title is symbolic of bridge supremacy throughout the world, with twenty-nine nations competing.

In annexing the Olympiad crown, the Italians captured their seventh world championship title, having dominated international bridge for the last decade. Italy has also won six times the Bermuda Bowl, another symbol of world bridge supremacy.

In billiards it is also an Italian who holds the title. Willie Mosconi has been the world's pocket billiards champion for more years than his many, frustrated challengers care to remember.

It would be impossible in a book of this size to cover every subject in which Italians have made notable contributions to America's greatness, a greatness which stands unrivaled. One can only hope to suggest by illustration what some of those contributions have been. Even the illustrations, however, cannot, because of space limitations, be numerous. The mention, therefore, of renowned individuals in any particular field of achievement is not to be interpreted as meaning there are not also other eminent persons in that same class of endeavor. I thus trust I will be forgiven by the admirers and friends of distinguished individuals whose names will not appear in this book simply because of lack of pages.

Of all the enterprises to which man has ambitiously dedicated himself in this most amazing age of all ages, none fires the imagination more than the Moon Project. In May 1961 President Kennedy declared we would have an American team on the moon this decade. At Merritt Island, Florida, the United States is building the world's first spaceport which, by 1966, will have developed launching sites from which astronauts may journey to the moon and planets.

At this nerve center of the astronomical universe we find Lieutenant Colonel Rocco Anthony Petrone, responsible for the planning, scheduling, and activation of NASA's launching facilities. Born of immigrant parents from the province of Potenza, Colonel Petrone was only twenty-five years of age when he was named project officer for the Redstone missile. Recalling that milestone in the evolution of rocketry, Colonel Petrone said:

> "Its liftoff moved this country into heavy rocketry. The Redstone and the Jupiter were forerunners of Saturn, at present the world's most powerful known rocket. In just eleven years, we have gone from the seventy-foot-tall Redstone, with 75,000 pounds of thrust at liftoff, to the 164-foot Saturn I, which last January generated one and a half million pounds of thrust—twenty times that of the Redstone, and boosted a record nineteen tons into orbit.
>
> "We are well on our way to Saturn V, the moon rocket, which will be a hundred times more powerful than that first Redstone. We used to come down to the Cape and set up a tent city for each launch. We ate, slept, and lived missiles."

When President Kennedy and Vice-President Johnson visited the Space Center in 1962 it was Colonel Petrone who gave the briefing on the Saturn rocket for these illustrious world figures.

Colonel Petrone is very enthusiastic about space travel and said recently: "I think the day will come when space travel will be so routine that astronomers, geologists, and other experts will make trips to the moon and beyond. And when that day comes, I'd like to be first in line."*

In the modern musical world the first Italian name that flashes before us is, naturally, Arturo Toscanini. Physically, Toscanini was a short man, but his magnetic personality filled whatever room, hall, auditorium, train, or ship in which he appeared. Never before or since has an orchestra conductor evoked such tumultuous, spontaneous admiration. This was a great tribute to Toscanini, of course, but it was also a manifestation of virtue in those who applauded and cheered because, through their emotional expression, they revealed appreciation of the human spirit in all its wondrous forms of harmony and concord. Toscanini symbolized what Mazzini said of music: it is "the harmonious voice of creation; an echo of the invisible world; one note of the divine concord which the entire universe is destined one day to sound."

* *Catholic Digest*, July 1964.

I attended Toscanini's final concert at Carnegie Hall with the New York Philharmonic in April 1936, when guards at the doors fought to keep out the crowds trying to push, buy, or beg their way into standing room privileges. When the maestro appeared, the vast audience rose en masse, the storm of applause seeming to shake the very foundations of the building. Not waiting until it should cease, Toscanini turned to the orchestra and lifted his baton. The miracle of that baton at once inundated and flowed over us and we felt ourselves hushed into the muteness of one viewing the vastness of the universe from a spaceship. Olin Downes, music critic of the New York *Times,* described the maestro as "pouring a veritable flood of energy from his eyes, his body, his fingers into an orchestra that shakes and reverberates to his commands, and proceeds from climax to climax of tonal splendor."

This was to have been Toscanini's final appearance in America. He was then sixty-nine years old, but he was to come back to lead the Symphony Orchestra to musical triumphs never attained by any other NBC group. He wielded his masterful baton until eighty-four. Ever since Toscanini had conducted at the Metropolitan Opera House, where he directed over one hundred operas without score, he was always accepted as a truly great conductor. By the time, however, that he climbed to the podium of the New York Philharmonic he was recognized as *the* conductor, with no others even within challenging distance. Until Toscanini appeared upon the American scene it was fashionable for conductors to "interpret," and, as a result, a Beethoven symphony might be bent almost wholly out of the composer's original concept. Toscanini refused to brook such tampering. He said, and his greatness proved it, that the task of a conductor was to bring to full flower the composer's intentions.

To attain this objective Toscanini's baton became a scepter. At rehearsals he stormed at his players, blasted them with ridicule, stamped off the stage and refused to return until assured that the piccolo player had achieved just the right meticulously accurate tone of a single note. Baton after baton splintered under his rage when his ear detected the slightest deviation from absolute accuracy. If a player entered his part a thousandth of a second late, the maestro would seize with both hands the clock before him, hurl it to the floor, and trample it to fragments as a release for the pent-up fury at such musical incompetence. In time the management learned to buy cheap clocks for the practice sessions.

It was a rare privilege for an outsider to be allowed in the rehearsal hall. I once attained this privilege through my acquaintance with Walter Toscanini, the maestro's son. This acquaintanceship later developed into the warmest and closest friendship. At this rehearsal something went wrong. I never knew what it could have been because the music pouring from the orchestra into my soul had lifted me into a heaven of mute and ecstatic serenity when suddenly Toscanini lifted the enormous and heavy folio of the score before him, ripped it apart and tore it to pieces.

As a result of this despotic insistence on perfection from his men, Toscanini's public concerts, which he always conducted without score, were perfect. His memory was simply staggering. He knew every note, pause, and nuance printed on the sheets before every player and every instrument. With his baton, then, which became a magic wand, he wove out of the air the lavish, lustrous tapestry of sound which caused people sitting in their homes at the radio and, later, before the television set, to leap to their feet, applauding. Toscanini's worshiping of perfection manifested itself in everything he attempted. Walter told me that when his father decided to learn English he first mastered the grammar and then selected for his lessons Shakespeare's sonnets.

Perfection! It was Toscanini's shibboleth. The music had to be exactly right. One does not look for a flaw in a Raphael painting, a Michelangelo statue, a rose or the North Star. Toscanini sought flawlessness in music and in human character as well.

The people applauded him and loved him for his courage. While directing at La Scala in Milan during Mussolini's regime, a Fascist chieftain directed him to play the Fascist hymn, "Giovinezza." Toscanini turned on him with scorn:

"I will not allow my orchestra to play 'Giovinezza.' The Scala is not a beer garden or Fascist propaganda territory. If you want to play it you can play it to your heart's content in the square outside the opera house or in the Galleria nearby. But not here!"

He defied Hitler's adherents. For years he had been conducting Wagnerian concerts at the Bayreuth festivals, but he refused even to enter Germany during the Nazi regime. The maestro also avoided the Mozart festivals at Salzburg when Austria went Nazi.

In his personal relationships Toscanini could almost purr with gentleness and sweetness. At the age of eighty-three he toured the country with his NBC Symphony Orchestra. When he came to Pittsburgh I was invited to dine with him and several others after the concert. It was my good fortune to sit next to him at his table at the Hotel Schenley. He was amiable, cheerful, even gay. We ate chicken and drank champagne and he regaled us with reminiscences. I particularly recall one. He told of having been invited to the home of a very wealthy man who had befriended some members of his orchestra. He recalled: "Everything was wonderful: the food was excellent, the wine superb, but my host insisted on talking music, of which he knew nothing. He was *ignorante*, in fact, *un imbecile*. Finally I could stand it no longer and I said to him: 'I thank you for your hospitality. You are a gentleman in every way, and for this, I take off my hat to you, but, for your knowledge of music, I put on eight hats!' " As he related this, he physically demonstrated his pulling off and jamming on hats, while everyone present howled with laughter.

Toscanini is now legendary and the legend of his supreme achievements in music will become even more luminous with the passing years, but there were and there are many other Italian musicians whose talents strike a full-toned chord on the harp of enduring fame. Alfredo Antonini, a composer in his own right, conducted brilliantly the Columbia Symphony Orchestra for many seasons. Dino Bigalli was conductor of the famous Chicago Grand Opera Company, as well as the Chicago Civic Opera Company. Victor de Sabata, one of the extraordinarily great conductors of the era, came to America from the La Scala in 1948 and electrified his audiences as he conducted the Pittsburgh Symphony Orchestra and other orchestras in the land.

As to Italian singers, their number and quality seem without limit. The Metropolitan Opera House has constantly echoed to famous Italian voices. In addition to those already mentioned in another chapter, one can name Rosa and Carmela Ponselle, Tito Schipa, Nino Martini, Dusolina Giannini, Licia Albanese, Ferruccio Tagliavini, Giuseppe di Stefano, Mario del Monaco, Cesare Siepi, Giulietta Simionato, Ettore Bastianini, Renata Tebaldi, Giorgio Tozzi, and Tito Gobbi. The great basso Ezio Pinza, after a distinguished career at the Metropolitan, became a matinee idol in the Broadway musical *South*

Pacific. And there is Ruggiero Ricci who makes his violin sing so divinely that one begins to understand what Paganini must have been like.

Gian Carlo Menotti, among modern opera composers, stands very high and is regarded by many as the regenerator of the nineteenth-century operatic tradition. He won Pulitzer prizes for his *The Saint of Bleecker Street* and *The Consul*. His operas also include *The Old Maid and the Thief, The Island God, The Telephone, The Medium, The Last Savage*, and his television perennial at Christmas time, *Amahl and the Night Visitors*. In addition to composing operas, Menotti writes plays.

Walter Piston, whose name veils his Italian ancestry, is Professor Emeritus of Music at Harvard University, and won a Pulitzer Prize in 1948 for his Symphony No. 3.

The complete assimilability of Italians in America cannot be better demonstrated than by the popular songs they have composed. What could be more completely American than "Wagon Wheels," "You Made Me Love You," "Then You've Never Been Blue," "Rain," "The Umbrella Man," "Row, Row, Row," "Deep Purple"? They all came from creative brains thumped out on the piano of creation by children of Italian immigrants.

The composer, Norman Dello Joio, well known as the commentator on broadcasts of the Metropolitan Opera, won, in 1957, the Pulitzer Prize for his distinguished creative work. Nicola Orlando Berardinelli, who has been conductor of four different opera companies and for a period of years was the leading baritone of the Denver opera company, is best known as a gifted composer, his creations listing "Ave Maria" and "My Rosary," among many others.

Guy Lombardo, band leader, is referred to in the entertainment world as the man who produces "the sweetest music this side of Heaven." Other well-known band leaders are Louis Prima, Ted Fio Rito, Joe Venuti, Frankie Carle, and Carmen Cavallero. Henry Mancini is a popular music composer who has won three Academy awards for songs he has written for motion pictures. Other Italian names in the entertainment world are Don Ameche, Frankie Laine, Dean Martin, Jerry Colonna, Anthony Franciosa, Connie Francis (born Constance Franconero), Joni James, Tony Arden, Tony Bennett, Vic Damone.

With the exception of Bing Crosby, no other American singer of live ballads has ever won such popular approval, and remained so durable, as Frank Sinatra. If a challenger existed, without doubt it would be Perry Como who refers to himself jokingly as "a retired Italian barber."

Less well known, but highly respected in the theatrical world, is Alfred Capurro Drake—singer and actor, who has starred in numerous Broadway musical comedies, earning high praise for his roles in *Kiss Me Kate* and *Kismet.*

The family name of Dennis James, actor and television personality, is Demisposa. Julius LaRosa achieved national fame as a popular singer with Arthur Godfrey. And of Jimmy Durante, singer, composer, and rollicking raconteur, it is enough to say that there never was a Jimmy Durante before and there never will be one again.

In the world of education one of the best-known Italians in America is Angelo Patri. For decades his name appeared in newspapers throughout the country as he imparted, in his widely syndicated column, advice and counsel to parents on what is the most important subject in any family, namely, how to raise children properly. He also wrote numerous books on child psychology. He was the first Italian-born educator to become a school principal in the United States.

The most famous Italian educator of modern times was Dr. Maria Montessori who dedicated herself to the education of defective children. She attained such remarkable success with her method, which has become known as the Montessori System, that she took up education of normal children, convinced that if backward children could be educated to overtake normal children, even more startling results could be attained with normal children. She proved her thesis. The heart of her method of instruction is that children should be allowed greater freedom in the pursuit of their studies, thereby gaining self-confidence. She said that children in a schoolroom should not be immobile like "rows of butterflies transfixed with a pin." When she visited America in 1913 she was hailed as a prophet of pedagogy, and after a triumphal tour of the East was feted at the White House.

Mario E. Cosenza, the first American of Italian birth to become dean of an American college—Brooklyn—launched the campaign to teach Italian language in the high schools and colleges of the nation. Joseph V. Calabrese, a former member of the Colorado Legislature, ranks high among the country's educators. He founded a school for exceptional children, then became President and Director of the National Association for Retarded Children. Peter Sammartino, President of Farleigh Dickinson University in Rutherford, New Jersey, was a member of the late President Kennedy's Commission on Higher Education and is the author of many educational texts. Dr. Neal V. Musmanno is Pennsylvania deputy Superintendent of Public Instruction. Dino Bigongiari, before his retirement, was a member of the Columbia University Faculty for more than half a century. Then there are Professors Andrew J. Chiappe, and Mario G. Salvadori of Columbia; Dr. John T. Rettaliata, President of the Illinois Institute of Technology, Dr. Edward J. Mortola, President of Pace College; Dr. Pasquale Porcelli, Professor of Mathematics at Indiana University and cited as one of the ten top research scientists in the United States; Dr. Roy Joseph Deferrari, who at the age of twenty-five was instructor in Latin and Greek at Princeton; Dr. Frederick D. Rossini, Dean of the College of Science of the University of Notre Dame; Antonio Ciocco, Professor of Biostatistics, University of Pittsburgh; Giuseppe Calabrese, Professor of Electrical Engineering, New York University; F. J. Bruno, Professor of Applied Sociology at Washington University; Andrew Bongiorno, Professor of English at Oberlin, Philip Romiti, Dean of the Law School of De Paul University, all of whom are guiding American students to the upperlands of intellectual solution of the problems facing the human race today. It has been said of Mario Pei, Professor of Romance Philology at Columbia University, that no one has done more to tear down the Tower of Babel than he. His command of numerous languages led George Bernard Shaw to say: "Professor Pei's prodigious memory and knowledge remind me of Isaac Newton."

Peter Riccio, Professor of Humanities at the Columbia University, where he has spent much of his scholarly lifetime, has exerted a profound influence on Italian students in America. He is now Director of the Casa Italiana, a unique and quiet cove of culture in the busy academic world. Dr. Grayson Kirk, President of Columbia, said that the Casa Italiana "exists to serve not only the University but the community as well. This city and this country owe so much to the people who have come here from the shores of Italy. We owe an unpayable debt to the cradle of culture which Italy has been for so many centuries, for so many people, in so many countries."

In the world of authorship, Italian writers have written high on the scroll of contemporary literature. Sergio Pacifici, Professor at the City University of New York, said recently: "Seldom before in modern times has the Italian literary landscape been as lush and productive as now."* Grazia Deledda of Sardinia won the Nobel Prize for Literature in 1926 for her novels *Elias Portolu* and *The Mother*. Giosuè Carducci, generally regarded as the national poet of modern Italy, had received the award in 1906. In 1959 it was conferred on Salvatore Quasimodo.

Luigi Pirandello was another Sicilian genius to win the Nobel Prize. His fame as master of the short story and dramatic prose will probably never fade away. Italian letters of today do not lack figures whose literary silhouettes are attracting popular enthusiasm. Ignazio Silone is a name known wherever books are read. *The Leopard* by Giuseppe di Lampedusa was an enormous success. Carlo Levi —*Christ Stopped at Eboli*—is a writer to be reckoned with. There are numerous other Italian writers who have received long and enduring welcome from book lovers in the United States. In spite of his quixotic adventures in war and peace, Gabriele d'Annunzio enjoyed an enormous audience in America. Giovanni Verga, a contemporary of d'Annunzio, is regarded by many as the best Italian writer since Manzoni.

The limited scope of this book will allow me only to enumerate a few of the successful Italian authors of today: Italo Calvino, Alberto Moravia, Mario Soldati, Carlo Cassola, Elsa Morante, Giuseppe Marotta, Elio Vittorini, Vasco Pratolini, Franco Fortini, Eugenio Montale, Giuseppe Ungaretti, Giorgio Bassani, Pier Paolo Pasolini, Carlo Emilio Gadda.

Giovanni Guareschi has delighted half the world with his continuing story, *The Little World of Don Camillo*, of the battles between an imaginary priest and an imaginary Communist mayor of an imaginary Italian town.

Among the literary titans of Italy, Benedetto Croce looms as one of the greatest humanist philosophic writers of all time. The products of his pen would crowd any large-sized bookcase. In addition to authoring a score of books, he produced the critical journal *La Critica*, in which for forty-one years he reviewed Italian and foreign litera-

* *Saturday Review*, February 11, 1961.

ture. He led the intellectual forces of the nation against the civil encroachments of Mussolini and, after the Duce's dethronement, was the foremost architect in building the new government of Italy. For a short period during the war I maintained military quarters in his villa in Sorrento because a British brigadier general, with little knowledge of the political realities of Italy, and with no knowledge at all of philosophical principles, insisted on evicting Croce from his villa to make room for an officers' club. Although Croce philosophically decried violence, he pragmatically cheered me when I stood at the door of his villa, with a Navy .45 Colt at my hip, and bade the British brigadier to be gone!

Croce well summed up his outlook on life when he said in 1952:

"I am often asked if I believe that the future belongs to Freedom. My answer is that freedom has no need of the future—it already possesses eternity."

A number of Italian writers in America have eloquently and even movingly described the life of Italian immigrants in America. We have already spoken of Pascal D'Angelo. Another Italian who toiled manually (bricklayer) and turned his experiences and observations into telling prose was Pietro DiDonato with his book *Christ in Concrete*, which was made into a film.

Jerry Mangone in his *Mount Allegro* captivates the reader with his story of Sicilian immigrants. John Fante wrote well in his book *Wait Until Spring, Bandini* on Italian immigrants who can obtain only seasonal employment and who suffer in dire poverty during the slack periods.

In practically every large metropolitan newspaper one sees by-lines with Italian names. The list would be too long for inclusion here but special mention should be made of Joseph Durso, writer and editor for the New York *Times*, television newscaster and assistant professor of journalism in the Columbia University graduate school. One of Detroit's best-known newspapermen is Frank Angelo, Managing Editor of the Detroit *Free Press*. And then there is Giuseppe Prezzolini, author, journalist, and professor emeritus of Columbia University, now living in Italy and commenting on the Italian scene.

Since the end of World War II, Italian studies have been given special attention in this country. Among the critics who regularly comment on Italian cultural events are such well-known persons as

Leslie Fiedler, R. W. B. Lewis, and Irving Howe. Several Americans have made their mark as outstanding teachers and scholars of Italian letters: Ernest H. Wilkins, the dean of Petrarch scholars in the world, Charles S. Singleton, Joseph Mazzeo, and Francis Ferguson, masterful *Dantisti* and prolific authors, as well as the younger John Freccero and Aldo S. Bernardo. Three reviews of Italian studies are also published at regular intervals: *Italica* (the scholarly bulletin of the American Association of Teachers of Italian), ably edited by Joseph G. Fucilla; *Italian Quarterly*, published at the University of California; and the lively *Cesare Barbieri Courier*, edited by Professor Michael R. Campo of Trinity College.

Considering the priceless heritage in sculpture every Italian can boast of, almost as his own property, it would be most extraordinary if Italian artists in America did not carve and cast figures worthy of that heritage. Among the large number who uphold the Italian artistic tradition, we can only list a few, as, for instance, Anthony De Francisci, who created the Independence Memorial at Union Square in New York and the embellishments of the façade of the United States Post Office at the nation's capital. Since 1924 he has been an instructor for young sculptors at Columbia College and the Beaux Arts Institute of Design. He designed, as already stated, the American silver dollar of 1921, and among the many medals and insignia he created for the Army and Navy was the familiar veterans' button of World War II.

Ralph J. Menconi, sculptor of Pleasantville, New York, designed the John F. Kennedy Memorial Medal. In 1964 he designed the President Johnson Medal, which has been struck in platinum, silver, and bronze. In all, he has produced more than three hundred medallion portraits, including those of fourteen Presidents and many signers of the Declaration of Independence.

America is populated with magnificent monuments fashioned into being by Italian sculptors. It is only natural that most of the statuary devoted to the discovery of America was carved by Italian chisels, two of the outstanding ones being the Columbus Monument in Columbus Circle, New York City, by Gaetano Russo, and the magnificent Columbus statuary by Frank Vittor in Schenley Park, Pittsburgh. There are Columbus statues also in Philadelphia, Boston, St. Louis, Chicago, Washington, Baltimore, New Haven, Scranton,

Pueblo (Colorado), Detroit, Newark, Hoboken, Richmond, St. Paul, Akron, Westerly (Rhode Island).

The superb monuments to the Battleship *Maine* and the Firemen's Memorial, both in New York, are the work of Attilio Piccirilli, assisted by his five artist brothers. It was this group of talented brothers who, working from a plaster model by the illustrious Daniel Chester French, carved the statue of Lincoln in the Lincoln Memorial in Washington. French's model was eight feet high. The Piccirilli brothers translated this into the present nineteen-foot-high statue, which is not monolithic but made up of twenty-eight blocks of marble carefully fitted together. Mr. French did the final work in the Memorial. This great sculpture hushes into reverence every person who looks upon it.

The works of S. Paolo Abbate, Curator of the Torrington Museum, Torrington, Connecticut, include the two Dante monuments in Newburgh, New York, and Providence, Rhode Island, the Lauricella Memorial in Calvary Cemetery in New York, and the Ruvolo Memorial in Torrington. Pietro Montana was awarded the Elizabeth M. Watrous Gold Medal in sculpture at the winter exhibit of the National Academy of Design. Among his celebrated plaques are the two of Mark Twain and Francis Cardinal Spellman. Bruno Beghè is not only a sculptor of renown in the United States but also a painter and violinist.

Virgil Cantini of the University of Pittsburgh is a dedicated and accomplished craftsman in painting, sculpture, art metal, and pottery. He is also an excellent teacher. The works of the talented Giuseppe Donato of Philadelphia have been on exhibit in Chicago, New York, Baltimore, and San Francisco.

Among architects, the name of Anthony J. DePace is outstanding. Pietro Belluschi is Dean of the Department of Architecture and Planning at the Massachusetts Institute of Technology. Mario E. Campiolo, who was born in Italy, but came to America at an early age, holds the eminent post of Assistant Architect of the Capitol in Washington. He is in charge of architectural, design and technical work of the Architect. The huge $12 million project for the Extension of the Capitol was his primary responsibility. From 1949 to 1957 he was Director of Architecture of the Colonial Williamsburg project. Mario C. Celli is chairman of the National Committee on School and College Architecture of the American Institute of Architects and represents the United States on the School Commission of the Union of International Architects.

Joseph Capolino has written impressively on the scroll of historical artists with his paintings in the Marine Corps building in Philadelphia. Albert Operti has immortalized on canvas many of the scenes he witnessed as a member of Peary's Arctic expeditions. Luigi Gregori executed, in the University of Notre Dame, the three magnificent murals depicting events in the life of Columbus. One of them, "Columbus' Return and Reception at Court," was reproduced by the United States Government on a commemorative stamp of the Columbian Exposition.

One of the greatest motion picture directors of all time whose smash hits are familiar to practically every movie fan in America, is Frank Capra. This directorial genius, who was born in Palermo and came to America at the age of six, won Oscars for his celebrated *It Happened One Night, Mr. Deeds Goes to Town,* and *You Can't Take It With You.* Other titles which one lists with fond nostalgia are *Lady for a Day, Broadway Bill,* and *Lost Horizon.*

Capra's films aim to entertain, which should be the primary objective of all theatrical media, but, while Capra in his pictures generously distributes wide smiles and booming laughter, he, at the same time, subtly underlines some good homespun philosophy, so that in the end, as one critic has remarked, "his audience's faith in mankind is restored."

Another Italian, Vincente Minnelli, of Metro-Goldwyn-Mayer, directed the musical *Gigi* which made an unprecedented sweep of nine Academy Awards.

Perhaps the greatest producer of motion pictures today is Dino De Laurentiis who gave to the world *War and Peace, Barabbas,* and *The Bible.* He has won two Academy Awards, *La Strada* and *Nights of Cabiria,* has produced more than one hundred films, and runs a $30 million studio in Rome. He is married to beautiful Silvana Mangano who stars in many of his pictures. Anna Magnani is another superb Italian actress. She won the Academy Award in 1955. The man who launched Anna Magnani and directed her in *Open City,* which took America by storm, was Roberto Rossellini. Overlooking the vagaries of his private life and some of the cinema failures he has registered, Rossellini is a great director who stands in the discriminating company of Luigi Zampa and Vittorio De Sica. De Sica is impressive as director, acting star, and writer. He achieved international fame in 1946 with his *Shoe Shine* and *Bicycle Thief*. Vittorio Gassman, who was married to the American motion picture star Shelley Winters, is a Shakespearean actor of talent. In 1963 he won the Italian Film Journalist Society Award for his role in the picture *The Easy Life*.

Two Italian actresses who are as well known to American audiences as Joan Crawford and Rita Hayworth are Sophia Loren and Gina Lollobrigida. Sophia Loren received the Academy Award Oscar for best actress of 1961 for her role in *Two Women*. Pier Angeli and her sister Marisa Pavan have also gained considerable acting recognition.

Anna Maria Italiano, whose professional name is Anne Bancroft, won the 1963 Oscar award for her work in *The Miracle Worker* as the teacher of the blind-deaf child, Helen Keller. Her portrayal was a tour de force which perhaps can never be surpassed for its dramatic emotional intensity.

Anna Maria Alberghetti, one of the newer of the Italian importations, has captured the heart of America with her lyric voice and sensitive beauty. It is my judgment that no one has ever sung "Torna a Sorrento" (my favorite) with more tenderness and melodic sweetness than has Miss Alberghetti.

The worlds of the motion picture and the theater are crisscrossed with Italian stars. Rossano Brazzi made some eighty films in Italy and was one of the leading screen heroes after World War II, in Europe and America. He played the lead in the film version of *South Pacific*.

Ernest Borgnine, who spent part of his boyhood in Italy, came to America, joined the Navy, and, after ten years as a sailor, turned to acting and stardom. He won the movie Oscar in 1955 for his role in *Marty*. Nor must we forget the stars of yesteryear whose images have disappeared from the silver screens but never from our fond memories: Mario Lanza, Henry Armetta, Elissa Landi, Bull Montana (Luigi Montagna), Edward Cianelli, Lou Costello, Monty Banks (Mario Bianchi).

In any discussion of prominent labor leaders, the name of Luigi Antonini is bound to be prominently mentioned. In September 1963,

Seventh Avenue in New York, in the heart of the garment district, was renamed, for a week, "Luigi Antonini Avenue" in honor of his eightieth birthday. The New York *Times* in reporting on the event said: "Antonini loves good food, hot peppers, good wine, grand opera, and work. He is the man who organized the city's Italian dressmakers, fought the sweatshops down, fought Fascism in his native land, fought the Communists who tried to take over his union when it was the biggest local in the country. His fights ended in victory. Yesterday, Mayor Wagner, on behalf of the city, gave him a gold medal at City Hall on his eightieth birthday. And during next week Seventh Avenue in the garment district will be called 'Luigi Antonini Avenue.'"

Other outstanding Italian labor leaders are James C. Petrillo, President of the American Federation of Musicians, United States and Canada; August Bellanca, Vice-President of the Amalgamated Clothing Workers of America; George Baldanzi, President of the United Textile Workers of America; Joseph Germano and Hugh Carcella, district directors in the United Steelworkers of America; Howard Molisani, Vincent LaCapria.

Armand D'Angelo, Deputy Commissioner of the New York Department of Water Supply, has also left an indelible mark on the rising graph of Labor's growth. Alfred A. Giardino, member of New York's Board of Education, is known as one of the nation's very able labor attorneys, and is a veteran labor arbitrator.

In the world of American business, Italian names are far too numerous for justice to be done to them in anything less than a book on the subject. We have already spoken of Amedeo P. Giannini (a book himself), the founder of the mighty Bank of America. Another great figure in the business, as well as the journalistic, world was Generoso Pope, publisher in his day of *Il Progresso* and *Il Corriere d'America*, the two most influential Italian newspapers in the history of the foreign press. He began his phenomenal career in America as a waterboy on a road gang, went into the sand and gravel business and became a multimillionaire. Nor did he forget the little Italian town of Arpaise, where he was born, installing there, as a gift, a whole electric light plant. His son, Fortune Robert Pope, carries on in the same splendid tradition of Italian journalism with the *Il Progresso* of today, its managing editor and chief editorial writer being the able Frank Cantelmo.

Louis R. Perini is a business executive to whom the overworked adjective "fabulous" can apply without exaggeration. Founder and president of one of the country's great construction firms, he bought, more as a hobby than anything else, the financially unprofitable Boston Braves, and transported them lock, stock, and barrel to Milwaukee. The baseball world was astonished. But while it was recovering from this spectacular innovation, Perini went on to set new attendance records in the league, win several pennants with his new Milwaukee Braves, and wrest the world's title from the seemingly unbeatable New York Yankees. Perini blazed the way, and now major league baseball extends from coast to coast.

There are very few people who (and I am no exception) do not reduce the tedium of waiting in a railroad station or an airport terminal by eating a handful or two of savory salted peanuts. When they do, the chances are nine to one that the peanuts they chew are Planters Peanuts, product of the Planters Peanuts enterprise, founded by Amedeo Obici, the "Peanut King" of America, who arrived from Italy at the age of twelve with about twelve cents in his pockets.

And one must not fail to mention Sebastiano Poli who, as a young immigrant, gathered pennies as he cranked a hand organ to a little monkey's dancing and eventually established a chain of theaters which he sold to William Fox for thirty million dollars.

In 1922 Melchiorre Pio Vincenzo Sardi opened in New York his Sardi's Restaurant which probably is unmatched in America as a rendezvous for luminaries of stage, screen, and radio. Another great Italian-American establishment is the fantastic Mamma Leone Restaurant on Forty-eighth Street. When Mamma Luisa Leone, who was born in Bazzano, Italy, opened her little eating place on April 27, 1906, she was told she would fail because there were already too many restaurants in New York. She replied: "I can cook good Italian food and I'll give people plenty. They'll come." The first day she served eighteen people. Now Mamma Leone's serves some four thousand people daily, in addition to handling some three thousand banquet-parties each year. Mamma Leone's has attained such phenomenal fame for the quality and quantity of food at reasonable prices that people queue up to sit and gourmandize in its large artistically decorated rooms vocal with fountains.

Other great Italian captains of industry have contributed to the daily enrichment of America, as the Vaccaros, the DiGiorgios, and the Scolios, fruit kings of America; the Angelo Petri family, wine producers; John Cuneo, President of Cuneo Press, the greatest printing establishment in the world; Pio Crespi, the cotton king of Waco; Antonio Giaccione, paper manufacturer; Ross Siracusa, head of Admiral Television; Louis Pagnotti, coal operator; Joseph A. Martino, President of National Lead Company; Salvatore Giordano, head of Fedders Air Conditioning; Paolino Gerli, industrialist; Vincent Riggio, President of the American Tobacco Company; Lee A. Iacoca, Vice-President of Ford Motor Company; Anthony G. De Lorenzo, Vice-President, General Motors; the LaRosa family and the Ronzonis, manufacturers of Macaroni Products; Uddo and Taormina, owners of Il Progresso Brand Products (a veritable empire in the food processing industry), Frank A. D'Andrea, head of the Great Andrea Television, who was the founder of FADO radio corporation (his initials); Bernard Castro, manufacturer of the famous "Castro Convertible" soft-bed, who started as a humble upholsterer and became the multimillionaire head of the greatest company of its kind in America.* Among builders, engineers, and architects who have built roads, tunnels, airports, and skyscrapers, there are men like the Gulls, DiNapoli, Rizzi, Corbetta, Del Balso, Paterno, Petrillo. Michael A. Rivisto on the Pacific Coast is one of the outstanding economic analysts of the country.

* *Il Progresso*, March 26, 1961.

The most publicized activity in America, as perhaps it is in any country, is government. Especially is this true where the people, through the medium of the ballot, choose their chief of state, subsidiary officials, and legislative representatives. Thus, a fair indication of the amalgamation into a homogeneous whole of any particular ethnic group is the extent to which that group participates in government. Obviously, if the majority of voters in any given political area are prejudiced against any specified grouping of citizens, persons within that grouping will not be elected to office. Prejudice does not necessarily mean animus and ill will, although most often it does. Prejudice might well be the synonym of unawareness or even ignorance, although when ignorance is persisted in, despite open avenues for ascertaining the truth, it can only be categorized as prejudice, bigotry, or one-mindedness, which of course is corroding to democratic society.

As I have already pointed out at length, the discrimination against Italians during the Ellis Island Era darkened the mind of many a person who either gained some personal advantage through its propagation or who was too intolerant to care that innocent persons suffered injustice. Thus, in those zones where stiff-necked bias prevailed, Italians could not hope to be elected or appointed to important office.

I have related how the people of Mt. Lebanon looked upon me in my first campaign for the Pennsylvania Legislature. And yet, after I was elected and had accredited myself in a manner which apparently pleased the voters in that municipality, the prejudice against my name disappeared. In succeeding elections the voters there honored me with the highest number of votes cast for the various candidates. I was elected twice to the Legislature and three times as Judge of Allegheny County. Then, in 1951, I announced my candidacy for the Supreme Court of Pennsylvania, an elective office. This time I had to go before the voters of the other sixty-six counties, in many of which I was more or less unknown.

Former United States Senator Joseph F. Guffey, who was supporting my opponent, declared that I could never win a statewide office because I was a Roman Catholic and I had what he called an "un-American name." I hired a station wagon, equipped it with phonograph and public address system, and campaigned throughout the state, speaking in public squares, at crossroads, at picnics, and wherever people might gather to listen to what I had to say. I dwelt on my boyhood on the banks of the Ohio, referred to my service in the Legislature, described the book I had written on the Constitution which Congress accepted as a congressional document, told of serving under the Stars and Stripes in two wars, related how President Truman had appointed me one of the judges representing the United States at the international war crimes trials in Nuremberg. And then I would end up, after this recital, with the rhetorical question: "If this does not make a name American, what does?"

In a statewide television appearance I concluded my speech with the declaration:

"If God in His infinite wisdom had my parents born in Italy and if He then transported them to America to give me birth, and if my angel mother placed a string of rosary beads in my cradle, it was all part of the divine plan for cooperation among all peoples of the world to bring a true spirit of tolerance and dignity to all mankind."

I was elected by an 88,000-vote majority.

It would appear that the first Italian to hold public office in America was Onorio Razzolini who hailed from Venice and settled in Annapolis where, in 1736, he was appointed Armourer and Keeper of the Stores of Maryland. Apparently the early Italian politicians made better progress in the South than in the North. In 1861, G. A. Pacetti became Mayor of St. Augustine, Florida. By 1880 two Italians were serving in the Texas Legislature and one (Antonio Ghio) was Mayor of Texarkana. In 1892 Constantine Lawrence Lavretta was elected to the Alabama Legislature, and in 1894 he became Mayor of Mobile. Frank L. Monteverde was Mayor of Memphis, Tennessee, from 1918 to 1921.

Nowhere, however, did Italians move at a more accelerated pace in public life than in the state of New York. Even in the early 1900s Italians were being elected as state legislators, congressmen, and judges. Then in 1933 Fiorello LaGuardia, after having served as congressman for fourteen years, won the election of Mayor of New York, and was re-elected in 1937 and 1941, giving to this largest metropolis in the world the longest and most progressive administration in New York's history.

Of an ebullient nature and of incessant energy, LaGuardia not only ran a highly efficient government but also enthusiastically participated in every phase of New York's super-busy life. He clanged to fires on speeding fire engines, conducted radio programs, and made the rounds at night with police. At times he held night court where the social elite often gathered, arrayed in white ties and tails, evening dresses and furs to see how the other half of the world lived. On one occasion Mayor LaGuardia fined a defendant ten dollars for vagrancy and then, turning to the wealthy audience, he said: "And I fine each of you as much as your conscience dictates for living in a city which permits economic conditions which compel able-bodied men to beg for a living." He collected $500, out of which he paid the defendant's fine, and then sent $490 to a charitable institution.

In 1941 President Franklin D. Roosevelt appointed him Chief of the United States Office of Civilian Defense and in 1946 he became director of the United Nations Relief and Rehabilitation Administration. In that year I was with him in Rome where he made a rousing speech in Italian to members of the Italian Parliament, bringing many of them to their feet cheering. LaGuardia's career was so colorful, dramatic, and exciting that a musical comedy, called *Fiorello*, was patterned on it.

The lack of voter prejudice against Italians in contemporary New York was never more marked than in 1950 when the three leading contenders for the mayoralty were all Italians: Vincent Impelliteri, Ferdinando Pecora, and Edward Corsi. Impelliteri, who had been

Major Rocco Anthony Petrone, responsible for the planning, scheduling and activating of NASA's launching facilities, world's first Spaceport, Merritt Island, Florida, is shown briefing an illustrious audience—including President John F. Kennedy, Vice-President Lyndon B. Johnson, and Secretary of Defense Robert S. McNamara—on the Moon Project.

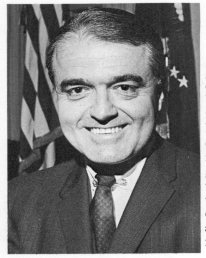

Jack Valenti, Special Assistant to President Johnson, as pilot of B-25s during World War II made fifty-one combat missions, flying from bases in Italy, the land of his grandparents. His numerous decorations include the Distinguished Flying Cross, Air Medal with five clusters. A graduate of the University of Houston, with a Masters Degree from Harvard University Business School, he brings to his distinguished post extraordinary talents and dynamic drive.

PHOTO BY CECIL W. STOUGHTON.

Anthony J. Celebrezze, United States Secretary of Health, Education and Welfare.

John O. Pastore, Senator of the United States and former Governor of Rhode Island.

John A. Volpe, Governor of Massachusetts. FABIAN BACHRACH.

Charles Poletti, Vice-President, New York World's Fair, former Governor of New York.

Joe DiMaggio, one of the greatest baseball players of all times. UNITED PRESS INTERNATIONAL PHOTO.

Rocky Marciano, retired undefeated World's Heavyweight Champion. UNITED PRESS INTERNATIONAL PHOTO.

Perhaps no one symbolized with greater affection the ties of sentiment between Italy and the United States than Enrico Caruso. His golden voice, continental courtliness, generous nature, and ever-friendly disposition endeared him to the American public as much as he was idolized by his people in Italy. His voice, recorded imperishably on records, will always recall the harmony between Italy and America. The lower picture shows Sorrento, close to his beloved birthplace Naples, and where he spent many vacations. The song "Return to Sorrento" aptly bespeaks the yearning to visit, in person or in spirit, the land which gave us modern civilization.

President of the Council and acting Mayor, was elected. At the end of his service in what has been called "the toughest job in the United States outside of the Presidency itself" he was appointed a Justice of the New York Supreme Court, a position to which he was later elected.

Ferdinando Pecora also entered the mayoralty race with an impressive background of public service. In 1933 he had achieved prominence for his brilliant work as counsel to the United States Senate Committee on Banking and Currency in its investigation of Wall Street activities. Later he was appointed by President Roosevelt to the Securities and Exchange Commission. He also later became a Justice of the Supreme Court of New York.

Edward Corsi's public achievements were equally noteworthy. For twelve years he was United States Commissioner of Immigration, establishing a magnificent record for humanitarian and efficient discharge of one of the most difficult and trying jobs in government. From 1943 to 1955 he was Industrial Commissioner for New York and then he became Assistant United States Secretary of State. His book on his experiences as Commissioner of Immigration, *In the Shadows of Liberty*, is an inspirational work.

In the 1964 Massachusetts elections the candidates for Governor on both the Democratic and Republican tickets were Italians, Francis X. Bellotti and John Volpe. Volpe emerged the victor.

Another popular Italian in New York, and a man of brilliant accomplishments, is Charles Poletti, who was a fellow student of mine at the University of Rome. After a successful career at the bar, he was elected to the Supreme Court of New York and then to the Lieutenant-Governorship. When Governor Herbert H. Lehman was elected to the U. S. Senate, Poletti became Governor. He also distinguished himself as an army officer during World War II, attaining the rank of Colonel and became Vice-President of the World's Fair in New York, 1964–65.

Political eminence among Italians has not been restricted to the East. One of the ablest and most popular of American mayors has been Angelo Rossi of San Francisco. There have been Italian mayors in cities throughout the country. Giovanni Schiavo lists the following: Maestri of New Orleans, Louisiana, Celentano of New Haven, Connecticut, DiSalle of Toledo, Ohio, D'Alesandro of Baltimore,

Maryland, Spagnola of Youngstown, Ohio, Addonizio and Villani of Newark, New Jersey, De Guglielmo of Cambridge, Massachusetts, Olgiati of Chattanooga, Tennessee, Fontana of Aliquippa, Pennsylvania, Levanti of Fitchburg, Massachusetts, DeSapio of Hoboken, New Jersey, Vaccarella of Mt. Vernon, New York, Ruffu of Atlantic City, New Jersey, Tedesco of Bridgeport, Connecticut, Martini and De Muro of Passaic, New Jersey, De Vita of Paterson, New Jersey, Casassa of Revere, Massachusetts, Paonessa of New Britain, Connecticut, Parente of Monessen, Pennsylvania, Quilici of Reno, Nevada, Imburgio of Melrose Park, Illinois, and there are scores of others.

Seven Italians have been elected Governor in four different states: Foster Furcolo and John Volpe in Massachusetts; Albert D. Rossellini in Washington; Michael Vincent DiSalle in Ohio; John Pastore, Christopher Del Sesto, and John A. Notte in Rhode Island.

The list of Italians who have been United States congressmen is a long and distinguished one. In the lower House the present members are: Peter W. Rodino, Jr., New Jersey; John H. Dent, Pennsylvania; Frank Annunzio, Illinois; Silvio O. Conte, Massachusetts; Emilio Q. Daddario, Connecticut; Dominick V. Daniels, New Jersey; Dante B. Fascell, Florida; Paul A. Fino, New York; Robert N. Giaimo, Connecticut; J. V. Vigorito, Pennsylvania; George P. Miller, California; Joseph G. Minish, New Jersey; Teno Roncalio, Wyoming; Joseph P. Addabbo, New York; Robert Leggett, California; and Carlton J. Sickles, Maryland. Previous members have been: Hugh J. Addonizio, New Jersey; Victor L. Anfuso, New York; Louis J. Capozzoli, New York; Anthony Cavalcante, Pennsylvania; Peter A. Cavicchia, New Jersey; Albert Cretella, Connecticut; Thomas D'Alesandro, Jr., Maryland; George A. Dondero, Michigan; Foster Furcolo, Massachusetts; Peter C. Granata, Illinois; Roland V. Libonati, Illinois; Albert P. Morano, Connecticut; Alfred E. Santangelo, New York; James P. Scoblick, Pennsylvania; and Anthony F. Tauriello, New York.

The Ohio Legislature contains the only father-son legislative team in the country. Anthony O. Calabrese occupies a seat in the State Senate while his son, Anthony O. Calabrese, Jr., represents his district in the House of Representatives.

In the Senate of the United States, John O. Pastore, former Governor of Rhode Island, is one of the ablest and most respected of the

solons. Despite the fact that twenty-seven Senators have more senior-
ity than this immigrant tailor's son, he is chairman of the all-impor-
tant Senate-House Atomic Energy Committee. A masterful orator
and keen debater, the Senator from Rhode Island is recognized and
admired throughout the country as one of the outstanding statesmen
of the era. His keynote speech at the Democratic National Convention in Atlantic City electrified the delegates and galleries, as well as
television viewers throughout the country.

Probably the most popular man of Italian lineage in Washington
today is Jack Valenti, Special Assistant to the President. From the
first day Vice-President Lyndon B. Johnson became President of the
United States, the personable and amiable Valenti has been at his
side continually. His abilities and capacities are phenomenal. He is a
combination speech-writer, diplomat, administrator, idea producer
and "spends more time with LBJ than any other staffer," said *News-
week* on March 1, 1965.

The high regard President Johnson bears toward Mr. Valenti has
been made evident many times and it was emphasized on June 2,
1964, when, in addressing an Italian group at the White House, he
said:

> "One of Italy's great artists said more than a hundred years ago:
> 'You may have the Universe if I may have Italy.' I feel that way my-
> self—about my favorite son of Italian descent, Jack Valenti. You may
> have anybody you want on your side if I can have Valenti on my
> side."

Another exceedingly popular high government official in Washington is Anthony J. Celebrezze, Secretary of Health, Education and
Welfare, appointed by President Kennedy and retained by President
Johnson. His career has been one to inspire any youth seeking a public career. Born in Italy of parents who raised thirteen children he
came to America and worked his way through college, becoming a
successful lawyer. He was elected to the State Senate of Ohio and
then Mayor of Cleveland. His administration was conducted with
such competence, skill, and regard for the people's welfare that he
was re-elected four times. He was just entering on his unprecedented
fifth term when President Kennedy selected him for his cabinet.

Frank Mercurio is a Commissioner in the United States Labor
Department. An outstanding diplomat in the service of the United

States is John J. Muccio who served as political advisor to the Supreme Allied Command in Germany at the end of World War II, and later became Ambassador Extraordinary to Korea.

Among other Italians holding high Federal posts are: Edward D. Re, chairman, Foreign Claims Settlement Commission; Eugene G. Fubini, Assistant Secretary of Defense; Michael V. DiSalle, member Advisory Commission on Intergovernmental Relations; John P. Botti, superintendent, Assay Office; Carmine S. Bellino, consultant to Senator R. Kennedy; G. Joseph Minetti, member Civil Aeronautics Board; Teno Rocalio, chairman, U. S. Section, International Joint Commission; Thomas D'Alesandro, member Renegotiation Board; Joseph A. Califano, Jr., Special Assistant to Secretary of Defense; Michael C. Barone, Assistant to Regional Director, Post Office Department.

On the New York scene again, the Italians can point with pride to the able Paul Screvane, deputy Mayor and President of New York City Council; John Travia, present Speaker and Joseph Carlino, former Speaker of the New York House of Representatives; State Senators Salvatore Cotillo and John J. Marchi; John P. Lomenzo, New York Secretary of State; Carmine DeSapio, former New York Secretary of State; Mario Cariella, President of Queens Borough, Albert Maniscalco, President of the Borough of Richmond; Sylvester J. Garamella, former New York City Deputy Police Commissioner, Emilio Mayer, President of the Italian Chamber of Commerce.

In Pennsylvania, Walter Alessandroni is Attorney General of the Commonwealth, Paul D'Ortona, President of Philadelphia City Council, and Adrian Bonnelly is President Judge of the County Court of Philadelphia. In Iowa the Attorney General is Lawrence F. Scalise. The list of Italian judges in the United States is too long to be included here. The list of Italian lawyers, doctors, and other professionals in America is endless. Among them I mention Melvin Belli, one of the ablest, most colorful, and well-known trial lawyers in the country. He was called the "King of Torts" by Life Magazine. In addition to his courtroom mastery he is an author of considerable distinction and is rated high among the most engaging lecturers in America. He has tried cases in all parts of the United States as well as in England, Japan, Italy, and Scandinavia. His defense of Jack Ruby, slayer of Lee Oswald, slayer of President Kennedy, was prominently covered in the American and world press. He has written a book on the subject.

In the face of the tremendous record of acknowledgment of Italian ability and character, no youth in America of Italian forebears should ever be reluctant about entering the lists for recognition of ability and idealistic objectives, out of any sense of "not belonging." Even President John Fitzgerald Kennedy, on Columbus Day, 1962, after being introduced by veteran, able Congressman Peter W. Rodino, told a cheering audience in Newark, New Jersey, that some Italian blood had, through his mother's ancestors, percolated into his veins. He said:

> "My grandfather, John F. Fitzgerald, who used to be Mayor of Boston, and was a Congressman, always used to claim that the Fitzgeralds were actually Italian, were descended from the Geraldinis, who came from Venice. I never had the courage to make that claim, but I will make it on Columbus Day here in this State of New Jersey today."

As soon as this statement was made, the United Press International initiated an intensive search into President Kennedy's genealogy. Reporters climbed the Kennedy-Fitzgerald family tree to its topmost twig and others dug down into the ground beneath the roots. From this arboreal expedition, the UPI turned in the following exciting and fascinating report:

DID AN ANCESTOR OF KENNEDY HELP COLUMBUS SHOVE OFF? ROME (UPI)—Christopher Columbus might never have discovered America if it hadn't been for one of President Kennedy's ancestors, the President's newly-discovered Italian relatives indicated here yesterday.

Kennedy startled Americans Friday by telling Columbus Day crowds he was descended on his mother's side from an Italian family named Geraldini.

He also startled five Romans named Geraldini, who had no idea they might be distant relatives of the American President.

The Roman Geraldinis are Arnaldo, 40, Rome correspondent of the Milan newspaper *Corriere Della Sera*; his son, Sergio, who also is a journalist; his daughter, Ornella, married to journalist Filippi Raffaeli; Count Gaetano Geraldini, a surgeon; and attorney Antonio Geraldini.

According to the Geraldini family archives, one of the early members of the family was Bishop Alessandro Geraldini, confessor of Queen Isabella of Spain and friend of Columbus.

At the Congress of Salamanca, when Columbus proposed to seek a new route to India by sailing West, the bishop sided with Columbus. He was among those who helped persuade Queen Isabella of Spain that it would be a good investment to finance the expedition of the Genoa sailor.

After Columbus made the voyage, and discovered America instead of a new route to India, he was so grateful to the bishop that he named one of the Antilles Islands after the bishop's mother, Graziosa.

President Kennedy said the Geraldinis hailed from Venice. The Geraldini family records bear this out, but show the family moved to Florence in the 14th century, where they were known as the Proud Ghibellines.

One branch of the family, the records show, migrated to France and then to Ireland. There they changed their name to Fitzgerald, the maiden name of the President's mother.

Another branch of the Geraldini family moved to Amelia, in the Umbrian Hills of central Italy, where they became part of the Italian nobility, with the title of counts.

They adopted as their family emblem an olive tree on a blue background with three gold stars—a symbol of peace. This branch of the family adhered to its symbol, striving to end the fratricidal wars which plagued Italy at the time.

One member of this family was a viceroy of Naples at the time of the Spanish domination.

The Geraldini family palace, built in 1470, still stands at Amelia. One of the streets of the town is named Allesandro [sic] Geraldini after the bishop. The tombs of many Geraldinis are found in the church of St. Francis of Amelia.*

* Courtesy of United Press International.

23 BONDS OF SENTIMENT

Americans climb the Alps in Italy and Italian mountain climbers revel in reaching for the peaks above the clouds in America. In July 1961 six Italian alpinists led by Riccardo Cassin carved an epic in ice and stone when they struggled up the "impregnable" south buttress face of 23,320-foot Mt. McKinley in Alaska. Bradford Washburn, Director of Boston's Museum of Science, described the ascent as the "most outstanding climb that has yet been made in North America." But this climb is merely a couple of steps upward in comparison to the political, commercial, and economic cliffs Italians have scaled with bare hands since the Ellis Island Era.

Sociological mountain ranges have been topped and respect-demanding plateaus have been occupied by Italians since those days when ships arrived in American seaports and nondescript immigrants surging down the gangplanks like waves of human cattle, were, for months or even years, treated with not much more care than that accorded cattle. Many years have passed since the day that melancholy vessel arrived in the New Orleans harbor to the accompaniment of jeers and cries denouncing the Italian voyagers for a crime which had been committed before their arrival. The superior and surly attitude that greeted the pilgrims from the Mediterranean, as if they were aggressors instead of eager allies, is happily now only a painful

260   THE STORY OF THE ITALIANS IN AMERICA

memory. No longer are immigrants regarded merely as potential laborers fit only for pick and shovel work or other menial tasks which
require no skill or training. Modern Italy is being appreciated as the
worthy successor of an earlier land which gave to the world the
mighty geniuses who laid the foundation of the edifice of western
civilization.

Today Italian engineers, industrialists, scientists, artists, musicians,
architects, and playwrights are invited to counsel with their American
counterparts in momentous American enterprises and projects. Italy
is no longer the land only of ancient Caesars and Renaissance
Raphaels. It manufactures planes, automobiles, electrical equipment,
engineering supplies, textiles, agricultural machinery. It is building
huge ocean liners, the most recent being the magnificent *Michelangelo* and *Raffaelo*. The Fiat firm in Turin organized and brought to
fulfillment the gigantic project that carried the Kariba Dam across
the Zambezi River in Africa. It is punching out the mammoth Great
St. Bernard and Mont Blanc Highway tunnels.

Italy is rolling out concrete superhighways which are as superior
to standard roadways as the Roman roads were to primitive foot and
animal paths. She is lifting buildings into the sky. In Milan the
Pirelli skyscraper gracefully soars for thirty-one stories and is tapered
at each horizontal end like a ship with two bows. Massive central
pillars of concrete and steel, rather than exterior walls, give it sturdi-
ness and majesty. It is an eye-filling, refreshing palace so resplendent
with numerous windows that fifty days are required to wash them
all, the lofty laundering being accomplished by attractive little cars
which travel on tracks over the shining surfaces like lightning bugs.
The building has no duplicate in the whole world.

Although Italy has long been regarded as a Cinderella nation, and,
indeed, she still remains poor in physical resources, she is not clad in
rags so far as fashions are concerned. Much of the fashion world of
today turns to Rome and Florence for the latest styles in wearing
apparel, jewelry, and other personal adornment.* The latest coiffures
for women, the contour and fabric of hats and shoes, the most modish
decor for home and garden come from designers in Italy. In motion
picture production Italy ranks second only to the United States.

* The fashion show in Florence, July 1964, was covered by fashion writers from
twenty-one countries, including those as far away as Japan, Uruguay, New Zealand,
Israel, and South Africa.

Most of today's mighty "spectaculars" with English-speaking performers are filmed in Italy.

Many Italian industrial designers are influencing shape and sweep in American cars. Adriano Olivetti, business machine magnate, startled the American commercial world when he bought out one of the oldest and most renowned of American establishments, the Underwood Typewriting Company. The Italian influence on American eating habits has been tremendous. It is reasonably estimated that there are at least thirty-five thousand Italian restaurants in the United States.

Food packing concerns vie with one another in putting up Italian foods in cans: minestrone, pasta e fagioli, ravioli, spaghetti and meatballs, hot and sweet peppers, pickled eggplant, frozen pizza. Edibles which at one time could be purchased only in Italian grocery stores are now attractively displayed in cellophane packages in supermarkets throughout the country: endive, broccoli, artichokes, garlic, oregano, zucchini, gorgonzola, cacciavallo, Italian tomatoes, pasta of many varieties.

Italian wines flood the liquor stores, Italian liqueurs grace every bar, Italian chefs with their high glittering white hats dominate hotel, restaurant, and private club kitchens. Necchi sewing machines lighten the needlework of many an American housewife. Italian fireworks paint the skies with explosive beauty, thunder, and fascinating designs. Italian operas are as melodious and popular as ever.

Technological Italy is now being respected as her artistic genius has always been ardently admired. One of the world's greatest engineer-architects today is the Italian Pier Luigi Nervi. But over and above Italy's enormous achievements in industrial, engineering, architectural, artistic, and commercial accomplishments, the world recognizes in her a special power greater than scientific, mechanical, electric, and nuclear energy. It understands and appreciates the universal moral force for preservation of the human race which resides in the Vatican in the person of the Pope. Non-Catholic as well as Catholic peoples realize that if the planet earth is to be spared an all-annihilating detonation, the salvation will come, not because of any one nation's, or combination of nations', superiority in destructive instrumentalities, but through understanding, sympathy, and love.

The person who perhaps in recent centuries accomplished more than anyone else to bring peoples together in closer harmony in the spiritual world was Angelo Giuseppe Roncalli, born in Sotto il Monte of peasant parents on November 25, 1881. He toiled in the vineyard of humanity as parish priest, medical sergeant in the Italian army in World War I, Prefect of Propagation of the Faith, Apostolic Visitor to Bulgaria, Apostolic Delegate to Turkey, and, as cardinal, Patriarch of Venice. A dedicated and serious worker, he did not see why religion had to be sad. To him it was joyous and he communicated that joyous vibrancy to all those about him. On October 28, 1958, he became Pope John XXIII, and at once inspired universal admiration and veneration because he regarded the human race as one human family. It was his task to restore faith in the brotherhood of man. In addressing a Jewish delegation he said:

"You of the Old Testament and we of the New must come closer and closer as brothers under God, to work for peace throughout the world."

His masterful encyclicals were addressed not alone to the 558 million Catholics in the world but to the entire world population. In his *Pacem in Terris* he spoke eloquently of the natural rights and "overwhelming dignity of man."

Justice then, right, reason, and humanity urgently demand that the arms race should cease; that the stockpiles which exist in various countries should be reduced equally and simultaneously by the parties concerned; that nuclear weapons should be banned; and that a general agreement should eventually be reached about progressive disarmament and an effective method of control. . . .

Patrick O'Donovan, writing in the *New Republic*, well said that Pope John's appeals to mankind effected "a sweet and reasonable change in the direction of peace. It is not a revolution. It is part of the endless process of trying to keep the world habitable. And it is the personal achievement of a marvelous old gentleman."

Pope John preached justice and lived it. When he discovered that Vatican employees were underpaid he at once ordered that salaries be raised according to the formula that the man who received the smallest wage yet supported the most numerous family should be granted the largest increase. He said that the Church which preached social justice "should set an example by paying its own help well, and trust to God for the needed income."

Putting into effect his preachments on racial equality he appointed the first Negro cardinal in church history. He also bestowed the red hat on a Filipino and a Japanese. The world loved John XXIII for his pulsating humanity. During the Christmas season of 1958 he visited the prison in Rome and smilingly said to the inmates: "You couldn't come to me, so I came to see you." He wished to talk to and offer comfort even to the most dangerous of the criminals. When the guards remonstrated, fearing for his safety, he replied: "They are all children of the Lord. Open up the gates." When he then, after five years of wise, courageous, humanitarian, and loving world steward-ship, himself stood at the threshold of eternity, one could almost hear St. Peter repeating Pope John's words: "Open up the Gates!"

Everyone remembers Pope John for his precious sense of humor. It was my ineffable honor to be received in private audience by him in December 1959, only a few days after there had appeared in the world's newspapers a photograph of himself and President Dwight D. Eisenhower laughing heartily. After I had knelt and received his blessing, the Pope engaged me in conversation and I said that every-body had greatly enjoyed that picture of him and President Eisen-hower in a most mirthful mood.

The Pope smiled and, with eyes twinkling, asked: "Would you like to know why we were laughing?"

I bowed to be accorded the privilege of listening. "As papal nuncio in Paris," he recounted, "I attended, shortly after the ending of World War II, an international conference where I saw General Eisenhower, supreme commander of the allied armies. Considering the greatness of his achievements and the fact that he was still com-paratively young, I remarked to people about me that General Eisen-hower would go on to reach greater heights.

"When President Eisenhower came here recently I told him how my prediction had come true and I said to him: 'I congratulate you on rising from second lieutenant in the army to President of the United States.' The President thanked me, and then I said to him: 'I didn't do so badly myself. I started as a sergeant in the army—and now I'm Pope!"

A Vatican official has told the following story of John XXIII. Learn-ing that the Pope desired to take a daily walk in his gardens, the official made arrangements to screen the path from the public. When the Pope saw the screen he said to the official: "Why this? Don't I look respectable?"

Pope Paul VI is extending the bridge begun by Pope John over the dark waters of misunderstanding and nationalistic, as well as religious prejudices. In a brave and unprecedented pontifical act he made a pilgrimage in January 1964 to the Holy Land and worshiped at the holy shrines of Christendom in the very heart of the disturbed Middle East, easing to a great extent, by his gracious presence, the tensions rife in that turbulent part of the world. In December 1964 he again shattered precedent by traveling to faraway India on a mission which he described as one of "love and peace." In Bombay over one million people—Hindus, Moslems, Sikhs, Parsees and Christians—greeted him with the cry of "Jai, jai! (Hail! Hail!)" With outstretched arms he replied: "We come as a pilgrim of peace, of joy, of serenity and love." In public and private audiences he urged Christians and non-Christians to come closer together in understanding and affection: "Are we not all one in this struggle for a better world?"

Presidents, kings, queens, prime ministers, senators, illustrious world leaders in government and civil life from all parts of the globe visit Rome and seek an audience with the Pope, an audience which is invariably granted. They never come away unimpressed. They know the Vatican seeks no material aggrandizement. They know also that the Roman Catholic Church, headed by the Pope, has been and continues to be the most potent spiritual force combatting Communism, which would destroy the freedom of man. Even though the Communist Party in Italy is larger than it should be, the vast majority of those who vote for that party's candidates have no identification with Soviet aims. Italian Communism, bad as it is, and though one would wish it did not exist, is still no insuperable threat to the democratic objectives of western civilization. One who prays in a Catholic church will never allow manacles to be slipped over his hands, or chains to be attached to his feet.

Ever since 1870 when the Vatican lost secular dominion over Rome, its territorial sovereignty extends over but 108 acres of land, but its spiritual influence is as vast as the soul itself. It seeks only to ring the bells, calling mankind to its obligations, the proper fulfillment of which will achieve the permanent peace for which all humanity consciously or unconsciously prays.

Italy itself is a land of church bells. Though the vault of heaven resounds with the music of carillons from the Alps to the Mediterranean, new bells are constantly being lifted into steeples and belfries. When Luigi Salzarulo, who had lived in America for fifty years, made a sentimental journey back to the place of his birth in Bisaccia, he shipped to the town, ahead of his arrival, a beautiful, clear-toned bell which was to be hung in the village campanile where it would sing of love and benediction in memory of Major Raymond Salzarulo, his son, who had been killed in World War II, fighting for the common cause of the United States and Italy. As the sacristan pulled the bell rope, Mr. Salzarulo shed a nostalgic and happy tear as he read the inscription on the bronze plaque at the base of the bell tower:

From the people of Richmond, Indiana, to the people of Bisaccia, Italy, in recognition of the high esteem in which we hold your native son and our fellow citizen, City Councilman Louis Salzarulo.

In April 1964 another bell voyaged across the same sea, but this time it traveled from Italy to America, instead of the other way around. The town of Sedegliano (sixty miles northeast of Venice) sent to John D'Appolonia in Penn Hills, Pennsylvania a bell from their own church campanile as an expression of gratitude for the generous assistance given by John and his father, who hailed from Sedegliano, in supporting the village nursery and church and helping to build the town hall.

This exchange of sentiment could be recalled hundreds, perhaps thousands of times, for on both sides of the ocean multitudinous bells are ringing out their joy in the bond of brotherhood between the United States and Italy, and between Americans and Italians.

The sentimental interdependency between Italy and America is charmingly illustrated in the delightful story of the Mayor of an Italian town who, welcoming a dignitary from afar, said: "I greet you in the name of four thousand of our citizens, three thousand of whom are in America."

In Northampton County, Pennsylvania, there is a small town made up entirely of immigrants or descendants of immigrants from the town of Roseto in the province of Foggia. Naturally the town is called Roseto. Thus, Italians exclusively run the government, till the soil, operate the small clothing factories within its borders, and keep it healthy. The excellent physical state and longevity of the inhabitants prompted the University of Oklahoma Medical School to

conduct a survey to determine how the people eat, drink, and work to
hold down the death rate, which is less than half that of the surrounding communities and where heart attacks are virtually non-
existent. Nancy Burden, writing in the Philadelphia *Bulletin,* says that
the medical experts who have moved into Roseto "are finding that
no small measure of this unusual health record is due to the home life
provided by the women of the town."

In Chicago, Mrs. Dominic Savino so carried on in the ways to
which she was accustomed in Italy that the political, commercial, and
social elite of that city met to do honor to her. She held no public
office, she had won no beauty contest, she had managed no publicly
advertised enterprise. A housewife of forty-nine, she gave of herself
to her neighbors, negotiating dark alleys and hallways, descending
into dank basements and climbing into dusty attics, helping all
those who needed someone to call the doctor, go for medicine, mind
the babies, wash a few clothes, order the landlord to fix that leak in
the roof, and put intoxicated husbands in their place. Without her
being aware of it, someone had added up the time she gave to her
neighbors in a year. It totaled 1589 hours. And she did all this without neglecting her home, husband, and four children.

And so, in the fall of 1949, she was invited to attend a ceremony,
not being advised the purpose of the event, thinking only it was
another neighborhood chore, although wondering why so many people were present. Fourteen hundred crowded the ballroom. Doctors,
lawyers, preachers, businessmen spoke on the age-long theme of good
neighborliness. She liked all this until she began to experience an
uncomfortable feeling that somehow she was involved in this oratory.
She was positively unhappy when one speaker looked at her and
spoke of "Symbol of good will. Real spirit of America. . . . Salute
this remarkable lady . . . the Little Saint of Erie Street." And then
when the Mayor, with another speech, presented her with a gold
medal, she broke down and wept. After sobbing into the numerous
bouquets of roses which had been piled before her, she answered the
question of a newspaperman who wanted to know why she cared so
much for others. She said: "Why I help neighbors? You gotta live
'til you die. So you live good."

In 1963 the government of the land in which Mrs. Savino was
born offered to the government of the land of her new home all the

marble that would be needed in the construction of the American National Cultural Center to be built in Washington. In accepting the gift, President Kennedy said:

"The gift will stand forever as a symbol of the old and intimate ties of friendship between Italy and the United States and the indispensable contribution the land of Vergil and Dante has made to our culture."

Those ties were never better symbolized than in the deed of Salvatore Catalano, the Sicilian sailor of 1804, who, as we have already related, guided Stephen Decatur's ship into the Tripolitan harbor and swung a cutlass with his American comrades in the daring exploit that destroyed the pirate-held frigate *Philadelphia*.

A half century later Americans repaid the debt to Catalano in his own Sicily. William DeRohan of Philadelphia, through private subscriptions and voluntary donations, obtained supplies and equipment for Garibaldi's expedition and shipped them to Genoa, where he transferred the cargo to three ships which sailed for Sicily under the American flag. The American minister, John Moncure Daniel, descendant of a signer of the Declaration of Independence, dispatched a message to Captain Palmer of the *Iroquois*, an American warship in the waters off Palermo, urging him to assure safe passage to these three vessels. They arrived in Palermo at the very moment that Garibaldi's need was the greatest, enabling him to continue the battle until he captured enough of the enemy's supplies to carry him to the ultimate triumph.

Another American ship, the *Charles and Jane*, laden with troops and supplies for Garibaldi, was stopped in midocean by a Bourbon man-of-war, whose captain demanded that the American vessel's papers be produced. Captain J. W. Watson of the *Charles and Jane* replied: "I refuse to consign my papers to pirates, who seize and cannonade without showing their own colors and who have insulted the American flag. I will cede only to force, and if I am compelled to cede, my government has a sufficient number of warships to reduce the whole Kingdom of Naples to ashes." The American ship was allowed to proceed and its cargo arrived in time to be of considerable assistance to Garibaldi at the battle of Milazzo.

Colonel Samuel Holt of Hartford, Connecticut, sent Garibaldi a quantity of self-loading revolvers and revolver-carbines, the newest invention in firearms up to that time. In explanation of this formidable gift he said: "America can never do enough for the nation which gave to the world Christopher Columbus."

It is not by chance that Columbus' statue appears in all parts of America, that there is a Columbia University, that a large organization is called the Knights of Columbus, and that the American continent boasts a Republic of Colombia.

It is not a matter of coincidence that the very seat of the American government is named the District of Columbia. It is not without meaning that American children thrill to the singing of *Hail, Columbia,* and *Columbia, the Gem of the Ocean.*

The bond of sentiment between Italy and America sometimes goes beyond life itself. There are Italians who want to be buried in America and Americans who ask to be laid to rest in Italy. Gennaro Sorrenti came to America and took up the humble calling of iceman. He saved enough pennies to accumulate twenty thousand dollars, which he bequeathed to New York City with the words: "In grateful appreciation for the opportunity the City gave me during my lifetime." He sleeps the eternal sleep in a Brooklyn cemetery.

Battista Mastroianni, who was a private in the United States Army in Korea,* was killed in action on November 8, 1951. Often, as he had wrapped his blankets tightly about him in the bone-freezing winds of the Korean mountains, he had expressed the wish that if he was to meet death in battle, he wanted to be buried in sunny Italy, where he was born. A grateful government saw to it that his wish became reality. The United States Army arranged for the transportation of his body across the Pacific, across the American continent and then across the Atlantic to Gizzeria in the province of Catanzaro where, also in accordance with his wish, there was placed above his grave the flag of the land of his choosing and for which he made the supreme sacrifice.

This intermingling of spirits between the two countries has found its counterpart in the physical fusion of families which a half century ago would have seemed incredible. In June 1953 many of the elite of New York turned out for the wedding of Sara Delano Roosevelt, granddaughter of President Franklin Delano Roosevelt, to Anthony di Bonaventura, son of a barber who had come from Italy. Anthony

* Some 300,000 Italian-Americans were in uniform during the Korean conflict.

lived in a neighborhood where laundry hangs on fire escapes and children use sidewalks for playgrounds. At the time of the engagement the foster parents of Sara, reputed to be worth $54 million, invited the di Bonaventura family to a sumptuous dinner at their 900-acre Long Island estate. The di Bonaventuras reciprocated by inviting the bride's parents to a lasagne dinner in their East Seventeenth Street flat.

Not every immigrant family has a son who marries a rich man's daughter, but every immigrant family has striven for the attainment of self-sufficiency which produces wealth in mutual happiness and human dignity. Alfonso LaFalce came to America in 1903, having no money, education, or trade. He still has no education and he still toils with his hands, but he and his wife have raised a family of eleven children, all of whom have done well in their respective fields of endeavor, which include music, storekeeping, salesmanship, barbering, baking, and acting. There are over thirty grandchildren. One of the daughters is a nun. A popular magazine recently devoted many pages to the illustrated story of the LaFalce family. One photograph showed the LaFalce clan at the dinner table which extended through the dining and living room, sparkling with such color that one almost smelled the fragrance of the *marinara* sauce on the spaghetti, the juicy meatballs, the hot sausages, fresh salads, glasses of red wine— and all decorated, festooned, and ornamented with the smiles of the joyous diners.

In the days of vaudeville, comedians always could be sure of a laugh by quipping on the ample size of Italian families, but this racial proclivity to numerous children was no small contribution to the latter-day development and progress of America. The country needed manpower and the Italians supplied brawn, as well as brain, in the industrial expansion of the nation. And, of course, the roster of every American regiment and ship in the days of war always carried a long list of Italian names.

Frank Maresca came to America in 1875 and settled in Jersey City, New Jersey. He raised a family of thirteen sons and three daughters. Three of his sons served in World War I, one making the supreme sacrifice in the Argonne offensive. Eight more served in World War II, one of them being wounded in Guam.

General Mark W. Clark, commander-in-chief of the Allied Armies in Italy, and whom I served as naval aide, paid tribute to the Italian-American soldiers under his command:

> "No one surpassed them in their devotion to American ideals and the American cause. Into their fighting spirit went their sense of gratitude for the great opportunities offered to them in America."

There were more Americans of Italian lineage than of any other ancestry in the Allied Armies which destroyed the Nazi armies in Italy, a destruction which led inevitably to the collapse of the western front and the ending of the war. The war in Italy was another manifestation of the complementary relationship between that country and America. Italy supplied the arena in which the Nazi menace could be vanquished and at the same time the war offered an opportunity for America to make a payment on its debt of gratitude to Italy for what it has given to civilization, by liberating Italy from its oppressors and bringing comfort and succor to a stricken land.*

In the fall of 1943, while military governor of Sorrento, I made arrangements to distribute flour to the war-starved civilian population. One of the priests of the town came to me and said: "Comandante, I would like to ask a grace. We have not had white flour in our town for many months and I have no more communion wafers in my church. I should like to purchase some of this snowy flour for the holy bread. May I send for it?"

"I'm sorry," I replied, "you may not buy the flour, nor may you send for it. The United States is *giving* you this flour and I shall deliver it myself."

That night I hoisted a small sack of the snow to my shoulder and stepped out to the streets of the blacked-out town. Unknown to me, a slight hole in the sack released a trickle of flour which powdered my whole blue uniform so that when I arrived at the church I gleamed

---

* Italian names appear in the casualty lists from Viet Nam. *Fra Noi* of Chicago, March 1965, reports: " 'Results were quite good,' said the jet pilot, Major Robert F. Ronca of Norristown, Pa., when he returned to Saigon after the retaliatory raid on North Viet Nam. But the price was high. American wounded during recent bleak days in that southeast Asia country have included Pvt. Leonard J. Barone of Pittsburgh and 1/c Dale A. Massa of Omaha. And among the dead: Pfc. John W. Malapelli of Burlington, Ky., during a raid on American billets; Sp/4 Carmine Cervellino of Patchogue, N. Y., in action; Sgt. L. C. Dominick Sansone of Wolcott, Conn., in a transport crash; 2nd Lt. Louis A. Carricarte of Miami, in a helicopter crash."

white from head to foot. In the light of the flickering candles, as I stepped across the sacred threshold, I thought to myself that if on the day of the Final Judgment I could be as white inside as I was then externally, I should have no difficulty in obtaining space at a window in Heaven. Overawed by this thought, added to a realization that this flour was to become holy communion, I proceeded directly to the altar and laid the precious burden on the lace-covered marble. I kneeled and was reciting a prayer when the parish priest invited me into the sacristy. He handed me a pen and asked me to sign a book. Almost in a trance I affixed my signature to the opened page before me and he explained: "This is the register for visiting priests. To-night you came here not as a navy officer, not as a man of battle, but as a messenger of the Lord, and you will be so recorded."

In many ways, the United States, in 1943 and since, has carried out the mandates of the Lord in aiding a stricken nation and in rendering assistance to a peace-loving, God-fearing nation. Italy bows in grati-tude to the United States, but the United States also has reason to be grateful to Italy, not only for her contributions to civilization but also for her tremendous sacrifices in behalf of the Allies in World War II, as well as World War I.

In 1925, after graduating from the University of Rome, I left Italy a temple of art, a garden of beauty, a poem of inspiration, and a song of joy. Nineteen years later, as an officer in the Navy, I was again in Italy. I found it passing through an ordeal of fire threatening to de-stroy its patrimony of culture and its treasure house of achievement. I saw the razing and crippling of cities and towns fabled in history, story, and song. I saw world-famous Cassino die. One thousand planes roared over that mountain town, each one dropping a package of inferno. And when the fiery explosion had ceased, hardly one brick rested on another. Jagged pieces of stone that once were the founda-tions of homes, which had sheltered loving hearts and laughing chil-dren—these stones thrust their piteous crests through the earth like amputated hands pleading for the mercy that no one knows in war.

I returned to Cassino ten years later. The town had been killed but its spirit had not died. Cassino rose again. Cassino, like all of Italy, has known countless invasions. Italy has been overrun by the Car-thaginians, Barbarians, Saracens, Vandals, Byzantines, Huns, by would-be conquerors from the north, east and west. They came in a tornado of fire and steel; they raised their flags of piracy, but they eventually departed with the ashes of defeat in their mouths.

And Italy lives. The glory and the grandeur which has been hers will go on and on because it has been strengthened and fortified by the physical rehabilitation of the land through the efforts of her people aided by the United States under the Marshall plan. Instead of wringing their hands in self-pity, the Italians used those hands in working the postwar miracle of reconstruction. Over one-half of her railroads and stock had been wrecked, the twisted and torn rails giving the appearance of enormous metallic pretzels. Nearly 6000 bridges had been destroyed; 67,000 kilometers of highways needed repairing; some 350 tunnels had been smashed; hundreds of thousands of homes had been leveled by bombs and artillery fire, two or three million were rendered uninhabitable; churches, commercial structures, and public buildings were phantom structures; factories were reduced to splinters, their machinery fragmentized; hundreds of towns had been literally wiped off the map; seaports had become cemeteries of ships, with their masts projecting above the water like tombstones. As I surveyed this structural and transportational chaos, I wondered if Italy would ever live again.

Today one can hardly believe that Italy had been crushed in the nutcracker of the fiercest war in history. The wrecked seaports have been rebuilt until they surpass what they were prior to the war; the ghost towns, wholly restored, live again as if nothing had happened; the skeletonized bridges are now fine steel and cement spans; the railroads glitter with new rails carrying the most modern and commodious of train equipment, railroad and air terminals have become the last word in scientific, architectural modernity. A few bombs in Milan had reduced the internationally famous *La Scala* opera house to a shambles. American architects and engineers worked with Italian architects and engineers and *La Scala* now blooms with musical and architectural beauty untarnished by any scar of the fiery ordeal through which it had passed.

Truly it can now be said of Italy that yesterday lives side by side with today. And it is probably this juxtaposition in chronology which makes Italy so attractive to Americans, who, while holding a candle to study the past, want to enjoy, with creature comfort, and even luxury, what the past reveals.

Italians, even greater worshipers of the past, still also take the scientific electronic age in stride. After all, it is this omnipresent progressive outlook on life which explains the Renaissance and the scientific marvels of da Vinci, Galileo, Volta, Malpighi, and Torricelli. It is because of this propinquity of ancient greatness to modern performance that tourists find Italy the favorite vacationland. England is historically fascinating, France is artistic, Germany is immaculate and its people courteous, and Switzerland is beautiful. But Italy has warmth. The sun is cheerful, the people more so. They are hospitable and friendly. In a day after arrival the foreigner feels he has returned to a land which was once his homeland. In 1964 more than twenty-three million tourists visited Italy.

Dr. Solomon B. Freehof, eminent clergyman and renowned scholar, wrote from Rome in 1953: "The Italians are the most lovable people in the world. They are friendly, patient, and endlessly kind. The visitor sees that fact in many ways, almost from the moment he enters the country."

And yet their friendliness is not the overflowing spirit of people who have had everything and therefore easily smile upon a world which has shown them only munificent bounty. No nation, with the possible exception of Ireland, has suffered so much in its history as has Italy. Wars, plagues, earthquakes, and tidal floods have ravaged the land and decimated its population, but with plow and trowel, hammer and shovel, and, above all, Faith, Italy has rebuilt itself and has made itself worthy of the compassion of the Traveler who spoke to St. Peter on the Appian Way.

In World War II, during a bombardment of Genoa, a naval shell penetrated the walls of a church filled with worshipers. When the rescuers rushed in among the wreckage they found fifteen hundred dead bodies. But the Genoese of today recall this tragedy not with bitterness but with an understanding of the unholiness of war and then point proudly to the rebuilt church with its soaring spire.

It was this kind of understanding which accompanied the Italian to America who, despite the bombardment of his spirit by discrimination, the attack on his dignity with insults and injustice, nevertheless continued to build the edifice of his faith in the ideals of America and the equality of opportunity which was the foundation of the New World.

And so excellently did he build, so thoroughly did he demonstrate his worthiness, and so loyal did he prove himself to the ideals, traditions, and objectives of America that when recommendation was made that the longest suspension bridge in the United States, in fact, in the world, be named after an Italian, this was done. Thus, the largest monument in the United States carrying the name of a European, has been dedicated to an Italian, Giovanni da Verrazano. President Johnson hailed the Verrazano-Narrows Bridge as "a bridge of breath-taking beauty." The New York *Times* said: "The bridge stretches like a fairy necklace across the gateway to America—an inexhaustible font of loveliness as full of dignity and inspiration as its neighbor, the Statue of Liberty."

I stood on that colossal span. It towers the height of a ten-story building above the sea so that the tallest ocean liner may pass beneath without scraping its masts. And as I leaned against the railing I looked out at the ocean whose bosom had borne the ship which had brought my father and mother to this land and I thought of the thousands of ships which had brought over millions of their co-nationals. The fleets carrying those Italian immigrants are not so numerous any more. The flood of immigration has dwindled to a trickle. The "old-timers" are passing away and it will be a sad day indeed when we will no longer see that breed of men who guided us and inspired us in our youth, and who, with other immigrants, made possible the Verrazano bridge of today.

The Italian of my boyhood wore corduroy trousers and a woolen shirt and carried heavy timbers on his back, not to build a Verrazano-Narrows Bridge, but a way across a wide creek, a deep gulley, or a depression in the earth, over which moved wheelbarrows and carts freighted with stones, shingles, planks, bricks, concrete and mortar for the building of roads, foundations, houses, schools, and every type of structure in the land. On Saturday night the Italian put aside his mortar-, mud-, and plaster-streaked clothes and the next day arrayed himself in his Sunday suit with its green vest across which stretched the heavy watch chain with a five dollar watch at one end and a figure of his patron saint at the other. A sprig of basil decorated his ear and he puffed at a Toscano cigar whose redolent, pungent smoke made me wish I would grow up fast so I could also smoke one of them, which was forbidden to me now. In those days children obeyed their parents and no one would ever dream of assuming he could know more than his father.

On Sundays we picnicked in the lush fields. I remember the large platters of spaghetti, the aromatic stuffed peppers, the enormous meatballs which we called cannon balls, the bowlfuls of tomato, pepper, and cucumber salad, and the bottles of colored carbonated pop with its delightful sting to the throat, while the men drank home-made ruby red wine gurgling from a jug. Then would come three youths with accordion, mandolin, and guitar, and I often wondered how they learned to play with such exquisite harmony since they had never seemed so smart to me in other things. And we would dance in the soft gloaming, and the stars were never so bright as then.

The green vest has disappeared but not the green memories of the immigrant's early years. On the day of the dedication of the Verrazano bridge I saw some of the old-timers and they crowded the rail and pointed in the direction of Italy. Nostalgia was in their eyes. Their children were now grown men and women with children of their own, and many of those children had children and they often objected to the Toscano smoke of the old-timer. And they would often ask him not to be so humble to others. This was America and everyone was equal to everyone else, they would say. It would be useless for the old-timer to explain that there was a difference between humility and subserviency. When he bowed, when he said, "Signor," and when he tipped his hat to a professor, a judge, or a doctor, he was showing respect for learning and for the dignity of man. He forbore explaining further that with human dignity go understanding, forbearance, and true brotherhood. He had learned all this in the little *paese* he had left so many years ago. This big Verrazano bridge seemed to transport him across the sea and across the years to that *paese*, to his boyhood before he looked to America for his future. His life was close to the end now and there would be just one more bridge to cross. He asked himself: Had he done his part? Would he leave the world a little better than when he came into it?

I approached one of the old-timers and helped him light his Toscano, which had gone out in the stiff wind sweeping through the steel girders. I asked him how old he was when he came to America. He said he was fifteen, but he remembered everything in Italy as if he had left it only yesterday. He said that America should allow more Italians to come to America. And it made me think of fifteen-year-old John Minadeo back in my home city of Pittsburgh. John, who was captain of the School's Safety Patrol back in 1954, and who had come to America only four years before, was leading his young comrades across Hazleton Avenue one day when an automobile roared down the street, its brakes not working and its steering wheel out of control. John leaped into action. He barked out orders and with outstretched arms forced his wards onto the protecting sidewalk. Several lagged behind and John pushed them out of the car's path. While shepherding the last one to safety the careening juggernaut was upon him. He had saved his adopted American brothers and sisters from death and serious injury but when the car finally came to a stop, John lay on the street dying of a fractured skull.

Many people live scores of years and never display one act of superb courage or offer one drop of sweat or blood in behalf of their fellow man. In a matter of seconds, John gave his all, and, in those few fragments of time, he revealed that he had the stuff of which Christopher Columbus, John Basilone, and the Drummer Boy of Shiloh were made. And thus the human race goes forward to the achievement of its grand and noble destiny.

Thousands filed by the little coffin at John's funeral, and a school, which was erected close to the spot where he offered his life for America's future, has been named the John Minadeo School. America— or any other country—will continue to need more John Minadeos. The restrictive immigration law has generally striven to keep them out. On the basis of national origin, the McCarran-Walter Immigration Act* reduced Italy's quota of immigrants to a penurious 5666 per year. Under its inhuman operation many families were permanently separated. Senator Robert F. Kennedy, who was then Attorney General, testifying before the House Subcommittee on Immigration on July 22, 1964, spoke of a case in Providence, Rhode Island, where a well-to-do Italian sought to bring to America his daughter who had lost her husband. He was notified that the existing immigration law required what amounted to an impossible choice: that of his daughter never joining her father again, and of being deprived of the protection and comfort of his home when she needed it desperately, or of coming to America without her three small children. Robert F. Kennedy commented:

* Representative Francis E. Walter, of Pennsylvania, co-author of the McCarran-Walter Immigration Act, as late as 1955 referred to Italians as "dagoes." *Evening Star*, Washington, D. C., March 27, 1955.

"What kind of humanity does this demonstrate to our millions of citizens of Italian descent, whose continued contribution to our common country is evidenced simply by a roll call of the Medal of Honor winners, or of political or economic or scientific leaders like Senator Pastore or Enrico Fermi or A. P. Giannini? . . . Are we to bar ourselves from the undoubted contributions of later generations of Italian immigrants and their descendants?"

President John F. Kennedy had recognized the need for a drastic revision of the McCarran-Walter Immigration Act and on July 23, 1963, strongly condemned the national origins system:

"The use of a national origins system is without basis in either logic or reason. It neither satisfied a national need nor accomplishes an international purpose. In an age of interdependence among nations, such a system is an anachronism, for it discriminates among applicants for admission into the United States on the basis of accident of birth."

On January 13, 1965, President Johnson characterized the national origins quota system "incompatible with our basic American tradition." He pointed out that:

"Violation of this tradition by the national origins quota system does incalculable harm. The procedures imply that men and women from some countries are, just because of where they come from, more desirable citizens than others. We have no right to disparage the ancestors of millions of our fellow Americans in this way."

He strongly urged Congress to "return the United States to an immigration policy which both serves the national interest and continues our traditional ideals. No move could more effectively reaffirm our fundamental belief that a man is to be judged—and judged exclusively—on his worth as a human being."

The New York *Times*, in editorially supporting President Johnson's message to Congress, said: "It is time to rekindle that lamp beside the golden door and banish forever those shadows that have dimmed its bright flame too long."

And it is time also to make Columbus Day a national holiday. The most important day in any person's life is his natal day. And yet the United States neglects to honor the day that America came into being. On October 12, 1492, like a mythical goddess, America rose from the mysteries of the deep, it burst from the infinite spaces, it emerged from the womb of time. It was destined to become a home for the homeless, the hope of the hopeless, the joy of the joyless. It became a temple of freedom and the land of opportunity. It became the shrine of all that is good in the aspirations of mortal man.

October 12 each year should be a day of great rejoicing, not only because it is the anniversary of the birth of the New World, but also because the life of Columbus is and can be a constant reminder of life's most powerful admonition: Never Despair. Go look at Christopher Columbus in painting and marble and talk with him. Study that countenance which never accepted defeat, no matter how crushing the forces against him. Take heart from him, never raise the flag of surrender. If you believe in your cause, a world of opportunity unfolds before you, as it did before the noble Genoese who never accepted No for an answer.

Oh noble Genoese, daring mariner, navigator of genius, and dreamer of worthy dreams. You have imparted the grandest lesson of all time—Never Despair. You will constantly be an encouragement, an inspiration, a constant urging to all of us to sail on and on until we too may find the San Salvador of our dreams, until we too may enter the port of Columbia in the realization of our fondest hopes of love, of peace, and of unbroken happiness.

BIBLIOGRAPHY

Abbott, John Stevens Cabot: *Italy*. P. F. Collier & Son, New York, 1882.
Adamic, Louis: *A Nation of Nations*. Harper & Brothers, New York, 1945.
Allen, Gardner W.: *Our Navy and the Barbary Corsairs*. Houghton Mifflin Co., Boston, 1905.
Andrews, Matthew P.: *The Founding of Maryland*. The Williams and Wilkins Co., Baltimore, 1933.
Antin, Mary: *The Promised Land*. Houghton Mifflin Co., Boston, 1912.
Arizona Historical Review, I.
Asbury, Herbert: *The French Quarter*. Alfred A. Knopf, Inc., New York, 1936.
Barzini, Luigi G.: *The Italians*. Atheneum Publishers, New York, 1964.
Beard, Annie E. S.: *Our Foreign-Born Citizens*. The Thomas Y. Crowell Co., New York, 1922.
Bernard, William S., and others, eds.: *American Immigration Policy*. Harper & Brothers, New York, 1950.
Bittner, Herbert, and Ernest Nash, eds.: *Rome*. Henry Regnery Co., Chicago, 1950.
Blackett, Patrick M. S.: *Fear, War, and the Bomb*. McGraw-Hill Book Co., 1949.
Bogardus, Emory S.: *Immigration and Race Attitudes*. D. C. Heath & Co., Boston, 1928.
Bolton, Sarah K.: *Famous Men of Science*. The Thomas Y. Crowell Co., New York, 1946.
Bosi, A.: *Cinquant' anni di Vita Italiana in America*. Bagnasco Press, New York, 1921.
Botta, Charles: *History of the War of Independence*. Nathan Whiting, New Haven, Conn., 1834. First edition published in Paris, 1812.
Bradsby, H. C.: *History of Vigo County*. S. B. Nelson & Co., Chicago, 1891.
Brady, Cyrus Townsend: *Stephen Decatur*. Small, Maynard & Co., Boston, 1900.

Brown, Francis J., and Joseph S. Rouček: *One America.* Prentice-Hall, Inc., New York, 1952.

Brown, Lawrence Guy: *Immigration.* Longmans, Green & Co., New York, 1933.

Burr, Clinton Stoddard: *America's Race Heritage.* The National Historical Society, New York, 1922.

Cadillac Papers, Michigan Historical Collection XXXIII, Lansing, Mich.

Cadogan, Edward: *The Life of Cavour.* Charles Scribner's Sons, New York, 1907.

Capitol, Art in U.S., by Italian Artists. Congressional Record, January 29, 1930, pp. 2630–34.

Carr, John Foster: *Immigrant and Library: Italian Helps.* Immigrant Education Society, New York, 1914.

Caruso, Dorothy: *Enrico Caruso: His Life and Death.* Simon and Schuster, Inc., New York, 1945.

Cauthorn, H. S.: *A History of the City of Vincennes.* M. C. Cauthorn, Vincennes, Ind., 1902.

Cellini, Benvenuto: *The Autobiography of Benvenuto Cellini.* Translated by J. Addington Symonds. Garden City Publishing Co., Garden City, N. Y., 1927.

Child, Irvin L.: *Italian or American?* Yale University Press, New Haven, Conn., 1943.

Clark, Francis E.: *Our Italian Fellow Citizens.* Small, Maynard & Co., Boston, 1919.

George Rogers Clark Papers: Edited by J. A. James. Vols. VIII and XIX. Illinois State Historical Library, Springfield.

D'Angelo, Pascal: *Pascal D'Angelo, Son of Italy.* The Macmillan Co., New York, 1924.

Davie, Maurice R.: *Refugees in America.* Harper & Brothers, New York, 1947.

DiDonato, Pietro: *Immigrant Saint: The Life of Mother Cabrini.* McGraw-Hill Book Co., New York, 1960.

Dunlap, Orrin E., Jr.: *Marconi: The Man and His Wireless.* The Macmillan Co., New York, 1937.

Fairman, C. E.: *Our Debt to Italy.* Congressional Record, January 28, 1925.

Fermi, Laura: *Atoms in the Family (My Life with Enrico Fermi).* University of Chicago Press, Chicago, 1954.

Foerster, Robert F.: *Italian Emigration of Our Times.* Harvard University Press, New Haven, Conn., 1919.

Garlick, R. C., Jr.: *Philip Mazzei, Friend of Jefferson. His Life and Letters.* Johns Hopkins Press, Baltimore, 1933.

Glazer, Nathan, and Daniel P. Moynihan: *Beyond the Melting Pot.* MIT Press and Harvard University Press, Cambridge, Mass., 1963.

Goggio, E.: *The Dawn of Italian Culture in America.* In *Romanic Review,* 1919.

————: *Italian Writers in American and Canadian Libraries.* In *Carroccio,* November 1924.

————: *Italian Influences in Longfellow's Works.* In *Romanic Review,* 1925.

————: *Benjamin Franklin and Italy.* In *Romanic Review,* 1928.

————: *Italy and the American War of Independence.* In *Romanic Review,* 1929.

————: *Washington Irving and Italy.* In *Romanic Review,* 1930.

————: *Italian Educators in Early American Days.* Reprinted from "Italica" in *Atlantica,* June 1931.

Grant, Madison: *The Passing of the Great Race.* Charles Scribner's Sons, New York, 1922.

Grant, Madison, and Charles Davison: *The Alien in Our Midst.* Galton Publishing Co., New York, 1930.

Guidi, Angelo Flavio: *Washington and the Italians.* In *Italy and the Italians in Washington's Time.* Italian Publishers, New York, 1933.

Hall, Prescott F.: *Immigration.* Henry Holt & Co., New York, 1906.

Handlin, Oscar: *The Americans: A New History of the People of the United States.* Little, Brown & Co., Boston, 1963.

Hart, Henry H.: *Venetian Adventurer.* Stanford University Press, Stanford, Calif., 1942.

Hearder, Harry, and D. P. Waley, eds.: *A Short History of Italy.* Cambridge University Press, New York, 1963.

Hubbard, Elbert: *Little Journeys to the Homes of the Great.* Edited by Fred Bann. William H. Wise & Co., New York, 1928.

Hume, Edgar Erskine: *Italy's Part in the World War.* In *Atlantica,* March–April 1935.

Irwin, R. W.: *The Diplomatic Relations of the United States with the Barbary Powers.* The University of North Carolina Press, Chapel Hill, N. C., 1931.

Jacobs, Bruce: *Heroes of the Army: The Medal of Honor and Its Winners.* W. W. Norton & Co., New York, 1956.

Josephson, Matthew: *Victor Hugo.* Doubleday, Doran & Co., New York, 1942.

Kaskaskia Records, edited by C. W. Alvord. Vol. V, Illinois State Historical Library, Springfield, 1909.

Kellogg, Louise P., ed.: *Early Narratives of the Northwest, 1634–1699.* Charles Scribner's Sons, New York, 1917.

Kennedy, John F.: A Nation of Immigrants. Harper & Row, New York, 1964.

Klein, Hermann: The Reign of Patti. Century Co., New York, 1920.

Kohler, Max J.: Immigration and Aliens in the United States. Bloch Publishing Co., New York, 1936.

Laffont, Robert: A History of Rome and the Romans. Crown Publishers, New York, 1962.

Lapp, Ralph E.: Atoms and People. Harper & Brothers, New York, 1956.

Laughlin, Clara E., and Betty Laughlin Sweeney: So You're Going to Italy! Houghton Mifflin Co., Boston, 1950.

Legler, H. E.: Henry Tonti. In Parkman Club Papers, I.

Levinger, Elma Ehrlich: Galileo, First Observer of Marvelous Things. Julian Messner, Inc., New York, 1952.

Lewis, Charles Lee: The Romantic Decatur. University of Pennsylvania Press, Philadelphia, 1937.

Lindsay, M. G.: Coronado: Searcher for the Seven Cities of Cibola. In Pan-American Magazine, October 1930.

Lissner, Ivar: The Caesars: Might and Madness. Translated by J. Maxwell Brownjohn. G. P. Putnam's Sons, New York, 1958.

Lord, Eliot: The Italian in America. B. F. Buck, New York, 1905.

McClellan, E. N.: How the Marine Band Started. U. S. Naval Institute Proceedings, Vol. 49, April 1923.

Magie, David: The Scriptores Historiae Augustae with English Translation. Vol. II and Vol. III. G. P. Putnam's Sons, New York, 1924.

Maisel, Albert Q.: The Italians Among Us. In Reader's Digest, January 1955.

————: They All Chose America. Thomas Nelson & Sons, New York, 1957.

Mangano, Antonio: Sons of Italy: A Social and Religious Study of the Italians in America. Missionary Education Movement of the U. S. & Canada, New York, 1917.

Mariano, John Horace: The Italian Contribution to American Democracy. Christopher Publishing House, Boston, 1922.

Mariotti, Giovanni: Here's Italy. Vallechi, Florence, Italy, 1945.

Markham, Sir Clements: Early Voyages to Magellan's Strait. Vol. 128. Cambridge University Press, New York, 1911.

Marraro, H. R.: American Opinion of the Unification of Italy. Columbia University Press, New York, 1932.

————: Philip Mazzei, Virginia's Agent in Europe. Bulletin of the New York Public Library, March and April 1934.

Martire, Egilberto: Il Padre Bressani. In La Tribuna, Rome, July 1, 1930.

Maynard, Theodore: *Too Small a World*. The Bruce Publishing Co., Milwaukee, 1953.

Mazzei's Memoirs. Translated by E. C. Branchi. *The Columbian Monthly*, May and July 1928. *William and Mary Quarterly*, July–October 1929, January 1930.

Moncada, F.: *Incidents in Garibaldi's Life in America*. In *Atlantica*, October 1932.

————: *The Little Italy of 1850*. In *Atlantica*, January 1933.

Morton, H. V.: *A Traveller in Italy*. Dodd, Mead & Co., New York, 1964.

The National Geographic Magazine, Vol. XXX. National Geographical Society, Washington, D. C.

Nelson, Gay H.: *Le Relazioni fra l'Italia e gli Stati Uniti, 1847–1871*. In *Nuova Antologia*, February 1907.

————: *Lincoln's offer of a command to Garibaldi*. In *Century Magazine*, November 1907.

Olson, Harvey S.: *Europe, Aboard and Abroad*. J. B. Lippincott Co., Philadelphia, 1960.

Panunzio, Constantine: *Immigration Crossroads*. The Macmillan Co., New York, 1927.

————: *The Soul of an Immigrant*. The Macmillan Co., New York, 1937.

Papini, Giovanni: *Laborers in the Vineyard*. Sheed & Ward, Inc., New York, 1930.

————: *Michelangelo*. E. P. Dutton & Co., New York, 1952.

Park, Robert E., and Herbert A. Miller: *Old World Traits Transplanted*. Harper & Brothers, New York, 1914.

Patri, Angelo: *A Schoolmaster of the Great City*. The Macmillan Co., New York, 1928.

Pellegrini, Angelo M.: *Immigrant's Return*. The Macmillan Co., New York, 1951.

————: *Americans by Choice*. The Macmillan Co., New York, 1956.

Pigafetta, Antonio: *Magellan's Voyage Around the World*. The Arthur H. Clark Co., Cleveland, Ohio, 1906.

Pisani, Lawrence Frank: *The Italian in America*. Exposition Press, New York, 1957.

Proctor, J. C.: *Marine Band History and Its Leaders*. In Washington *Sunday Star*, May 8, 1932.

Pulver, Jeffrey: *Paganini*. Herbert Joseph Ltd., London, 1936.

Randall, H. S.: *The Life of Thomas Jefferson*. J. B. Lippincott, Philadelphia, 1888.

Riis, Jacob: *The Making of an America*. The Macmillan Co., New York, 1937.

————: *How the Other Half Lives.* Sagamore Press, Inc., New York, 1957.

Roberts, Kenneth L.: *Why Europe Leaves Home.* Bobbs-Merrill Co., New York, 1922.

Rose, Philip M.: *The Italians in America.* George H. Doran Co., Garden City, N. Y., 1922.

Ross, Edward Alsworth: *The Old World in the New.* Century Co., New York, 1914.

Salvatorelli, Luigi: *A Concise History of Italy.* Oxford University Press, New York, 1940.

Schermerhorn, R. A.: *These Our People.* D. C. Heath & Co., Boston, 1949.

Schiavo, Giovanni: *The Italians in Missouri.* Italian-American Publishing Co., New York, 1929.

————: *One of America's Founding Fathers.* Vigo Press, New York, 1951.

————: *Four Centuries of Italian-American History.* Vigo Press, New York, 1957.

————: *The Truth About the Mafia and Organized Crime in America.* Vigo Press, New York, 1962.

Sforza, Count Carlo: *Italy and Italians.* E. P. Dutton & Co., New York, 1949.

Smith, Denis M.: *Italy.* The University of Michigan Press, Ann Arbor, Mich., 1959.

Smith, Ken: *Baseball's Hall of Fame.* Grosset & Dunlap, Inc., New York, 1963.

Smith, Robert: *Heroes of Baseball.* The World Publishing Co., New York, 1952.

————: *Baseball in America.* Holt, Rinehart & Winston, Inc., New York, 1961.

Smith, William Carlson: *Americans in the Making.* D. Appleton-Century Co., New York, 1939.

Sondern, Frederic, Jr.: *Brotherhood of Evil: the Mafia.* Farrar, Straus & Cudahy, New York, 1959.

Starritt, S. Stuart: *Garibaldi the Liberator.* The Religious Tract Society, Manchester, England, 1929.

Stella, Antonio: *Italian Immigration to the United States.* G. P. Putnam's Sons, New York, 1924.

Symonds, J. A.: *The Debt of English to Italian Literature.* In *Fortnightly Review,* Vol. 17, New Series, 1875.

Taft, L.: *The History of American Sculpture.* The Macmillan Co., New York, 1924.

Trevelyan, Janet Penrose: *A Short History of the Italian People.* G. P.
    Putnam's Sons, New York, 1920.
Trimble, Joe: *Yogi Berra.* A. S. Barnes, New York, 1952.
The Unity of Italy. The American Celebration of the Unity of Italy at
    the Academy of Music, New York, January 12, 1871.
Venturi, L.: *Pitture Italiane in America.* U. Hoepli, Milan, 1931.
Villa, Silvio: *The Unbidden Guest.* The Macmillan Co., New York, 1923.
Walsh, James J.: *What Civilization Owes to Italy.* Stratford Company,
    Boston, 1930.
Warne, Frank Julian: *The Immigrant Invasion.* Dodd, Mead & Co., New
    York, 1913.
Winship, G. P.: *The Coronado Expedition.* 14th Report of the U. S.
    Bureau of Ethnology. Washington, D. C., 1896.
Young, Donald: *American Minority Peoples.* Harper & Brothers, New
    York, 1932.

INDEX